Front View of the Presidents House in New Jersey.

H Dawkins Sculp

John Witherspoon

AND THE FOUNDING OF THE

AMERICAN REPUBLIC

John Witherspoon

AND THE FOUNDING OF THE
AMERICAN REPUBLIC

JEFFRY H. MORRISON

University of Notre Dame Press
Notre Dame, Indiana

Endsheets: engraving, "Nassau Hall and the Presidents House" by Dawkins.
Printed with permission of the Princeton University Library, University
Archives, Department of Rare Books and Special Collections.

Manufactured in the United States of America

Library of Congress Cataloging-in-Publication Data
Morrison, Jeffry H., 1961–
    John Witherspoon and the founding of the American
republic / Jeffry H. Morrison
        p.   cm.
    Includes bibliographical references and index.
    ISBN 0-268-03485-0 (cloth : alk. paper)
        1. Witherspoon, John, 1723–1794.   2. Witherspoon, John, 1723–1794—
Political and social views.   3. Statesmen—United States—Biography.
4. United States. Declaration of Independence—Signers—Biography.
5. Presbyterian Church—United States—Clergy—Biography.   6. United
States—Politics and government—1775–1783.   I. Title.
    E302.6.W7M677   2005
    973.3'092—dc22

                                                            2005004931

∞ This book is printed on acid-free paper.

for melissa

If we could go right back to the elements of societies and examine the very first records of their histories, I have no doubt that we should there find the first cause of their prejudices, habits, dominating passions, and all that comes to be called the national character. . . . America is the only country in which we can watch the natural quiet growth of society and where it is possible to be exact about the influence of the point of departure on the future of a state.

—Alexis de Tocqueville

contents

acknowledgments

William Wilberforce once remarked that a man he had just met was sadly in need of "the chastening hand of a sound classical education." The same can be said of me; but fortunately I had the benefit of many chastening hands (and brains) along the way to writing this book. To begin with, there were my teachers at Georgetown University: Walter Berns, George Carey, and Joshua Mitchell. Carey, that most enlightened person, made especially trenchant suggestions. There were also these colleagues and mentors who helped me in innumerable ways: Daniel Dreisbach of the American University; my former colleagues in the Department of Political Science at the United States Air Force Academy, particularly Paul Carrese and Stephen Knott (now at the University of Virginia); John Witte, Jr., of Emory University Law School; Mark Hall of George Fox University; Garrett Ward Sheldon of the University of Virginia's College at Wise; Michael Novak of the American Enterprise Institute; Barry Ryan of Regent University; and Robert George of Princeton University. I owe a special debt to my editor (now friend) at the University of Notre Dame Press, its associate director, Jeffrey Gainey. Of course, as academic authors are compelled to say, none of these people is to be held accountable for the book's shortcomings and errors, though I do recall Publius saying something like "I never expect to see a perfect work from imperfect man."

I received help from a number of archivists and librarians while researching. Among these I am especially grateful to: Whitfield J. Bell, Jr., of the American Philosophical Society, for making available to me his files on Witherspoon; Marvin W. Kranz of the Manuscript Division, Library of Congress; Ben Primer and Margaret Sherry at the Princeton University Library; and Dr. Elizabeth Stone, archivist of the National Presbyterian Church in Washington, D.C.

Last, I wish to acknowledge the extraordinary generosity of the Bradley Foundation of Milwaukee, Wisconsin; the Earhart Foundation of Ann Arbor, Michigan; the Intercollegiate Studies Institute of Wilmington, Delaware; and the Witherspoon Institute of Princeton, New Jersey, all of whom underwrote my efforts; and the faculty and staff of the James Madison Program in American Ideals and Institutions in the Department of Politics at Princeton University, which hosted me and provided a visiting professorship during the academic year 2003–2004.

Spring 2004   Princeton, New Jersey *preface*

〰️ In the northwest quadrant of that monumental city, Washington, D.C., a bronze statue of John Witherspoon towers over traffic between Connecticut Avenue and N Street: stately, imposing, and altogether ignored. Most people who work or live in Washington, even residents of fashionable Northwest, are equally ignorant of its existence (it is a stone's throw from a well-known statue of Longfellow) and the man it memorializes.

That monumental statue, now one of three in the U.S. to Witherspoon—another, equally ignored, is in Philadelphia's Fairmount Park—was erected in the early twentieth century in front of the Presbyterian Church of the Covenant, whose members wished to commemorate one of their own denomination who had signed the Declaration of Independence and had earned, they thought, a distinguished place in American history.[1] Those Presbyterians wished to memorialize Witherspoon both as a churchman and as a statesman. A Witherspoon Memorial Association was formed; private donations were solicited from Andrew Carnegie and others; the sculptor William Couper, creator of the Longfellow statue in Washington and the heroic likeness of John Smith at Jamestown, was commissioned; and in 1909 the statue was unveiled and dedicated. At the dedication ceremony addresses were given by Lord James Bryce, the English ambassador, and by President Woodrow Wilson, a son of Witherspoon's Princeton, whose address was titled a "Review of the Life and Services of Witherspoon."[2] Around that time the statue became, as so many things eventually do become, the property of the federal government.[3] Years passed, the Church of the Covenant was torn down, and in 1976, during the bicentennial of the Declaration, a committee of Presbyterians was formed to have the Witherspoon statue moved to the National Presbyterian Church on Nebraska Avenue. In the event, the statue remained where it had always been, and Witherspoon himself continued to fade from memory.

I began this project in 1994, the bicentennial of Witherspoon's death. In the decade I have been studying Witherspoon I have conceived a fondness for that statue, partly because I like underdogs, but mostly because it teaches two telling object lessons. First, it illustrates how thoroughly Witherspoon has been ignored in the century since its commissioning; second, it shows up the confusion that sometimes exists in modern America over the proper degree of separation between church and state. Apparently the proposed transfer of the statue in 1976 occasioned some hand-wringing over the constitutionality of the federal government honoring a minister with a statue in the first place. Two bills (H. R.12778 and S.2996)[4] were introduced in Congress that year authorizing the relocation of the Witherspoon monument, but the project died a quiet death, lost in the welter of bicentennial activities and what a contemporary wag called "tons of red-white-and-blue junk." Nevertheless, because he was a preeminent churchman and statesman, Witherspoon still affords an ideal point of departure, to appropriate Alexis de Tocqueville's language, for addressing questions about religion and politics and, more broadly, about the American founding.

But Witherspoon scholarship remains, as one writer put it in 1990, "astonishingly thin."[5] The best book on Witherspoon is still Varnum Lansing Collins's *President Witherspoon: A Biography*, a two-volume work from 1925 that was reprinted in 1969. There have been several other biographies of varying quality besides the Collins work. Of these, two repay attention: a portrait of Witherspoon by his former pupil, Ashbel Green, probably written in 1840–1841 and finally published under the editorship of Henry Lyttleton Savage in 1973; and one by Witherspoon's descendant, David Walker Woods.[6] In 2001, L. Gordon Tait published *The Piety of John Witherspoon*, a solid study of his religiosity that devotes little space to his political life.[7] Beyond these books Witherspoon has merited chapters in edited volumes such as Richard B. Sher and Jeffrey R. Smitten's *Scotland and America in the Age of the Enlightenment*, and histories such as Mark Noll's *Princeton and the Republic, 1768–1822*.[8] Usually, however, he has merited pages rather than chapters, and nothing to speak of by a political scientist.[9] So far as I know, this is the first comprehensive treatment of Witherspoon's political thought and career.

Much of the scholarship on Witherspoon has dealt with his pre-American life in Scotland from 1723 to 1768 and has emphasized, in one way or another, his Scottishness. I focus instead on Witherspoon as an American political thinker and have relatively little to say about his Scottish career, although I suggest how the Scottish common sense philosophy helped make him and his students into practical American politicians. I have attempted throughout to relate Witherspoon's political thought and even his moral epistemology to that of the key founders, particularly that curious pair of rivals-turned-friends: the northern Federalist John Adams and the southern Republican Thomas Jefferson, the "North and South Poles of the American Revolution," as Benjamin Rush called them. (Indeed, Rush — who helped reconcile the two in their old age — wrote to Adams that while others may have done more, he and Jefferson *"thought* for us all" during the Revolution.)[10] The final chapter is devoted to placing Witherspoon in the context of American political thought during the founding era, particularly in relation to the three dominant ideologies associated with British liberalism, classical republicanism, and Protestant Christianity.

John Witherspoon

AND THE FOUNDING OF THE
AMERICAN REPUBLIC

chapter one

Forgotten Founder

He was a man of a great and luminous mind. . . . His works will
probably preserve his name to the end of time.

—Benjamin Rush on John Witherspoon

It is one of the little ironies of American history that Benjamin Rush, who once predicted that the accomplishments of his old friend the Rev. John Witherspoon would "probably preserve his name to the end of time," should himself be more famous at present than Witherspoon. Rush no doubt thought that of the two men Witherspoon had the better purchase on lasting fame. He complained to John Adams that "my friends have often told me I must throw sixes (to use an allusion from the dice board) to eclipse the ruin of my reputation."[1] By contrast, their contemporaries had all been impressed by Witherspoon. In 1774, Adams himself (never one to suffer fools gladly) found him not only a "clear, sensible" preacher, but "as high a Son of Liberty, as any Man in America."[2] Nearly forty years later Adams wrote to Rush, who by then was remembering Witherspoon as "our old Scotch Sachem," that "Witherspoon had *Wutt* [wit] and sense and taste" and recalled him as a wise old Scot.[3]

By the time of his first meeting with Adams in 1774, Witherspoon had been president of the College of New Jersey at Princeton for half a dozen years since relocating from his native Scotland. He went on in the remaining two decades of his life to draw the attention of other prominent men on both sides of the Atlantic for the roles he played in the American Revolution and the nation's political birth. In fact, Witherspoon's American years from 1768 to 1794 perfectly overlaid those commonly referred to as "the founding," and his political career from 1774 to 1789 covered the most decisive years of that period.[4]

The American Career, 1768–1794

John Witherspoon, D.D., LL.D. (1723–1794) lived a remarkable life that spanned the last three quarters of the eighteenth century. Born the same year as Adam Smith, at the beginning of the Scottish Enlightenment, Witherspoon was educated at its heart at the University of Edinburgh.[5] At the urging of Benjamin Rush, the trustees of the College of New Jersey at Princeton, and George Whitefield,[6] the Anglican evangelist who helped touched off the First Great Awakening, Witherspoon emigrated to Princeton in 1768 to become sixth president of the College. He remained there during the crucial founding years of the republic until his death in 1794, during the second term of George Washington's presidency. Witherspoon's political career was spent at the founding's epicenter in and around Philadelphia during its crisis years. He served periodically in the New Jersey provincial and state legislatures (1774–1789), in the Continental and Confederation Congresses throughout the Revolution (1776–1782),[7] and in the New Jersey convention that ratified the federal Constitution (1787).

In point of fact, John Witherspoon had three careers, any one of which should have guaranteed him the prominent and lasting place in American history that he has been denied.[8] Pastor, college president, and politician, his careers combined in interesting ways. He was the sole clergyman and college president to sign the Declaration of Independence, which secured him a place that is literally unique among the founders at the crossroads of religion, education, and politics.[9] Witherspoon was also an amateur scientist, political economist, rhetorician, and philosopher; in short, he was a kind of polymath, or aspired to be one. His interests and abilities made him the sort of well-rounded man we associate with American Enlightenment characters such as Thomas Jefferson or Benjamin Franklin. Like those two, Witherspoon was an intellectual handyman, though he lacked their talent with gadgetry. As a man of science he was clearly inferior to both Franklin, whom the French delighted in calling the "Electrical Ambassador,"[10] and Jefferson, but he did share their keen interest in furthering scientific study in America. (He was elected an officer in the American Philosophical Society the same year as Jefferson and the astronomer David Rittenhouse, for instance.) As a theologian and, more important, as a moral philosopher, Witherspoon was their superior. But above all it is his political career that most clearly marks Witherspoon as a founder of the republic, and it is to this career that we first turn our attention.

Witherspoon, along with many others, has long been overshadowed by his more verbose brother founders. Those famous men—Washington, Adams, certainly Jefferson (who wrote, and preserved, 20,000 letters during his long life), James Madison, Alexander Hamilton, and Franklin—have continued to hold the spotlight, while lesser characters such as Witherspoon have remained in the shadows.[11] As it was, Witherspoon had a noteworthy political career, and he nearly had an immortal one. Had one or two situations turned out differently, he would surely rank alongside the most celebrated founders. Still, there is plenty in Witherspoon's political career as it actually unfolded to attract more than the scant attention he has been shown in the scholarly and even popular literature. By any fair measure he deserves to be classed among the founders of this republic. By signing the Declaration of Independence and the Articles of Confederation and by ratifying the Constitution, he had a direct hand in passing three of the four Organic Laws of the United States,[12] and the two most celebrated founding documents, the Declaration and Constitution—the "apple of gold in the frame of silver," as Abraham Lincoln (borrowing from Proverbs) called them.

By the summer of 1776 when he led the New Jersey delegation to the Second Continental Congress in Philadelphia, Witherspoon had already been active in provincial politics for several years. He had been on the Committee of Correspondence for Somerset County since its inception and had been a delegate to the New Jersey provincial congress from 1774 until his appointment to the Continental Congress in June 1776. His record in Congress reveals that, excepting part of the year 1780, Witherspoon was scrupulous in his attendance and almost preternaturally active. The *Journals of the Continental Congress* record his appointment to 126 committees in six years of service (said to be more than any delegate of his time), including two crucial standing committees, the Committee on Foreign Affairs and the Board of War.[13]

Witherspoon got the attention of his congressional colleagues early and held it throughout the next six years. Sometime during the debates on July 1 and 2, 1776, a member of the conservative faction (probably John Dickinson of Pennsylvania) argued that the country at large was not yet ripe for independence. Witherspoon shot back that in his judgment the colonies were not only ripe for independence but also "in danger of becoming rotten for the want of it."[14] By so replying, he helped prod Congress toward passing Richard Henry Lee's Resolution for Independence on July 2, and the Declaration of Independence two days later. Appointment to a prodigious number of committees followed immediately and did not abate until Witherspoon retired from Congress at the end of 1782 with the end of the War in plain view. It is a further measure of the confidence other congressmen placed in him that Witherspoon was tapped to draw up the instructions to the American peace commission in France in 1781. That commission originally consisted solely of John Adams but had been expanded to include John Jay, Franklin, Jefferson, and Henry Laurens. The instructions Witherspoon wrote on June 15 "were asked for . . . as a means of curbing John Adams," according to constitutional historian Edward Corwin.[15] Witherspoon himself complained of what he called Adams's occasional "stiffness and tenaciousness of temper."[16]

Witherspoon also made less formal, though no less important, contributions to the founding. He preached a number of politically influential sermons and was a productive pamphleteer, especially during the Revolutionary period.[17] Several of his political pamphlets and speeches have been preserved in the *Works,* including "Reflections on the Present State of Public Affairs"; "On Conducting the American Controversy"; "On the Contest Between Great Britain and America"; "On the Affairs of the United States"; a piece on Thomas Paine's *Common Sense* over the pseudonym "Aristides"; and a series of periodical essays, which he signed "the Druid."[18]

Nor did Witherspoon's political influence end with his own retirement from politics in 1789. The list of his Princeton graduates reads like a roll of early American notables. Among these were twelve members of the Continental Congress; five delegates to the Constitutional Convention; one U.S. president (Madison); a vice president (the notorious Aaron Burr); forty-nine U.S. representatives; twenty-eight U.S. senators; three Supreme Court justices; eight U.S. district judges; one secretary of state; three attorneys general; and two foreign ministers. In addition to these national officeholders, twenty-six of Witherspoon's graduates were state judges, seventeen were members of their state constitutional conventions, and fourteen were delegates to the state conventions that ratified the Constitution.[19] Chief among Witherspoon's graduates was James Madison, "Father of the Constitution" and reluctant architect of the Bill of Rights. Madison stayed on at Princeton for an extra term following his graduation to study Hebrew under the "old Doctor's" direction and then proceeded to carry certain elements of

Witherspoon's political-theological creed into his own public career, culminating in two stormy terms as president from 1809–1817.

So intertwined were Witherspoon's political and pastoral careers, not to mention his political theory and his theology, that his political career cannot adequately be appreciated without understanding his status as a clergyman. Witherspoon came from a long and distinguished line of Reformed (that is, Calvinist) pastors, and his mother claimed lineal descent from the Scottish reformer John Knox. In Britain and Europe he had gained fame as the outspoken leader of the democratic and evangelical Popular party that opposed the more traditional (though theologically liberal) Moderate party of Francis Hutcheson in the Scottish Presbyterian church, and as the author of two widely cited pieces written during his Scottish ministry. The first, titled *Ecclesiastical Characteristics,* was a satire on the urbane Moderate clergy; the second, *A Serious Enquiry into the Nature and Effects of the Stage,* was an indictment of the theater for its bad effects on public morals. Thus, by the time he received the call to Princeton in 1768, Witherspoon was already something of an international figure in ecclesiastical circles.

His star continued to rise in America. He quickly formed powerful connections throughout the colonies, from fellow pastors such as Ezra Stiles and Timothy Dwight in New England to family (one of his daughters married Madison's friend the Reverand Samuel Stanhope Smith,[20] who founded what became Hampden-Sydney College in Virginia) and Presbyterian colleagues in the Carolinas and Georgia. Witherspoon was a fixture in the joint conventions the Presbyterians had with the Congregationalists of the General Association of Connecticut.[21] These conventions were originally called to ally the two denominations against a potential Anglican establishment, that perennial bugaboo of dissenting colonial Protestants. There his lifelong friendship with Stiles, the president of Yale College who found Witherspoon "a very learned divine" but complained privately that he was too much of a politician, was strengthened.[22] (Yale conferred an honorary Doctor of Laws on Witherspoon in 1785 just as Princeton had on Stiles in the previous year.)[23]

From 1785 through 1789, Witherspoon was the leading figure in nationalizing the American Presbyterian Church. Out of that effort came catechisms, a confession, a directory of worship, and an ecclesiastical constitution called "the Form of the Government," portions of which were written by Witherspoon. His Introduction to the Form of the Government set out the first principles of church polity for the new national church. Due primarily to his influence, the Form of the Government contained articles that strongly

upheld religious liberty, and in fact liberalized the Westminster Confession of
Faith of 1647.

Being the most eminent American Presbyterian of the late eighteenth
century in turn made Witherspoon one of the most eminent clergymen in all
America at that time.[24] In 1776, Presbyterians had nearly 600 congregations,[25]
mostly in the middle and southern colonies, and they were a powerful force
among the Reformed churches. The Reformed bloc included Presbyterians,
Dutch and German Reformed, and Congregationalists; according to Fred
Hood, the Reformed denominations in the middle and southern states alone
made up "the largest religious sector of the United States in 1780."[26] As a key
leader of this largest sector, Witherspoon was put near the top, and perhaps at
the very top, of the ministerial heap in founding-era America.

His denominational and indeed national prominence gave Witherspoon's
sermons, many of which were printed and circulated extensively, considerable
weight. Weightiest of all was his first explicitly political one, "The Dominion
of Providence Over the Passions of Men," preached on May 17, 1776, a congressional Fast Day. The first edition of the "Dominion of Providence" was
printed that year by Robert Aitken of Philadelphia. Second and third editions were reprinted in Glasgow in 1777, accompanied by annotations in
which the author was called a rebel and a traitor;[27] a fourth was reprinted in
Philadelphia and London in 1777; and a fifth was brought out in London
in 1779.[28] The favorable American response to the sermon helped rally support for independence, especially in New Jersey, which was not keen on
independence just then, and vaulted Witherspoon into the Continental Congress in late June of 1776. As the de facto head of the New Jersey delegation
in Congress, and of all colonial Presbyterians, Witherspoon was ideally po-
sitioned to spur the independence movement forward.

In fact, what we now call the Revolutionary War was known by many
in Europe and England—even by George III—as the "Presbyterian Rebellion."[29] A Hessian soldier wrote from America, "[c]all this war, dearest
friend, by whatever name you may, only call it not an American Rebellion.
It is nothing more nor less than an Irish-Scotch Presbyterian rebellion."[30]
Although this was hyperbole from a frustrated soldier on foreign soil (Tom
Paine—no Presbyterian, he—would have thought it a gross overstatement),
it nevertheless reflected the active participation in the Revolutionary effort
by Witherspoon and by so many of his denomination.

In addition to the "Dominion of Providence" and his other political sermons,[31] Witherspoon was the author of one congressional Fast Day proclamation and two Thanksgiving Day proclamations, fully one-third of Con-

gress's religious proclamations during the years he was a member.[32] These proclamations are quintessential expressions of the theological-political ethos of the Revolutionary years. Many of their themes — the Almighty's providential care for the United States, the necessity of religion and morality for civic health — were the stock-in-trade of late-eighteenth-century American political orations such as Washington's Farewell Address. Witherspoon incorporated those proclamation themes into his sermons and lectures to upperclassmen and divinity students.

The presidency of a college, and the most national of the colonial colleges to boot, gave Witherspoon the chance to put his broad mind and training to good use. In those days, and especially in the early stages of Princeton's history (the College had been founded in 1746), the president had to be a man of wide competence who could raise funds, oversee day-to-day operations, and be the principal instructor as well. By all accounts, Witherspoon was an excellent professor. In disciplines such as the sciences, which he did not feel qualified to instruct, he did what he could to keep abreast of recent developments in both theory and practice.

Like virtually all of the political founders, Witherspoon was a dabbler in what was called "natural philosophy" in the eighteenth century, and what we simply call "science" today. He experimented with horticulture at his country home, Tusculum (he liked to style himself a "scientific gardener"), and, more important, was elected a member of the scientifically minded American Philosophical Society of Philadelphia in 1769 and kept up his membership until his death in 1794. Witherspoon was appointed to the Committee on Mechanics and Architecture and the Committee on Husbandry and American Improvements, and he was twice elected councillor of the Society.[33] On at least one occasion he lectured before the Society, on the subject of American improvements.[34] And Witherspoon was at least familiar enough with contemporary physics that he took it upon himself, too rashly it now appears, to question certain assertions of Newtonian theory such as the infinity of space and the infinite divisibility of matter, in the public press.[35] His own interest, if not expertise, in natural science led President Witherspoon to beef up scientific studies at Princeton and to lay out unheard-of sums for scientific apparatus. Most notable of these was Rittenhouse's famous Orrery, an intricate working model of the solar system and probably the most celebrated mechanical device of the age. But it was in the humanities, or "letters," that Witherspoon's pedagogical talents were best utilized.

It is commonly acknowledged that the Lectures on Eloquence, first given in class by President Witherspoon and later published in his *Works* beginning in 1800–1801, were "the first American rhetorical treatise."[36] Indeed, Witherspoon was responsible for a number of firsts in America. In his series of essays from 1776 to 1781 over the pseudonym "the Druid," which included observations on the American language, he coined the word "Americanism"—a term that, as Martin Diamond pointed out, has no counterpart in any other nation's vocabulary.[37] Witherspoon has also been attributed with introducing the Latin word "campus" into the American lexicon, when he used it to describe the grounds at Princeton in 1774.[38]

Witherspoon wrote on political economy as well, with lasting consequences for the infant republic. In October 1789, Alexander Hamilton, Washington's newly appointed secretary of the treasury, asked Witherspoon, according to Witherspoon's return letter, for advice on "a proper provision for the public Debt" and "public Credit."[39] In the fall of 1789, Hamilton sought information and opinions from a select handful of persons "on various aspects of public finance" for use in preparing his "Report Relative to a Provision for the Support of Public Credit." These advisers included James Madison and John Witherspoon, and their responses were, according to the editors of the Hamilton *Papers*, "undoubtedly used by Hamilton in drawing up the Report" of January 1, 1790.[40] In fact, both the Report of January 1 and Hamilton's "Second Report of the Further Provision Necessary for Establishing Public Credit" or "Report on a National Bank" of December 13, 1790, bear the marks of Witherspoon's influence. Interestingly, "Hamilton's opinions on [economic] discrimination in the Report closely resemble the ideas advanced by John Witherspoon in his letter to the Secretary of the Treasury."[41]

In 1786, prompted by congressional admirers, Witherspoon had drawn together materials from his various speeches and brought out an *Essay on Money as a Medium of Commerce, with Remarks on the Advantages and Disadvantages of Paper Admitted into General Circulation*, one of the earliest American free-market economic treatises. (It seems that Witherspoon was always a die-hard free marketeer: after a visit to the beleaguered Continental army in the field, he published a pamphlet "On the Proposed Market in General Washington's Camp," addressed to "His Excellency General Washington, and the Officers of the American Army," which argued against price fixing.)[42] The *Essay on Money* was then reprinted in separate editions in 1787 and 1788. It was probably the reputation of that essay as well as his own high opinion of Witherspoon that prompted Hamilton to solicit Witherspoon's advice, and then to incorporate that advice into two of his most famous state papers.[43]

President Witherspoon's Lectures on Moral Philosophy marked another first in American education: a systematic treatment of moral philosophy, which was then coming into vogue in the colonial colleges.[44] Derived largely, though not uncritically, from Francis Hutcheson's *System of Moral Philosophy* (1755), these lectures — in oral, manuscript, and published forms — were vastly influential.[45] Manuscripts of the lectures, which were copied verbatim from a syllabus by each member of the senior class at Princeton for a quarter century, circulated widely throughout the colonies, and one historian even claims they influenced Hamilton's draft of Washington's Farewell Address.[46] In 1820 the University of Pennsylvania was still listing "Witherspoon," along with "Hutcheson, Paley [and] Smith," as a text on "natural and political law."[47]

Witherspoon's broad mind was, if not exactly "luminous" as Benjamin Rush held, at least capable of refracting the light of others, especially the Scottish philosophers such as Hutcheson (1694–1746) and Thomas Reid (1710–1796), whom he helped introduce into America. One of Witherspoon's first tasks was to root out the philosophical idealism that was a legacy of his short-lived predecessor at Princeton, President Jonathan Edwards, and that thoroughly dominated the College in 1768. A year after he assumed the presidency, all of the tutors who professed this system (including Jonathan Edwards, Jr.) had been harried out of the Princeton land. Witherspoon had succeeded in substituting Scottish realism for the New England idealism of Edwards, Samuel Johnson, who had tutored the elder Edwards at Yale, and Bishop George Berkeley.

Given the wide range of subjects that Witherspoon was capable of engaging, it is little wonder that Rush, Whitefield, and the Princetonians were anxious to see him transplanted to America. His mental abilities, coupled with a happy administrative talent and forceful personality, virtually assured him the place he assumed among its leading politicians and citizens. Carrying a substantial reputation from Great Britain with him, in 1768 Witherspoon was straightaway initiated into the leadership of New Jersey society and, because of the strategic importance of nearby Philadelphia, into a wider circle of influential Americans as well. He quickly became one of the foremost figures, not only in New Jersey but also in all America, during the formative 1770s and 1780s. His unquestioned skills in overlapping careers in religion, education, and public affairs were rewarded not only with early success in all three but also with the confidence of the most notable of the founders — from orthodox Christians such as John Jay to the heterodox such as John Adams, Franklin, Jefferson, and Washington.

Contemporary Americans of all religious persuasions were taken with Witherspoon from the start. Shortly after his installation at the head of "Jersey-College," as it was sometimes called, the president embarked on two fund-raising circuits: one north to New England in 1768, and another through the South in 1769. During this second trip, Witherspoon stopped in Williamsburg to preach in that Anglican stronghold, drawing a crowd that forced him to speak in the Capitol yard since no building in town (let alone Bruton Parish Church) could accommodate it.[48] (Afterward a collection for the College was taken, in which 86 pounds sterling were given, including 20 pounds from the governor.) Witherspoon's first biographer, Ashbel Green (1762–1848), recalled how the "knowledge that he was to conduct a public service, usually filled the largest churches in our cities and populous towns"; this is confirmed by Witherspoon himself, who acknowledged the "unusual throng" gathered to hear his sermon on the "Dominion of Providence" in 1776.

Witherspoon had a personal quality that eighteenth-century people called "presence," and Americans today call "gravitas." Green, who had been Witherspoon's student (B.A. 1783) and eventually became president of Princeton himself, described Witherspoon in these words: "His public appearance was always graceful and venerable: and in promiscuous company, he had more of the quality called *presence*—a quality powerfully felt, but not to be described—than any other individual with whom the writer has ever had intercourse, Washington alone excepted."[49] Perhaps this was true, but like Washington (and Jefferson, for that matter), Witherspoon had no gift for self-deprecation. Green forgot, or chose to forget, that the president saw collegiate pranks as personal challenges to his authority, and was defensive about his marriage late in life to a twenty-four-year-old widow. (Though what sixty-nine-year-old man would not be?)[50] And what Green called Witherspoon's gracefulness sometimes gave way to prickliness, which his pupil failed to record. Still, that did nothing to tarnish the favorable impression that Witherspoon made on John Adams. A month after their first meeting, Adams recorded a second encounter in his diary (September 1774): "Dr. Witherspoon enters with great spirit into the American cause. He seems as hearty a Friend as any of the Natives—an animated son of Liberty."[51] This was no small concession from Adams, who had a lifelong distrust of the clergy. "My friend," he wrote Benjamin Rush in 1809, "the clergy have been in all ages and countries as dangerous to liberty as the army."[52] Nor was Adams easily awed, even by great men: to him, Hamilton was always "the bastard brat of a Scotch pedlar" and Washington was "old muttonhead." It is true that Adams begrudged Witherspoon his financial status, but then he complained about almost everyone who appeared to out-earn him. (Like Jefferson, Adams always worried that his farm would not pay.) Writing about a pastor who made too much money for his taste, he asked, "[p]ray how comes Parson Caldwell to be so very rich? I suppose he was another Witherspoon or another [Alexander] MacWhorter who thought a part of Christ's kingdom was of this world." (For the record, Witherspoon's estate was valued at $2,495 at his death, Adams's at nearly $100,000.)[53] Even Franklin and Washington—who served without pay during the War—were not beyond the reach of Adams's envy. "You know there were but two whigs in the Revolution, Franklin and Washington," he again wrote Benjamin Rush. "Franklin's sacrifices we learn in your account of Richard Bache's [Franklin's son-in-law] fortune of 530,000 dollars; and Washington's sacrifices we learn from his will, in which it appears he left four or five hundred thousand dollars to his nephews; and from the Federal City, by which he raised the value of his property and that of his family a thousand per cent, at an expense to the public of more than his whole fortune."[54]

A number of Adams's colleagues, notably Franklin, Jay, Jefferson, and Washington, also had high estimates of Witherspoon's patriotism and character. Franklin, who had reason to nurse a grudge toward Witherspoon if he had chosen to, used his diplomatic connections to help free John Witherspoon, Jr., when the young man was imprisoned in England in 1781.[55] Franklin referred in his diplomatic correspondence to the elder Witherspoon as a "friend," even though Witherspoon had helped depose and arrest Franklin's bastard son William, the royal governor of New Jersey, in June 1776. On April 5, 1784, when he was serving as an American representative in France, Franklin wrote what a pleasure it would be for him to see Witherspoon while the latter was on the Continent.[56] The next day (April 6), John Jay, who was in France with Franklin, wrote to Witherspoon, "[i]f . . . you should visit Paris, I assure [you] it will give me great pleasure to see you, and to be instrumental in rendering it agreeable to you. We have been fellow laborers in the same field, and if you come we will rejoice together in celebrating 'Harvest Home.'"[57] (Jay's brother-in-law was Henry Brockholst Livingston, a Witherspoon graduate and an associate justice of the Supreme Court.)

Even Jefferson, ordinarily a vicious anti-cleric (he was always harping about the "irritable tribe of priests" and clergy who were "a very formidable engine against the civil and religious rights of man"),[58] was able to put aside his biases when dealing with his old colleague from Congress. Despite his belief that Presbyterians were "the loudest, the most intolerant of all sects, the most tyrannical, and ambitious,"[59] in 1783 when Jefferson needed a tutor for a fledgling academy in Virginia's Albemarle County, he sought out Witherspoon, hoping to snatch up one of his Princeton pupils. (Even before the Revolution, Witherspoon's reputation as an educator was substantial; in 1774, Philip Vickers Fithian wrote a friend who had just been made a professor that the best way to impress his students was to tell them he had "gone through the usual Course in the noted College of New-Jersey, under Dr[.] Witherspoon, so universally known & admired.")[60] Told by Witherspoon that the College was "just getting together again" since the War's end and that no one could be spared, Jefferson advised a friend in Albemarle that he should instead "interest some person in Scotland to engage a good [tutor]" because "[f]rom that country we are surest of having sober attentive men."[61] In 1800, when the first edition of Witherspoon's *Works* was published posthumously, Jefferson bought two volumes, one for his personal library and the other for a gift.[62]

George Washington, although he would hardly have considered Witherspoon his "closest friend," as claimed by one of Witherspoon's hagiographers,[63] nevertheless held the Jerseyman in high regard as a patriot, religious leader, and educator. Washington personally paid twenty-five pounds sterling per year to Witherspoon so that a friend's son, William Ramsay the younger, could afford to study under him at Princeton.[64] Washington took time in 1784 to write Witherspoon what turned out to be one of his longest personal letters, concerning the settlement of his own western landholdings by religious communities.[65] He stated that "it would give me pleasure to see these Lands seated by particular Societies, or *religious Sectaries with their Pastors.*"[66] And in late April 1789, on the way to New York for his first inauguration, the president-elect stopped over in Princeton to receive an address from Witherspoon on behalf of the Princeton faculty, and he may have spent the night — he seems to have slept everywhere else — at the Witherspoon home.[67]

British contemporaries also ranked Witherspoon high among Americans, and especially among traitors. Adam Ferguson, his old Edinburgh classmate who was a British commissioner to the colonies in 1778, wrote a letter that year placing Witherspoon in select company:

It is the fashion to say that we have lost America. . . . I am in great hopes that nothing will be lost, not even the continent of North America. We have 1200 miles of territory occupied by about 300,000 people of which there are about 150,000 with Johnny Witherspoon at their head, against us — and the rest for us. I am not sure that if proper measures were taken but we should reduce Johnny Witherspoon to the small support of Franklin, Adams and two or three more of the most abandoned villains in the world, but I tremble at the thought of their cunning and determination opposed to us.[68]

Another British officer, writing to Major General Sir Guy Carleton in 1783, singled out *"Dr. Witherspoon . . .* the political firebrand, who perhaps had not a less share in the Revolution than Washington himself. He poisons the minds of his young students and through them the Continent."[69] (During the early years of Witherspoon's tenure the College was known, with good reason, as a "seminary of sedition": 138 of Witherspoon's Princeton men—including two of his sons—held some rank in the Continental army, while there were only five professed loyalists.)

On July 30, 1776, British soldiers on Long Island also paid Witherspoon the left-handed compliment of burning an effigy of him preaching to Generals Washington, Charles Lee, and Israel Putnam, whose likenesses were also put to the torch.[70] And after the battle of Trenton a Hessian jäger bayoneted the Presbyterian minister John Rosborough, supposing he was Rev. Witherspoon.[71] Witherspoon himself referred to this "barbarity," which had "happened in one of the streets of this place," in his "Sermon Delivered at a Public Thanksgiving After Peace" (1782), reminding his listeners that Rev. Rosborough "received his death wound while on his knees begging mercy."[72] (However, the assumption, repeated by all of Witherspoon's biographers, that Horace Walpole was referring to Witherspoon when he lamented that "Cousin America has eloped with a Presbyterian parson" is unfounded; Walpole was referring to the physician Dr. Joseph Warren, whom he mistook for a dissenting clergyman.)[73] When the Frenchman François Barbé de Marbois wanted information on the state of New Jersey, he chose Witherspoon for a correspondent, just as he had favored Governor Thomas Jefferson in Virginia. Jefferson's reply became his only book, *Notes on the State of Virginia;*[74] Witherspoon's briefer response was titled "A Description of the State of New Jersey."[75]

Thus, Witherspoon's contemporaries—friend and foe, American and European—ranked him high among that generation we call the founders. A small but growing number of modern scholars has likewise recognized Witherspoon's importance, and a few have mused on his relative obscurity. In 2001, Arthur Herman realized that "[m]ost Americans are totally unaware of John Witherspoon's role in the making of their revolution and the Declaration of Independence. Even scholars rarely include him among the

charmed company of 'Founding Fathers.'"[76] Marci Hamilton (2000) found
the influence of Witherspoon and Calvinism at the Constitutional Convention "surprisingly untouched."[77] James Hutson (1998) gave Witherspoon,
whom he calls a "colossus," an appropriate place in his *Religion and the
Founding of the American Republic*, a book accompanying an exhibit of the
same name at the Library of Congress.[78] In 1992, William Safire included an
abridgement of Witherspoon's "Dominion of Providence" in *Lend Me Your
Ears: Great Speeches in History*.[79] The provocative Garry Wills, convinced
that the Scottish Enlightenment was the key to understanding the founding,
looked into Witherspoon's record at Princeton and proclaimed in 1981 that
"Witherspoon was probably the most influential teacher in the entire history
of American education."[80] Douglass Adair (1974, posthumous) recognized
that "since James Madison became one of the chief architects of our political
democracy . . . his sojourn at Nassau Hall under the tutelage of the learned
Dr. John Witherspoon was of incalculable importance to the destiny of the
United States."[81] Henry Lyttleton Savage, in his edition of Ashbel Green's biography of Witherspoon (1973), acknowledged him as "a man who stood out
among the men of his time."[82] Lyman H. Butterfield (1953), associate editor of
Jefferson's *Papers* and director of the Institute of Early American History and
Culture at Williamsburg, declared that Witherspoon was "unquestionably a
great man."[83] But perhaps the single best assessment belongs to Madison's biographer, Ralph Ketcham (1985): "[a]n examination of Witherspoon's writings combined with his record at Princeton marks him as an incredible and
perhaps somewhat overlooked figure in the growth of America."[84]

Rediscovering John Witherspoon

Assessments such as these beg the question of how such an "incredible" figure as Witherspoon came to be overlooked. Three reasons come readily to
mind. The first is simply a lack of available material. True enough, Witherspoon's *Works* comprise nine volumes (some 2,500 pages) in the 1804–1805
edition, but they are exceedingly difficult to find (the last edition was published in 1815), and key primary materials — a diary or journal, correspondence, records of the New Jersey ratifying convention — are either lost or
never existed.[85] The absence of these primary materials is due to the sack-
ing of Nassau Hall and the president's home after the Battle of Princeton, to
Witherspoon's own wishes, and finally to plain bad luck.

The British were in an uncommonly foul mood by the time they arrived at Princeton on the January 3, 1777, between having lost the humiliating engagement at Trenton on Christmas Day and having failed once again to destroy the colonial army that morning. Although all of the records are not clear, some histories of the Battle of Princeton allude to British vandalism of Nassau Hall (Witherspoon himself confirmed this) and the president's home.[86] According to one account related to Thomas Jefferson, Witherspoon's library was burned by "free booters" and the old man was said to be so furious, especially at losing his "tracts" (possibly his political pamphlets), that he was tempted to lay aside his clerical robes and send the looters to the devil.[87]

While many of his more famous peers were scrupulous diarists, the only extant Witherspoon diary consists of a printed almanac from 1768 (the year of his removal to America) with a few pages of expenses in his none-too-legible hand at the beginning and end. Even worse, from among the thousands of letters he received and wrote—in his later years Witherspoon devoted two days of every week entirely to correspondence—only a handful have survived. For reasons known only to himself, he ordered "a large collection of his papers," apparently including his correspondence, "to be burned a little before his death."[88] For a famous man, Witherspoon was refreshingly, if somewhat maddeningly, unconcerned with his future fame. He seems to have taken no thought at all to preserving it, in contrast to contemporaries such as John Adams, for instance, who constantly fretted about his place in history.

The trustees of Witherspoon's surviving papers were not as careful as they might have been, either. David Walker Woods, a descendant and biographer, wrote in 1906 of having "my own collection of his manuscripts," which have since vanished.[89] Worse yet for Witherspoon's political reputation, there is only a bare record of the New Jersey ratifying convention of 1787. It seems that people in New Jersey were less interested in recording the arguments in their convention—perhaps because there was less dissension—than were their counterparts in Virginia and New York. Still, it would be helpful to have a record of the debate for several reasons, not least of which is that Witherspoon was by all accounts a leading voice in that convention, which so quickly ratified the proposed federal Constitution (third behind Delaware and Pennsylvania).

Witherspoon ratified the Constitution in 1787, and he might very well have signed that document himself had he not been otherwise employed during the early summer. By an odd turn of fate ("Providence," Witherspoon would have called it), May of 1787 found the Reverend Doctor in Philadelphia drawing up a new constitution for the fledgling Presbyterian Church in the United States, instead of sitting in the Federal Convention that was meeting at the same time a few blocks away.[90] The annual Synod of New York and Philadelphia had been gathering in Philadelphia beginning the third week in May every year since consolidation of the two synods in 1758.[91] Witherspoon was therefore committed a year in advance to the Synod meeting in mid-May and was unavailable to answer the call for state delegates to assemble in the Pennsylvania State House. On May 18 he took his seat in the Synod in the Second Presbyterian Church,[92] four days after "the day fixed for the meeting of the deputies in Convention for revising the federal system of Government," according to Madison's notes of the Federal Convention debates.[93] Witherspoon also knew that work on the new Presbyterian constitution might possibly go on for weeks, which in fact it did. The New Jersey delegation to the Federal Convention, consisting of the "honorable David Brearly, William Churchill Houston, and William Patterson Esquires," appeared on "friday the 25th of the said month [May 1787]," while Witherspoon and the Synod were still sitting,[94] and while the Society of the Cincinnati were also meeting. The *Pennsylvania Packet* newspaper of May 31 rhapsodized on this coincidence of conventions:

> Perhaps this city [Philadelphia] affords the most striking picture that has been exhibited for ages. Here, at the same moment, the collective wisdom of the continent [the Constitutional Convention] deliberates upon the extensive politics of the confederate empire, a religious convention [of Presbyterians] clears and distributes the stream of religion throughout the American world, and those veterans whose valour accomplished a mighty revolution [the Society of the Cincinnati], are once more assembled to recognize their fellowship in arms, and to communicate to their distressed brethren the blessings of peace.[95]

Witherspoon would doubtless have been chosen as a delegate from New Jersey to the Federal Convention if he had been available.

It is difficult indeed to think that Witherspoon — for years a vocal proponent of a strong permanent union among the states, probably the leading character in New Jersey society, signer of the Declaration of Independence and the Articles of Confederation, not to mention a man of international reputation — would have been overlooked. And based on his political writings and speeches, he would have been a signer and a forceful advocate of the stronger civil government created by the Constitution. Thus, a prior commitment to his ministerial duties denied him his place among the "demigods," in Jefferson's overblown phrase.[96] Even so, it was a remarkable political accomplishment for Witherspoon to have signed the Declaration of Independence, the Articles of Confederation, and ratified the Constitution. And he was present, in a manner of speaking, at the Federal Convention: five of his Princeton students, including James Madison, attended as delegates.

Witherspoon almost placed a sixth delegate in the Convention, in the person of Alexander Hamilton, who came very close to attending the College of New Jersey along with Madison and his future (and fatal) rival, Aaron Burr. Hamilton was anxious to attend Witherspoon's Princeton, which he found "more republican" than royalist King's College (now Columbia University), where he eventually matriculated, and Witherspoon was anxious to have him. In 1772 he wrote an "Address to the Inhabitants of Jamaica, and other West-India Islands, in Behalf of the College of New-Jersey" recruiting students like the West Indian–born Hamilton.[97] The following year, Hamilton made a trip to Princeton to see about enrolling, accompanied by his landlord, one Hercules Mulligan, a man "well acquainted" with the president by his own account. Hamilton was introduced to Witherspoon, who examined the young man orally and was favorably impressed—he had been educated at Elizabethtown Academy by Francis Barber, a Princeton man and former Witherspoon student. However, Hamilton tacked a presumptuous qualification onto his application: he must be allowed to bypass the standard curriculum and graduate at his own pace. The Princeton trustees balked at Hamilton's rider and ordered Witherspoon to inform him that no such arrangement would be allowed; Hamilton went to King's College instead.[98] Had Hamilton gone to Princeton alongside Madison, this would have meant that the two principal authors of *The Federalist Papers,* and six of the delegates to the Philadelphia convention, would have been trained by John Witherspoon, and scholars would no doubt be making a good deal of hay out of that.

As it turns out, modern scholars have not made much out of Witherspoon one way or another. In many books where one might reasonably expect to find a chapter about him, there is no mention of the New Jersey "colossus." *The Forgotten Leaders of the Revolution* (1955), for example, forgot John Witherspoon, although it contained chapters on such worthies as Jeremiah Wadsworth of Connecticut and Thomas Rodney (youngest brother of Caesar) of Delaware.[99] On the whole, modern writers have been content to toss off a paragraph or two — or at best a chapter — on Witherspoon and be done with him.[100] There seems to be a positive prejudice against Witherspoon's intellectual abilities among modern writers, which is a second possible reason for his obscurity. Almost every scholar in the twentieth century, in marked contrast to those of the nineteenth century and especially to Witherspoon's own contemporaries in the eighteenth, seems convinced that because he was intellectually unoriginal, he could not have been profound.[101] This despite the fact that even William Smith (1727–1803), provost of the rival Academy of Philadelphia (now the University of Pennsylvania), had to admit that Witherspoon possessed "a greater Share of Erudition than I believe any Man in this Country."[102] Another indictment of his mental powers that crops up with regularity is that since he was an eclectic thinker, Witherspoon was at best inconsistent and at worst confused. (This, as I shall be arguing later, is wholly beside the point: all of the founders were eclectic.) The impression given to would-be students of Witherspoon's thought is that he is not worth the effort it would take to read through the multivolume *Works*, provided a circulating copy could even be found.

There is a third possible reason why Witherspoon has been so universally ignored, and it has to do with his status as a clergyman-turned-politician. Even in his day some Americans were made uneasy by the idea of clergymen as legislators, and present-day Americans have become ever more scrupulous about keeping church separate from state. Thus, Witherspoon, a man who, as we shall see, insisted on wearing his clerical garb to the Continental Congress, who composed religious proclamations in the name of that Congress, who scoffed at the suggestion that clergy were somehow disqualified from holding high public office, and who has been accused of embracing a general establishment of Protestantism, can be an uncomfortable reminder of a less "separated" age. Although he actually advocated non-establishment,[103] Witherspoon can thus appear as a sort of political dinosaur, a relic of an American species long extinct, who is not worth the trouble of digging up.

All of the foregoing has resulted in a lamentable forgetfulness on the part of modern scholars, to say nothing of the public, concerning John Witherspoon. James Bryce once remarked that "Hamilton, alone among the founding fathers, had not been done full justice by Americans,"[104] but the number of underappreciated founders, including Witherspoon, has increased since Lord Bryce's time.[105] That forgetfulness may be, and probably is, accidental, or it may be willful. In any event the neglect has not been, to steal a phrase from Edmund Burke, salutary. His remarkable accomplishments, coupled with his unique position at the junction of politics, religion, and education during the founding, require that Witherspoon be removed from the roll of forgotten founders.

chapter two

"The Public Interest of Religion"

Virtue, Religion, and the Republic

The practice of true and undefiled religion . . . is the great foundation
of public prosperity and national happiness.
    —John Witherspoon, Thanksgiving Day Proclamation, 1782

In the momentous year 1776, Edward Gibbon published the first volume of his *Decline and Fall of the Roman Empire,* in which he had little good to say about Christianity and even less about clerics. "The influence of the clergy," he wrote, "might be usefully employed to assert the rights of mankind; but so intimate is the connection between the throne and the altar, that the banner of the church has very seldom been seen on the side of the people."[1] But Gibbon was wrong about that, as even the editors of his magnificent history note,[2] and as the career of his contemporary the Reverend John Witherspoon illustrates. In 1776, Gibbon (1737–1794) himself was a member of Parliament, implacably opposed to the American Revolution, while Witherspoon (d. 1794) was sitting in the Continental Congress pushing for independence from Gibbon's King George III. Witherspoon was a member of the so-called Black Regiment, American clergy who agitated and sometimes even fought for independence.[3]

Among the founders there was no better representative of the intertwining of religion and politics than Witherspoon. In fact, if we wished to invent a figure who at once represented America's early commitments to these two, we could hardly do better than to invent the parson-politician from

New Jersey. As the lone clerical signer of the Declaration, he occupied a place genuinely unique at the nexus of religion and politics during the founding. Witherspoon himself never shrank from this dual role: he conspicuously wore his large Geneva collar to sessions of Congress,[4] and he ridiculed a provision in the Georgia constitution of 1789 forbidding ministers from holding public office.[5] That episode from his career was duly noted by the United States Supreme Court in *McDaniel* v. *Paty et al.* (1978).[6] Witherspoon was able to move gracefully between the two arenas of activity, one secular and the other sacred, because his beliefs regarding the role played by religion in supporting civil government were perfectly synchronized with those of nearly all the founders — even non-Christians such as Benjamin Franklin, and probably John Adams and George Washington.

Religion and Politics

Witherspoon's status as the "prototype of the political parson during the Revolutionary War"[7] inevitably led him to the crossroads of religion and politics in the important Confederation period. Derek Davis has argued, in *Religion and the Continental Congress, 1774–1789: Contributions to Original Intent*, that a careful examination of the thought of Continental Congressmen from 1774 through 1789 can elucidate the constitutional framers' original intent regarding the interplay of religion and the civil state. Studying the work of those Congressmen, he says, can shed light "on the intended meaning of the Constitution and the First Amendment as they relate to the desired relationship between religion and government in the United States."[8]

On the Fast Day of May 17, 1776, Witherspoon preached what became his most famous sermon, "The Dominion of Providence Over the Passions of Men." That same day, John Adams wrote to his wife Abigail, "Great Britain has at last driven America to the last step, a complete separation from her; a total absolute independence, not only of her Parliament but of her crown."[9] Witherspoon's sermon, by his own admission the first overtly political expression from his pulpit, was dedicated to "the Honourable JOHN HANCOCK, Esq., President of the Congress of the United States of America," and it turned out to be one of the most important of the revolutionary political sermons.

The "Dominion of Providence" was, as its title implies, a predictable Calvinist discourse on the general sovereignty of God, inspired by Psalm 76:10: "surely the wrath of man shall praise thee; the remainder of wrath

shalt thou restrain." Witherspoon's decidedly Calvinist illustration of the
biblical text was that

> all the disorderly passions of men, whether exposing the innocent to pri-
> vate injury or whether they are the arrows of divine judgment in public
> calamity, shalt in the end be to the praise of God; or, to apply it more par-
> ticularly to the present state of the American colonies and the plague
> of war, the ambition of mistaken princes, the cunning and cruelty of op-
> pressive and corrupt ministers, and even the inhumanity of brutal sol-
> diers, however dreadful, shall finally promote the glory of God, and in
> the meantime while the storm continues, his mercy and kindness shall
> appear in prescribing bounds to their rage and fury.[10]

The sermon also contained a large section (an "improvement" of the text,
in the sermonic language of the day) in which Witherspoon applied the general scriptural teaching to the particulars of the American situation and par-
tially laid out his thoughts on the proper relationship between religion and
civil government.

Late that same year, Witherspoon was tapped to draft a proclamation
in the name of Congress recommending a "day of solemn fasting and humiliation." This proclamation, issued on December 11, 1776, was the first of
three religious proclamations composed by Witherspoon between 1776 and
1782. It recommended to all the United States "to implore of Almighty God
the forgiveness of the many sins prevailing among the ranks, and to beg the
countenance and assistance of his Providence in the prosecution of the present just and necessary war," and recommended to both civil and military officers "the exercise of repentance and reformation."[11]

Witherspoon also drafted Thanksgiving Day proclamations issued by
Congress on October 26, 1781, and October 11, 1782, as Congress followed its
practice of issuing Thanksgiving Day proclamations each October throughout the War.[12] These days of fasting, humiliation, prayer, and thanksgiving,
though recommendations to the states, were often strongly worded. Witherspoon's Fast Day Proclamation of 1776 proposed that a fast be appointed
"as soon as possible" and advised "in the most earnest manner" that persons
in authority encourage repentance and reformation and discourage immorality in those under them. These proclamations employed the language
of the covenant theology held by Witherspoon and other Reformed Protestants, according to which God had made a covenant with the people of the
United States to bless them as long as they were holy and to curse them when

they were sinful. Engaged as they were in a desperate war with Great Britain, "*public bodies,* as well as private persons," were urged by Witherspoon and Congress "to reverence the Providence of God, and look up to him as the supreme disposer of all events."[13] Even on days of thanksgiving the people were "to confess our manifold sins; to offer up our most fervent supplications to the God of all grace, that it may please Him to pardon our offences, and incline our hearts for the future to keep all his laws . . . and cause the knowledge of God to cover the earth, as the water covers the seas."[14]

In September 1782, Dr. Witherspoon was a member of a three-man congressional committee appointed to consider a petition of support for Philadelphia printer Robert Aitken's translation and printing of the Holy Bible.[15] The committee returned a resolution on September 12, drafted by Witherspoon and approved by Congress, which said: "The United States in Congress assembled, highly approve the pious and laudable undertaking of Mr. Aitken, as subservient to the interest of religion . . . and being satisfied . . . of his care and accuracy in the execution of the work, they recommend this edition of the Bible to the inhabitants of the United States."[16] His efforts on this committee turned out to be among Witherspoon's final acts in Congress. Bibles from England were hard to come by in the autumn of 1782, and with the support of Witherspoon and Congress, Aitken's work became the "first English language Bible published on the North American continent."[17] The Confederation Congress was acting on the prevalent belief that the ready availability of Bibles was an important prerequisite to personal and public happiness, just as they had on March 19 of that year, when they asked God to "make us a holy, that so we may be an happy people."[18]

In the autumn of 1782, Witherspoon delivered what has erroneously been labeled the "Sermon Preached at a Public Thanksgiving After Peace" (it was actually delivered during the War)[19]—a sermon which, like the better-known "Dominion of Providence," captures his thinking on the proper relation between religion and politics. This sermon is particularly interesting because he gave it just after his retirement from Congress, in response to a congressional Thanksgiving Day proclamation he had written himself. The proclamation asked the states to "command" those citizens under their authority to observe a day of "solemn thanksgiving to God for all his mercies" and recommended a "cheerful obedience to his [God's] laws, and . . . the practice of true and undefiled religion, which is the great foundation of public prosperity and national happiness."[20] Witherspoon began his sermon by thanking God for "the goodness of his providence to the United States of America, in the course of a war, which has now lasted seven years," and then suggested that "[t]hose who are vested with *civil authority* ought also, with much care, to promote religion and good morals among all under their government."[21]

In this Thanksgiving Sermon we have one of the clearest examples of the linking of Christian morality, the role of ministers in divine service, and public order. Witherspoon's hearers knew by "sad experience, that the regular administration of divine ordinances, the observation of the Sabbath, and the good order of the country in general, have been much disturbed by the war." Of course, the founders' writings are replete with allusions to the usefulness of religion to the country. But in Witherspoon's Thanksgiving Sermon we see a spelling out of the relationship between true religion and the public order in a more explicit fashion than was customary by the founders. John Adams, for example, may have argued that "[o]ur Constitution was made only for a moral and religious people,"[22] but he seldom elaborated on the precise relationship between religious teaching and public order. Witherspoon, on the other hand, made just such an explicit elaboration in his Thanksgiving Sermon of 1782, and it was clear what was to be expected from clergy and their flocks. Religious leaders were to play a vital role, perhaps even more important than the laws themselves, in a republican society.

> The return which is expected from them to the community is, that by the influence of their religious government, their people may be the more regular citizens, and the more useful members of society. I hope none here will deny, that the manners of the people in general are of the utmost moment to the stability of any civil society. When the body of a people are altogether corrupt in their manners, the government is ripe for dissolution. Good laws may hold the rotten bark some longer together, but in a little time all laws must give way to the tide of popular opinion, and be laid prostrate under universal practice. Hence it clearly follows, that the teachers and rulers of every religious denomination are bound mutually to each other, and to the whole society, to watch over the manners of their several members.[23]

In 1789, after reading a provision in the new Georgia constitution barring ministers from the general assembly, Witherspoon lampooned it in the local broadsheet. Writing ironically in the character of a confused parson, he suggested that the following section be substituted for the one proposed, to clear up certain "ambiguities" in the constitution:

No clergyman, of any denomination, shall be capable of being elected a member of the Senate or House of Representatives, because [here insert the grounds of offensive disqualification, which I have not been able to discover] Provided always, and it is the true intent and meaning of this part of the constitution, that if at any time he shall be completely deprived of the clerical character by those by whom he was invested with it, as by deposition for cursing and swearing, drunkenness or uncleanness, he shall then be fully restored to all the privileges of a free citizen; his offence shall no more be remembered against him; but he may be chosen either to the Senate or House of Representatives, and shall be treated with all the respect due to his *brethren*, the other members of the Assembly.[24]

Once again, Witherspoon leveraged his national clout as a pastor and politician to insist that religion's voice be heard in public councils.

Public Religion

The preceding examples underscore Witherspoon's commitment to a proper role for religion in public life short of establishment, which we might conveniently call "public religion."[25] But his public religion was not the kind of civil theology that Abraham Lincoln contemplated a half-century later, when he suggested that "reverence for the laws" become the "political religion" of the land.[26] Lincoln's political "religion" was, if it can be put this way, a purely secular affair: it was a religion without a god, though Lincoln himself was a deeply religious man in his own way. But to Witherspoon this kind of political religion would not do; in order to be most useful in public affairs, religion had to be rooted in sincere belief in and worship of God. He did occasionally refer to the cause of independence as "sacred"[27] but that is as close as he ever came to Lincoln's brand of civil theology or political religion. He sometimes spoke of "visible religion,"[28] or "the public credit of religion," but Witherspoon more frequently used the phrase "the public interest of religion."

Just what sort of religion was in "the public interest"? This is not a trivial question because, as Gibbon observed, "a prudent magistrate might observe with pleasure and eventually support the progress of a religion which diffused among the people a pure, benevolent, and universal system of ethics, adapted to every duty and every condition of life, recommended as the will and reason of the supreme Deity, and enforced by the sanction of eternal rewards and punishments," regardless of whether it were true or sincerely believed.[29] We ought therefore to ask how Witherspoon, who was a magistrate as well as a minister, defined religion, and whether it mattered to him if the religion were true or if its adherents sincerely believed it.

The only kind that concerned Witherspoon was what he habitually referred to as "true religion." He preferred compound terms such as "true religion" or "true and undefiled religion" to naked "religion," and he supplied precise definitions of those terms. First (and we would expect nothing less from an ordained minister of the gospel), true religion had to be Christian. As he said in the "Dominion of Providence," "[t]here can be no true religion till there be a discovery of your lost state by nature and practice and an unfeigned acceptance of Christ Jesus as he is offered in the gospel."[30] Second, it had to manifest itself in good works. "True religion," he continued, "is nothing else but an inward temper and outward conduct suited to your state and circumstances in providence at any time."[31] True religion thus had both inward and outward components: the inward was the soul's "temper," the outward was the expression of that temper in personal conduct. This understanding of true religion was in keeping with the New Light theology of the day that stressed personal regeneration and held that holy conduct would necessarily accompany saving faith. By true religion, Witherspoon meant something like genuine or sincere religion—a kind of Christianity that was marked by genuine conversion and that changed a person inside and out.

It is not entirely clear, however, that Witherspoon was a thorough-going New Light pastor. According to the memoirs of Aaron Burr, Witherspoon passed off the revival that swept the Princeton campus during his presidency as "not true and rational religion, but fanaticism."[32] And Ebenezer Bradford, a student during the Princeton revival of 1772, wrote to Joseph Bellamy that Witherspoon and Rev. Elihu Spencer were "great enemies to what they call Eastward, or New Divinity. . . . The Dr. has lately been conversed with upon these things since they have made such progress in the College, and declares that he is neither for nor against them; however, he both preaches and converses in contradistinction to them."[33] Bellamy, a Connecticut New Light revivalist and associate of Jonathan Edwards, had written a well-known booklet, *The Nature of True Religion Delineated* (1750), which Witherspoon owned and appears to have read closely. Bellamy wrote that part of being made in the image of God included having a "temper of mind or frame of heart perfectly answerable to the moral law; the moral law being, as it were, a transcript of the moral perfections of God."[34] In his fourth lecture on moral philosophy, Witherspoon concluded that "[t]he result of the whole is, that we ought to take the rule of duty from conscience enlightened by reason, experience, and every way by which we can be supposed to learn the will of our Maker, and his intention in creating us such as we are. And we ought to believe that it is as deeply founded as the nature of God himself, being a transcript of his moral excellence, and that it is productive of the greatest good."[55] While noncommittal (or even skeptical) toward the religious enthusiasm associated with the New Divinity of Edwards and Bellamy, Witherspoon was nevertheless in their camp on matters of theology.

Whenever he spoke of "true religion," and especially when his topic had anything to do with public life, Witherspoon meant orthodox Christianity. I say "orthodox Christianity," and not "Reformed Christianity," because I am not certain that he meant anything more narrow than that. It is a natural temptation to read Reformed Protestantism back into the language of a staunch Calvinist like Witherspoon, but his works do not necessarily warrant it, and there are other facts that suggest the broader meaning. Chiefly, there is his manifest Christian ecumenism. Witherspoon was on good terms with individual Anglicans such as George Whitefield, whom, as we saw, he considered a minister of "great zeal and discernment."[56] More than once he complimented Catholic sects such as the Jansenists, whose "admirable practical treatises" he commended to his divinity students, and this in an age of anti-Catholic bigotry. True, he sometimes used prejudicial-sounding language — he referred to "papists" and "Popery" — but then, what Protestant did not? Witherspoon was more tolerant than most, and he gestured toward increased religious liberty for Roman Catholics: "we ought in general to guard against persecution on a religious account as much as possible . . . . Papists are tolerated in Holland without danger to liberty. And though not properly tolerated, they are now connived at in Britain."[57]

Surprisingly, Witherspoon did not use the word "true" in a way that emphasized the truth of Christianity over other religions, as Montesquieu did in his *Spirit of the Laws*, though Witherspoon certainly assumed its truth, particularly in his sermons.[38] (Montesquieu wrote: "In a country so unfortunate as to have a religion that God has not revealed, it is necessary for it to be agreeable to morality; because even a false religion is the best security we can have of the probity of men.")[39] In his public addresses, Witherspoon focused more on Christian behavior than on the "peculiar distinctions" of doctrine that divide sects when defining true religion. Put differently, he often stressed universal Christian *practice* rather than the deep and frequently divisive fine points of *faith.* "Do not suppose, my brethren," he preached in the "Dominion of Providence," "that I mean to recommend a furious and angry zeal for the circumstantials of religion, or the contentions of one sect with another about their peculiar distinctions. I do not wish you to oppose anybody's religion, but everybody's wickedness. Perhaps there are few surer marks of the reality of religion than when a man feels himself more joined in spirit to a true holy person of a different denomination, than to an irregular liver of his own."[40]

Lines such as these give the impression that Witherspoon felt brotherly affection for any Christian who was sincere of heart and a "regular liver," regardless of denomination. Yet we should not infer that he ranked faith or doctrine, in an absolute sense, lower than practice, or that he had a merely instrumental view of Christianity. Of course, Witherspoon did think true religion was useful: on one occasion he told an audience, "[b]e assured that true religion is the way to health, peace, opulence and public esteem."[41] On another, he claimed that Christianity was "the great polisher of the common people."[42] It was not uncommon for eighteenth-century thinkers to speak of the common folk as needing "polishing"; the Tory (and religious skeptic) David Hume referred to commerce, rather than Witherspoon's religion, as the great polisher of the common folk.[43]

Witherspoon could also sound a little like his heterodox colleague Benjamin Franklin at times. Franklin was an unconcealed skeptic when it came to Reformed doctrine, and he valued Christianity exclusively for the good behavior it produced. In the *Autobiography,* Franklin used language nearly identical to Witherspoon's about "peculiar doctrines" and sects to record his disgust at a Presbyterian pastor's preaching, because "his discourses were chiefly either polemic arguments, or explications of the peculiar doctrines of our sect, and were all to me very dry, uninteresting, and unedifying, since not a single moral principle was inculcated or enforced, their aim seeming to be rather to make us Presbyterians than good citizens."[44]

But unlike Franklin, Witherspoon continually brought his audiences back to the state of their own souls, despite his emphasis on Christian behavior. Even in the "Dominion of Providence," which was preached on an explicitly political occasion, Witherspoon reminded his listeners that the eternal state of their souls was to be their crucial concern. Important as the political questions of the day were (and in May of 1776 they were important indeed), still Witherspoon had to ask, "is it of less moment my brethren whether you shall be the heirs of glory or the heirs of hell?"[45] In less political settings he was even more emphatic about the centrality of individual salvation and the importance of right doctrine. Lecturing divinity students at

Princeton, the president insisted that "[r]eligion is the grand concern to us all, as we are men;—whatever be our calling and profession, the salvation of our souls is the one thing needful."[46] In sum, Witherspoon left behind a good working definition of true religion: sincere, orthodox Christianity that results in virtuous behavior.

He supplied an equally explicit definition of the public interest of religion in the "Dominion of Providence." "Suffer me to recommend to you an attention to the public interest of religion, or in other words, *zeal for the glory of God and the good of others.* I have already endeavored to exhort sinners to repentance; what I have here in view is to point out to you the concern which every good man ought to take in the national character and manners, and the means which he ought to use for promoting public virtue; and bearing down impiety and vice."[47] Here again, Witherspoon emphasized the public or "visible" nature of religion by recasting the two tablets of the Decalogue as "the glory of God and the good of others." Having exhorted his listeners to attend to the private or individual component of religion, that is, to the state of their own souls, he then turned to the public or corporate component—the "public interest" of religion. True religion must have a keen interest in "the national character and manners," and its role must be nothing less than the promotion of public virtue and the prevention of public vice. Profanity, impiety, and "immorality of every kind" must be ridden down *for the political good of the republic.* "Nothing is more certain than that a general profligacy and corruption of manners make a people ripe for destruction. A good form of government may hold the rotten materials together for some time, but beyond a certain pitch, even the best constitution will be ineffectual, and slavery must ensue. On the other hand, when the manners of a nation are pure, when true religion and internal principles maintain their vigour, the attempts of the most powerful enemies to oppress them are commonly baffled and disappointed."[48]

It was axiomatic for Witherspoon, and in fact for nearly all the founders, that virtue *and therefore religion* were necessary conditions for republican government. This was so because virtue was thought to be necessary for maintaining republican liberty, and religion in turn was thought to be necessary for virtue. "[I]f we go to the history of mankind," Witherspoon said, "we shall find that . . . the knowledge of divine truth . . . certainly is the way to virtue."[49] In a protracted section of the Thanksgiving Sermon (1782), he elaborated on what he had said in the "Dominion of Providence" concerning the place that virtue, and hence religion, had in holding a republic together.

It is a truth of no little importance to us in our present situation, not only that the manners of a people are of consequence to the stability of every civil society, but that they are of much more consequence to free states, than to those of a different kind. In many of these last, a principle of honour, and the subordination of ranks, with the vigour of despotic authority, supply the place of virtue, by restraining irregularities and producing public order. But in free states, where the body of the people have the supreme power properly in their own hands, and must be ultimately resorted to on all great matters, if there be a general corruption of manners, there can be nothing but confusion. So true is this, that civil liberty cannot be long preserved without virtue. A monarchy may subsist for ages, and be better or worse under a good or bad prince, but a republic once equally poised, must either preserve its virtue or lose its liberty.[50]

It was religion, and especially the virtues that flow from true religion, that gave vigor to the republic.

Let us endeavour to bring into, and keep in credit and reputation, everything that may serve to give vigour to an equal republican constitution. Let us cherish a love of piety, order, industry, frugality. Let us check every disposition to luxury, effeminacy, and the pleasures of a dissipated life. . . . And in our families let us do the best by religious instruction, to sow the seeds which may bear fruit in the next generation. We are one of the body of confederated States. For many reasons I shall avoid making any comparisons at present, but may venture to predict, that whatsoever State among us shall continue to make piety and virtue the standard of public honour, will enjoy the greatest inward peace, the greatest national happiness, and in every outward conflict will discover the greatest constitutional strength.[51]

"Piety, order, industry, frugality": here is a longhand version of what, since Max Weber, has been called the Protestant work ethic.[52] But Witherspoon was certainly not alone in linking these virtues together in such a way. John Adams, who was descended from a long line of Puritans and continued to adhere to the Protestant social ethic despite moving toward Unitarianism in his personal theology, proposed the following thought experiment. "Suppose a nation," he wrote, "in some distant region should take the Bible for their only law-book, and every member should regulate his conduct by the precepts there exhibited! Every member would be obliged, in conscience, to temperance and frugality and industry; to justice and kindness and charity toward his fellow men; and to piety, love, and reverence, towards Almighty God. In this commonwealth, no man would impair his health by gluttony, drunkenness, or lust; no man would sacrifice his most precious time to cards or any other trifling and mean amusement."[53] Adams also included a moralistic section in his draft of the Massachusetts constitution of 1780, in which he made it the "duty" of the Massachusetts legislature to inculcate "industry and frugality, honesty and punctuality" in the people.[54] Franklin, too, coupled industry and frugality, although at times he omitted piety: "[t]he way to Wealth is as plain as the Way to Market. It depends chiefly on two words, *Industry* and *Frugality*."

By insisting that religion was a necessary condition for republican government, Witherspoon was swimming in the mainstream of eighteenth-century American political thought. We can again turn to John Adams for support. "Statesmen," he wrote, "may plan and speculate for liberty, but it is religion and morality alone, which can establish the principles upon which freedom can securely stand. The only foundation of a free constitution is pure virtue."[55] George Washington was more explicit still in connecting virtue to religion. In a familiar section of the Farewell Address, we find: "[o]f all the dispositions and habits which lead to political prosperity, Religion and morality are indispensable supports. . . . And let us with caution indulge the supposition, that morality can be maintained without religion."[56] (Historian Fred Hood has even written that an "amazing similarity" of language between Hamilton's draft of the Farewell Address and Witherspoon's Lectures on Moral Philosophy makes the influence of the Lectures on that address "immediately apparent.")[57] In this regard, Witherspoon was typical of not only the political founders but of American Presbyterians as well. The Presbytery of Hanover, Virginia, acknowledged in 1784 that

> it is absolutely necessary to the existence and welfare of every political combination of men in society, to have the support of religion and its solemn institutions, as affecting the conduct of rational beings more than human laws can possibly do. On this account it is wise policy in legislators to seek its alliance and solicit aid in a civil view, because of its happy influence upon the morality of its citizens. . . . It is upon this principle alone, in our opinion, that a legislative body has a right to interfere in religion at all, and of consequence we suppose that this interference ought only to extend to the preserving of the public worship

of the Deity, and the supporting of institutions for inculcating the great fundamental principles of all religion, without which society could not easily exist.[58]

Witherspoon's formulation of the relationship between religion and republicanism was typical of the thinking of nearly all the founders, even the heterodox such as Washington. His formulation might be put this way: no republic without liberty, no liberty without virtue, and no virtue without religion. The Continental Congress itself found it appropriate "humbly to approach the throne of Almighty God" to ask "that he would establish the independence of these United States upon the basis of religion and virtue."[59] Still, by insisting that "true religion" meant orthodox Christianity, Witherspoon was nearer the right bank of the mainstream, to push that watery metaphor a bit further, than the political elite like Adams and Washington. On this particular point, Witherspoon was closer to the sentiments of the Antifederalist Charles Turner, who was careful to emphasize that "without the prevalence of *Christian piety and morals,* the best republican Constitution can never save us from slavery and ruin."[60]

Not only was religion a necessary support of republican government, for Witherspoon it was more important even than acts of the legislature. The public credit of religion was "more powerful than the most sanguinary laws."[61] Because he considered religion such an indispensable and powerful support of a republic, Witherspoon recommended that "[m]agistrates . . . are called to use their authority and influence for the glory of God and the good of others."[62] Those civil authorities who "would have their authority both respected and useful, should begin at the source, and reform or restrain that impiety towards God, which is the true and proper cause of every disorder among men."[63] In fact, so important was religion in Witherspoon's estimation that he could say, "[w]hoever is an avowed enemy to God, I scruple not to call him an enemy to his country."[64] Such a conclusion shocks the modern ear, but it is understandable (if not acceptable) given the premise with which he began, namely, that religion is a necessary and healthy support of republican government. Besides, the belief that civil magistrates should have power to advance true religion and punish impiety had an ancient pedigree in Reformed Scottish thought. The Scotch Confession of Faith (1560) contained an article that read, "to . . . Magistrates, we affirm that chiefly and most principally the conservation and purgation of the Religion appertains; so that not only they are appointed for Civil policy, but also for maintenance of the true Religion, and for suppressing of Idolatry and Superstition

whatsoever."[65] Washington himself came to a similar conclusion in the Farewell Address, warning: "[i]n vain would that man claim the tribute of Patriotism, who should labor to subvert these great Pillars of human happiness
[religion and morality], these firmest props of the duties of Men and citizens."[66] If, as Witherspoon claimed, religion is critical to the survival of free
government, it is no wonder that he would grant civil authorities a hand in
promoting piety or at least in preventing impiety.

This was his conclusion in the fourteenth of his Lectures on Moral Philosophy, on "Jurisprudence," in which he took up the thorny issue of church-
state interaction. Witherspoon's first preliminary remark regarding jurisprudence, or "the method of enacting and administering civil laws," was that
"a constitution is excellent, when the spirit of the civil laws is such as to have
a tendency to prevent offences and make men good, as much as to punish
them when they do evil." This in turn begs the question, "what can be done
by law to make the people of any state virtuous?" Since "virtue and piety are
inseparably connected, then to promote true religion is the best and most
effectual way of making a virtuous and regular people." "Love to God, and
love to man, is the substance of religion; when these prevail, civil laws will
have little to do." But this is too easy: it sidesteps "a very important disquisition, how far the magistrate ought to interfere in matters of religion." That
disquisition is supremely important because "[r]eligious sentiments are very
various — and we have given it as one of the perfect rights in natural liberty,
and which ought not to be alienated even in society, that every one should
judge for himself in matters of religion."[67]

Like the authors of the Westminster Confession before him, and James
Madison after him, Witherspoon always acknowledged that the conscience
must be left free. The Westminster divines had written that "God alone
is lord of the conscience";[68] Madison quoted the Virginia Declaration of
Rights of 1776 in his Memorial and Remonstrance to illustrate that "the
Religion then of every man must be left to the conviction and conscience of
every man; and it is the right of every man to exercise it as these may dic-
tate."[69] Madison also sounded eerily like Witherspoon's Presbyterian colleagues in Hanover in his Memorial. Arguing against religious establishments, he wrote, "[w]ho does not see that the same authority which can
establish Christianity, in exclusion of all other Religions, may establish with
the same ease any particular sect of Christians, in exclusion of all other
Sects?"[70] The Presbytery of Hanover had sent up a petition in 1776 arguing against establishment, to this effect: "[c]ertain it is, that every argu-

ment for civil liberty, gains additional strength when applied to liberty in the concerns of religion; and there is no argument in favor of establishing the Christian religion, but what may be pleaded, with equal propriety, for establishing the tenets of Mahomed [*sic*] by those who believe the Alcoran."[71] Thus, Madison echoed a position long held by Witherspoon and other Presbyterians, namely, that the church did not need or want government establishment.

Still, for Witherspoon, non-establishment and liberty of conscience left room for civil magistrates to promote religion and even to "make public provision for the worship of God." There were three "particulars" that civil magistrates were free to do regarding the promotion of public religion without violating individual religious liberty. "(1.) The magistrate (or ruling part of any society) ought to encourage piety by his own example, and by endeavoring to make it an object of public esteem. . . . Magistrates may promote and encourage men of piety and virtue, and they may discountenance those whom it would be improper to punish. (2.) The magistrate ought to defend the rights of conscience, and tolerate all in their religious sentiments that are not injurious to their neighbors." As if to underscore the point, Witherspoon even argued for toleration of a sect (such as Catholics) that was thought to hold "tenets subversive of society and inconsistent with the rights of others" on the grounds that such sects perhaps "are never dangerous, but when they are oppressed."[72] But freedom of conscience did not mean freedom to *act* in any way sects or individuals pleased. "(3.) The magistrate may enact laws for the punishment of acts of profanity and impiety. The different sentiments of men in religion, ought not by any means to encourage or give a sanction to such acts as any of them count profane." Then, smuggled in between two numbered points about toleration, came the strongest accommodationist statement he ever made:

> Many are of opinion, that besides all this, the magistrate ought to make public provision for the worship of God, in such manner as is agreeable to the great body of the society; though at the same time all who dissent from it are fully tolerated. And indeed there seems to be a good deal of reason for it, that so instruction may be provided for the bulk of common people, who would, many of them, neither support nor employ teachers, unless they were obliged. The magistrate[']s right in this case seems to be something like that of a parent, they have a right to instruct, but not to constrain.[73]

This was a subtle position to hold, neither wholly separationist nor wholly accommodationist, to use the rhetoric of present-day church and state controversies. For Witherspoon the relationship between civil government and religious piety was crucial, and the two could be balanced so that the demands of public order and individual conscience could both be satisfied without doing violence to either. His stress on the importance of piety helps explain why Witherspoon objected so vigorously to John Adams's nomination of Thomas Paine for secretary of the Committee on Foreign Affairs in 1777. Witherspoon, a member of the Committee, accused Paine, who had mocked original sin and other doctrines of orthodox Christianity in *Common Sense*, of having "bad character" and questionable patriotism. But this was not just prejudice from a sanctimonious cleric. Paine had in fact struck out several pro-colonial passages from Witherspoon's political essays as editor of the *Pennsylvania Magazine*, claiming they were "too free"; and Witherspoon had, despite its anti-Christian passages, defended the political arguments of *Common Sense*, showing that he, for one, knew how to separate religion and politics.[74] Besides, by 1805 Adams had come round to Witherspoon's opinion of Paine, and with a vengeance: "I do not know whether any man in the world has had more influence on its inhabitants or affairs for the last thirty years than Tom Paine. There can be no severer satire on the age. For such a mongrel between pig and puppy, begotten by a wild boar on a bitch wolf, never before in any age of the world was suffered by the poltroonery of mankind, to run through such a career of mischief."[75]

But for all of his recommendations that magistrates "use their authority for the glory of God" and "reform and restrain impiety," Witherspoon was no theocrat. Nor does his talk of making "public provision for the worship of God" prove that he advocated "active state support of Protestant Christianity," as one commentator has claimed,[76] let alone any sort of establishment, as others have claimed.[77] To begin with the obvious, Witherspoon did not stipulate "Protestant Christianity," only public worship that was agreeable to the "great body of the people." Presumably this could have meant Roman Catholicism in the case of Maryland, a historically Catholic colony, or other traditions at more local levels such as counties or townships. Furthermore, "public provision for the worship of God" could admit of any number of government actions, all short of promoting Protestantism or any sectarian version of Christianity whatever. Witherspoon himself wrote three recommendations for days of prayer and thanksgiving on behalf of the Continental Congress that were so nonsectarian that none even mentioned Christ by name. This sort of public provision for worship through religious proclamations is a far cry from establishment, and in fact it was engaged in by Thomas Jefferson and James Madison at the state level, and by Madison at the federal level, as we shall see.

Witherspoon held the axiomatic view of his day that republican government and civil liberty (as he said in the Thanksgiving Sermon) relied on religion for their very existence. But then he turned the proposition back on itself and argued that religion relied on civil liberty as well. The two had in fact been so closely related throughout history that they were nearly inseparable. "The knowledge of God and his truths have from the beginning of the world been chiefly, if not entirely, confined to those parts of the earth where some degree of liberty and political justice were to be seen . . . . There is not a single instance in history in which civil liberty was lost, and religious liberty preserved entire."[78] (One can hear a faint echo of Rousseau, who claimed in the *Social Contract* that "[t]hose who distinguish between civil and theological intolerance are mistaken, in my opinion. Those two types of intolerance are inseparable.")[79] When we examine history, Witherspoon insisted, we find that "knowledge of divine truth . . . has been spread by liberty."[80] The two liberties, in other words, are not so easy to separate in practice as they may be in theory. That is why he ended the "Dominion of Providence" with a prayer that "God grant that in America true religion and civil liberty may be inseparable, and that the unjust attempts to destroy the one, may in the issue tend to the support and establishment of both."[81] A convenient way of stating Witherspoon's position on church and state or religious and civil liberty would be that the two were theoretically distinct but practically indistinguishable.

Good Presbyterian that he was, Witherspoon agreed with the Westminster Confession of Faith that "God alone is Lord of the conscience,"[82] and indeed he had repeated that language when he drafted the Introduction to the Form of the Government of the Presbyterian Church in the United States. The Form of the Government (1788) read as follows: "The Synod of New-York and Philadelphia are unanimously of opinion[:] I. That 'God alone is Lord of the conscience; and' . . . they consider the rights of private judgement, in all matters that respect religion, as universal and alienable [*sic*]: They do not even wish to see any religious constitution aided by the civil power, further than may be necessary for protection and security, and, at the same time, equal and common to all others."[83] Witherspoon therefore had no desire to see any particular Christian denomination, even his own, formally established as an official religion (in fact he was opposed to establishment of the Anglican Church throughout the colonies), because such an establishment would violate dissenters' rights of conscience. He did not take this to mean, however, that the state could play *no role whatever* in promoting true religion. Witherspoon acknowledged that there was "a good deal of reason" to suppose that "the magistrate ought to make public provision for the worship of God, in such manner as is agreeable to the great body of the society; though at the same time all who dissent from it are fully tolerated."[84]

For Witherspoon, religion was most powerful as a pre-political or, more properly, a sub-political force. Although sub-political and informal, true religion was more powerful than either the laws or the form of government or, what is the same thing, the constitution. True religion was to act as a sort of leaven, working its healthy influence throughout the political body without benefit of formal establishment but with equal aid and protection from the state.

Witherspoon and Madison

John Witherspoon presented a case for public religion that could have been articulated, and indeed was articulated, by any number of founders; in this respect he was an archetype of the late eighteenth-century political theorist. He used his leverage in religion, politics, and especially education to introduce his theological-political creed to the hundreds of well-placed young men who came within his orbit, and to reinforce that creed in those who had already learned it apart from him. One of those young men, James Madison, went on to a position of unparalleled influence that had far-reaching effects — they are still with us today — for public religion in America. Madison, known as the Father of the Constitution and the Bill of Rights, probably produced the initial draft of what became the First Amendment,[85] and certainly produced the oft-cited Memorial and Remonstrance of 1785 that helped defeat Patrick Henry's bill for the support of Christian ministers in Virginia, along with some of the best-known *Federalist* papers. His public and private actions and correspondence revealed a perennial interest in religion. During his postgraduate sojourn during the autumn and winter of 1771–1772 when he studied Hebrew under Witherspoon, Madison was likely positioning himself for a career in the ministry.[86] His behavior fits a pattern of ministerial candidates of that era: Ebenezer Bradford, who was at Princeton during Madison's time, "remained at Princeton after his graduation to read theology with Witherspoon in preparation for the ministry," and Peter Fish (class of 1774) stayed two extra years to study with the president. (However, Madison himself claimed that it was his ill health as much as anything that convinced him to stay on at Princeton those extra months, "employing his time in miscellaneous studies; but not without a reference to the profession of Law; He availed himself of this opportunity of acquiring a slight knowledge of the Hebrew, which was not among the College Studies.")[87] Madison remained throughout his long life one of the most theologically literate of the early American political figures.[88] A letter to Robert Walsh in 1819 contained a lengthy discussion of religious instruction and the benefits to both clergy and laity of separating church from state;[89] part of the "Detached Memoranda" (1819?) consists of Madison's private ruminations on appointing federal chaplains, issuing religious proclamations, and other activities he engaged in as president.[90] In 1821, at age seventy, he ordered an *Apocryphal New Testament,* and at seventy-five he was still corresponding about the merits of arguments for God's existence.[91] As late as 1833 he wrote Rev. Jasper Adams about the proper relationship between American civil government and "the best & purest religion, the Xn [Christian] religion."[92]

Madison caught his theological bug from Witherspoon, though his evangelical fever appears to have broken by the time he entered public life. As we know, the relationship between President Witherspoon and Madison that began at Princeton seems to have been "unusually strong," as the latter's biographer puts it.[93] Confirmation can be found in a letter from Madison to Jefferson from 1791 (the year of the ratification of the Bill of Rights) in which Madison expressed his dismay at missing Witherspoon at Princeton, where he had made a special trip to see old "Docr. Witherspoon."[94] For his part, Witherspoon told Jefferson: "during the whole time he was under [my] tuition [I] never knew him to do nor to say an improper thing."[95] (Robert Rutland has noted that Madison at least *wrote* some improper things while at Princeton, including ribald verse for the amusement of his fellow Whig Society members.)[96]

Just how indebted Madison was to Witherspoon for his church-state theory is difficult to say precisely. Madison is difficult to pin down on such matters,[97] and he had a flexibility in his political thought and behavior that bordered on inconsistency. For instance, one can ask, Who was the real Madison—the presidential author of religious proclamations, or the private citizen of the "Detached Memoranda" who thought them ill-advised and dangerous to the rights of religious minorities? But as Ralph Ketcham notes, "there is more evidence than might be expected at first glance" regarding Witherspoon's influence on Madison.[98] And at least two recurring themes in Witherspoon's church-state teaching seem to have implanted themselves permanently in his student's mind. The first was a robust notion of religious liberty; the second was a political realism descended from Saint Augustine's, and especially Calvin's, skeptical view of human nature.[99] A third theme of Witherspoon's, that civil magistrates could provide for public worship of God while tolerating dissenters, manifested itself throughout Madison's public career, though he privately repudiated it after his retirement.

Madison left Princeton in the spring of 1772 and returned to his native Virginia, where, for several years, he spun his vocational wheels. But in 1774 he saw Baptists being carted off to jail for preaching in Orange County, which reinforced his appreciation for religious liberty and perhaps stirred his political ambitions. He promptly fired off a letter to his friend and fellow Princetonian William Bradford (later U.S. attorney general), complaining of that "diabolical Hell conceived principle of persecution" at work in his home county.[100] Two years later, Madison was elected to the provincial convention that met in Williamsburg. There, in his first public act, he offered a successful amendment to George Mason's proposed Virginia Declaration of Rights, which replaced Mason's recommendation for religious "*toleration*" with more robust language that declared "the freedom of conscience to be a *natural and absolute* right," as he recounted in his Autobiography.[101] Mason's proposal recommended "that all Men shou'd enjoy the fullest Toleration in the Exercise of Religion"; Madison's initial proposal replaced Mason's phrasing with this fateful language: "all men are equally entitled to enjoy the free exercise of religion."[102]

Madison's substitution of liberty for toleration was quintessential Witherspoon. Recall that Witherspoon had questioned whether religious liberty could even exist without civil liberty, and he scoffed at the notion that ministers should be excluded from political office in Georgia simply because of their vocation. He demanded to know how a religious profession somehow stripped ministers of a civil right in that state.

> Now suffer me to ask this question: Before any man among us was ordained a minister, was he not a citizen of the United States, and if being in Georgia, a citizen of the state of Georgia? Had he not then a right to be elected a member of the assembly, if qualified in point of property? How then has he lost, or why is he deprived of this right? Is it by offense or disqualification? Is it a sin against the public to become a minister? Does it merit that the person who is guilty of it should be immediately deprived of one of his most important rights as a citizen?[103]

Madison was faced with an identical situation in Virginia. Seeing that Thomas Jefferson's draft for a new state constitution barred ministers from holding public office, Madison, like a model Princetonian, asked his mentor, "[d]oes not the exclusion of Ministers of the Gospel as such violate a fundamental principle of liberty by punishing a religious profession with the privation of a civil right? Does it [not] violate another article of the plan itself which exempts religion from the cognizance of Civil power? . . . does it not in fine violate impartiality by shutting the door agst [*sic*] the Ministers of one religion and leaving it open for those of every other."[104]

The modern constitutional scholar Mark DeWolfe Howe has asserted that "the framers of the Constitution," of whom Madison was foremost, "were willing to incorporate some theological presuppositions in the framework of federal government. I find it impossible to deny that such presuppositions did find their way into the Constitution."[105] More to the point, a number of commentators (Lord James Bryce, for one) have remarked that there is a Calvinistic realism, perhaps even pessimism, concerning the frailty of human nature explicit in *The Federalist Papers* and implicit in the Constitution.[106] Such realism seems especially to permeate those numbers — *Federalist* 51, to take an obvious example — written by Madison. In a familiar passage in that essay, Madison, writing as "Publius," insisted: "[a]mbition must be made to counteract ambition. The interest of the man must be connected with the constitutional rights of the place. It may be a reflection on human nature, that such devices should be necessary to control the abuses of government. But what is government itself but the greatest of all reflections on human nature?"[107] To Madison, human nature reflected an unmistakable depravity, that favorite word of the Calvinist. "[T]here is," he wrote, "a degree of depravity in mankind which requires a certain degree of circumspection and distrust."[108] After all, "[i]f men were angels, no government would be necessary."

But men most assuredly are not angels (though neither are they mere brutes, as Hobbes would have us believe). Madison had absorbed the biblical account of human origins, namely, that mankind was created a little lower than the angels and yet raised from the dust of the earth, and he took for granted the mixture of noble and base qualities in human actions. Witherspoon had taught him that although "man now comes into the world in a state of impurity or moral defilement," it is a mistake to conclude that "every act in every part of it is evil," and he warned against going "to an extreme on the one hand or on the other, in speaking of human nature."[109]

Madison internalized this teaching, and as an apologist for the new Constitution, he argued that the trick to constructing a government for men who are tinctured with depravity is to plan for a lack of "better motives":

> In framing a government which is to be administered by men over men, the great difficulty lies in this: you must first enable the government to control the governed; and in the next place oblige it to control itself. A dependence on the people is, no doubt, the primary control on the government; but experience has taught mankind the necessity of auxiliary precautions. This policy of supplying, by opposite and rival interests, the defect of better motives, might be traced through the whole system of human affairs, private as well as public.[110]

The dark underside of human nature must always be kept in mind when ordering a government, especially one that is concerned, as the American constitutional system is, with protecting minority rights. Not to compensate for the evil in human nature would be foolish, because, as Madison glumly admits in *Federalist* 10, "[t]he latent causes of faction are . . . sown in the nature of man."[111] In *Federalist* 51, too, one can feel a reverberation of Witherspoon's doctrine of the interdependence between civil and religious liberty: "[i]n a free government, the security for civil rights must be the same as that for religious rights."[112]

Douglass Adair implies that Madison drew from Witherspoon's Lectures on Moral Philosophy, and the Scottish Enlightenment texts that formed the core of those lectures, his "very early and strong impressions in favor of Liberty both Civil & Religious," as Madison himself put it.[113] In the first of those Lectures, Witherspoon suggested that when considering human nature one was forced toward "a strong presumption of the truth of the Scripture doctrine of the depravity and corruption of our nature."[114] Nor should we forget that in those Lectures Witherspoon had suggested that the magistrate "ought to make public provision for the worship of God," which Madison in fact did as a delegate in Virginia and then as president of the United States. Although we are apt to remember his famous Memorial from 1785 to the exclusion of all else, in October of that year Madison sponsored "A Bill for Appointing Days of Public Fasting and Thanksgiving" in the General Assembly that authorized religious proclamations and also required ministers to "attend and perform divine service and preach a sermon" on days of public fasting and thanksgiving "on pain of forfeiting fifty pounds for every failure."[115]

Years later, as president, Madison issued religious proclamations that were criticized, according to his own account in the "Detached Memoranda" (ca. 1819?), for "using general terms" and for "not inserting particulars according with the faith of certain Xn sects." Perhaps that is why Madison came to regard executive proclamations as "shoots from the same root" as other ill-advised legislative acts, such as congressional chaplaincies, that he also criticized in the Memoranda. "Altho' recommendations only," executive proclamations "imply a religious agency, making no part of the trust delegated to political rulers. . . . They seem to imply and certainly nourish the erronious [*sic*] idea of a *national* religion. The idea just as it related to the Jewish nation under a theocracy, [having] been improperly adopted by so many nations which have embraced Xnity, is too apt to lurk in the bosoms even of Americans, who in general are aware of the distinction between religious & political societies." Thus, the practice of federal executive religious proclamations, "if not strictly guarded naturally terminates in a conformity to the creed of the majority and a single sect, if amounting to a majority."[116]

In Madison's church-state theory, and most especially in his behavior as a public official in Virginia and as president of the United States, the influence of Witherspoon may be discerned. First and foremost, Madison was scrupulous in protecting the liberty of religious minorities. As Witherspoon put it, "one of the most important duties of the magistracy is to protect the rights of conscience," which Madison did consistently throughout his public life. Second, as a Virginia legislator and then as president, Madison provided for public worship without violating the principle of freedom of conscience. Recall that Witherspoon had admitted that it seemed reasonable that "the magistrate ought to make public provision for the worship of God, in such manner as is agreeable to the great body of the society; though at the same time all who dissent from it are fully tolerated." When he issued his presidential proclamations suggesting religious observances, Madison was providing for public worship, and in a way that was so "agreeable to the great body of the society" and nonsectarian that some religious groups criticized him for being too general. (Madison pleaded that he was just following the precedent set by President Washington.) Third, Madison carefully ensured that no theocracy on the model of ancient Israel would ever develop in the United States. Even Americans, he noted, were apt to hanker after a theocracy "just as it related to the Jewish nation under a theocracy," like the liberated children of Israel hungered for the leeks of Egypt. Witherspoon had pointed out in his Lectures on Moral Philosophy that while "[t]he political

law of the Jews contains many noble principles of equity, and excellent examples to future lawgivers; yet it was so local and peculiar, that certainly it
was never intended to be immutable and universal."[117]

Still, Madison was his own man on questions of church-state separation,
and it would be a mistake to think of him as Witherspoon on a wider stage.[118]
It is difficult, for example, to imagine Witherspoon objecting to the general
assessment bill in Virginia, let alone objecting as vehemently as Madison
did. Furthermore, it is doubtful that the bland religious proclamations issued by Madison as president would have struck Witherspoon as "no part
of the trust delegated to political rulers," as the Virginian concluded in his
later years. Nor does it seem likely that Witherspoon would have objected to
congressional chaplains, whose appointment Madison thought a "palpable
violation of equal rights, as well as of Constitutional principles."[119] Although
Madison comes off as the more strict separationist by comparison, the two
men did share a church-state theory that was complex and supple rather than
simple and rigid. Madison's metaphor of a "line of separation"[120] between
church and state was, as one commentator points out, more "subtle" than
Jefferson's blunt image of a wall, and it better acknowledged the "complex
and shifting intersection of church and state."[121] Perhaps Madison would
not have come away from his college years with comparable subtlety had
he studied under a doctrinaire tutor such as Timothy Dwight at Yale, who
wanted explicit religious language in the federal Constitution, instead of
under John Witherspoon at Princeton. And when we consider the realism—
even Puritanical pessimism—in Madison's political thought, we can presume that this attitude was only reinforced by Witherspoon's relentless Calvinism during his years at Princeton.[122]

We can do more than presume in the case of Witherspoon's political theology, which can be reconstructed clearly from his political sermons and
other writings. Witherspoon had a clearly defined and not uncharacteristic
view of public religion during the founding, in which orthodox Christianity
was a necessary condition for republican government, and civil and religious
liberty were mutually dependent. Religion was not only compatible with
republican government, it was also literally indispensable to it, as Washington (and Hamilton, who drafted much of it) said in the Farewell Address. Yet
for all this, Witherspoon was not a theocrat: church and state were to be kept
separate to the extent that no particular denomination was to be established
by law, and the state could not have power over any ecclesiastical body. To
be sure, civil magistrates could encourage religion by example and legiti-
mately could punish profanity and impiety. Certainly there was no reason

why clergy should be forbidden in Georgia—or in Virginia, as Madison pointed out to Jefferson—from holding civil office. Although civil liberty and religious liberty could be separated conceptually, in practice the interests of one were bound to the interests of the other. There was, to use Jefferson's now irresistible phrase, a "wall of separation" between church and state, but for Witherspoon that wall was not "high and impregnable," as the Supreme Court has since held,[123] but low and permeable. In short, Witherspoon subscribed to a sort of theological-political creed in which there could be no civic happiness without holiness, and according to which there was a very definite "public interest of religion."[124]

chapter three

"Plain Common Sense"

Educating Patriots at Princeton

*Nassau Hall. May she again flourish and continue the nursery of
statesmen, as she has been of warriors.*
                                        —Toast raised at Princeton, 1783

*Call upon the rulers of our country to lay the foundations of their
empire in knowledge as well as virtue. . . . Let the law of nature
and nations, the common law of our country, the different systems
of government, history, and everything else connected with the
advancement of republican knowledge and principles, be taught
by able professors.*
                                        —Benjamin Rush, 1786

Second only to religion, the founders believed in the importance of education to the success of their American experiment in self-
government. Of course to men of their generation, religion and education
went hand-in-glove, and we need look no further than the Northwest Ordinance of 1787 for proof of that. Article III of the Ordinance (the third
of our Organic Laws) states: "Religion, morality, and knowledge, being necessary to good government and the happiness of mankind, schools and
the means of education shall forever be encouraged."[1] Thus, the founders
viewed religion (which produced morality) and education as the two legs
that would support the formal structure of the government. They may not

all have been as dewy-eyed as Jefferson ("Enlighten the people generally, and tyranny and oppressions of body and mind will vanish like evil spirits at the dawn of day"),[2] but they all believed that education was vitally important.

Their belief found collective expression in a proposal at the Constitutional Convention to "establish and provide for a national University at the Seat of the Government of the United States,"[3] and in individual founders such as George Washington and Benjamin Rush. We associate Washington more with actions than with thought, and yet he spent considerable energy in the last decade of his life futilely advocating creation of a national university. Washington suggested, in his final annual message to Congress (1796), in letters to Jefferson (1795) and Hamilton (1796), and even in his will (1799),[4] erecting a university on the Potomac where students could learn the moral and intellectual virtues necessary in a republic by reading books and observing public figures. In short, he wanted a distinctly American institution where future statesmen could obtain "political education in the principles and practice of self-government: the same kind of education he had given himself."[5] Rush, another booster of the national university (and of Witherspoon), even suggested a curriculum.

> We have changed our forms of government, but it remains yet to effect a revolution in our principles, opinions, and manners so as to accommodate them to the forms of government we have adopted. This is the most difficult part of the business of patriots and legislators of our country. . . . Call upon the rulers of our country to lay the foundations of their empire in *knowledge* as well as virtue. . . . Let us have colleges in each of the states, and one federal university under the patronage of Congress, where the youth of all the states may be melted (as it were) together into one mass of citizens after they have acquired the first principles of knowledge in the colleges of their respective states. Let the law of nature and nations, the common law of our country, the different systems of government, history, and everything else connected with the advancement of republican knowledge and principles, be taught by able professors in this university. This plan of general education alone will render the American Revolution a blessing to mankind.[6]

But the efforts of the founders fell stillborn, and there never has been a de jure national university. There was, however, a de facto one during the founding, and it was the College of New Jersey under John Witherspoon.

The early trustees of the College expressed their desire that "[t]hough our great intention was to erect a seminary for educating ministers of the Gospel, yet we hope it will be a means of raising up men that will be useful in other learned professions—ornaments of the State as well as the Church. Therefore we propose to make the plan of education as extensive as our circumstances will admit."[7] Princeton was ideally situated to realize such a desire. Midway between the northern and southern colonies, the College of New Jersey was not easily identifiable with the religious zeal that ignited the First Great Awakening in Massachusetts and Connecticut, or the Anglicanism and secular philanthropy that respectively characterized Virginia and Georgia, for example. New Jersey itself had never had an established religion, and the founders of the College incorporated the principle of nonestablishment and even cited the New Jersey charter of 1664 in their own charter of 1746. Since "no Freeman within the said Province of New Jersey, should at any Time be molested, punished, disquieted, or Called in Question for any difference in opinion or practice in matters of Religious Concernment, who do not actually disturb the civil Peace of the said Province," the Princeton founders "have also expressed their earnest Desire that those of every Religious Denomination may have free and Equal Liberty and Advantage of Education in the Said College."[8]

Witherspoon himself played up the nonsectarian nature of the College in his "Address to the Inhabitants of Jamaica, and other West-India Islands, in Behalf of the College of New-Jersey" (1772): "[t]his college was founded, and hath been conducted upon the most catholic principles. . . . Accordingly there are now, and have been from the beginning, scholars of various denominations from the most distant colonies," some of whose religious affiliations Witherspoon did not even know or care to know.[9] Under his leadership, Princeton became the most nationally minded of the nine colleges in existence by 1776. Evidence of this is found in the 1771 Commencement address, an epic poem with an equally epic title, "The Rising Glory of America." Jointly written by Philip Freneau, the future "father of American poetry," and Hugh Henry Brackenridge, it was delivered by Brackenridge before James Madison and his graduating classmates.[10] What is significant about the address is its national scope (it was not, after all, an "Ode to Nassau Hall" or about "The Rising Glory of the Jerseys")—a scope that was encouraged by Witherspoon and the general climate at the College.

Witherspoon made the most of Princeton's fortunate location and circumstances, so that at the end of the Revolution he was able to realize the hopes of the early trustees. By 1783 toasts were being offered to "Nassau

Hall. May she again flourish and continue the nursery of statesmen, as she has been of warriors."[11] We have already seen the extraordinary list of Witherspoon's protégés in public office. Reflecting on that record in 1896, Woodrow Wilson concluded that the College seemed "a seminary of statesmen rather than a quiet seat of academic learning" during the founding.[12] In fact, it is safe to say that no single educator in early America matched Witherspoon's record of making politicians and patriots.

Witherspoon fed his developing politicians a curriculum laced with republican theory, and he also led by example — precisely the combination that Washington had suggested for a national university. He had always insisted that "[e]xample is itself the most powerful and successful instruction; and example is necessary to give meaning and influence to all other instruction."[13] Yet throughout his years of public service, Witherspoon always reserved a good part of his considerable energies for teaching and the administration of the College because he shared the founders' lofty view of the importance of education for future statesmen. We would know this even if he had not said so in plain language: his entire life in America, twenty-six years in all, was spent as the president of the College of New Jersey, although in his later years as his health declined he had half of his salary paid to Samuel Stanhope Smith (1751–1819),[14] who was in effect his co-president. Writing to recruit students from the West Indies in 1772, Witherspoon appealed to their sense of public duty: "[higher education] is also of acknowledged necessity to those who do not wish to live for themselves alone, but would apply their talents to the service of the Public and the good of mankind. Education is therefore of equal importance, in order either to enjoy life with dignity and elegance, or employ it to the benefit of society in offices of power or trust."[15] Even while sitting in the Continental Congress during the War years, Witherspoon continued to direct the College, never missing a Board of Trustees meeting, presiding over every Commencement, and returning to Princeton at every opportunity.[16] Perhaps his most permanent and wide-reaching contribution as president of the College was the Lectures on Moral Philosophy, whose influence on early American political thought (and practice) is difficult to overestimate.

The Lectures on Moral Philosophy

Witherspoon was not the first professor to teach moral philosophy in the colonies, or even at the College of New Jersey. Moral philosophy — a catchphrase for political theory, political economy, ethics, formal philosophy, and jurisprudence — was introduced into the curriculum under Witherspoon's predecessor, Samuel Finley.[17] However, the "distinction of being the first college head in America to set forth in his classroom lectures a definite *system* of ethics" rightly belongs to Witherspoon.[18] The creation of the Lectures on Moral Philosophy was done, like so much else in his life, under the pressure of time. It was primarily for this reason that he relied heavily on the *System of Moral Philosophy* of Francis Hutcheson, his old liberal rival from the Scottish kirk and chair of moral philosophy at Glasgow. The Lectures thus occupy an odd position in the Witherspoon corpus: they are among the best-known and most important of his writings, yet the least original and least polished. The Lectures read less like a full-blown treatise on moral philosophy than lecture notes, which in fact they were. (In this respect they were like Aristotle's *Politics*, which some modern scholars believe were used in a similar fashion.) Through them, he introduced concepts and arguments and then proceeded to move "off text" into more detailed discussions and give-and-take with his students. This accounts for the sometimes cryptic references in the Lectures, such as "They are also very apt to choose a favorite and vest him with such power as overthrows their own liberty, — examples, Athens and Rome,"[19] which obviously mark points that Witherspoon intended to backfill with more detail.

The Lectures were delivered by the president annually to Princeton upperclassmen and were considered the capstone of their education. Ashbel Green, who had studied under Witherspoon, recounts that in addition to working through them in the classroom, each member of the senior class copied out his own set of Lectures from a master manuscript[20] that was "required to be accurately studied, and every leading idea fixed in the memory. Then at recitation, which was always taken by the author himself," extemporaneous additions "enlivened by anecdotes and remarks" were made by Witherspoon. "These enlargements, at the time of recitation were indeed often very considerable, and exceedingly interesting."[21] Although on the whole they are written in a style that is logical and succinct, Witherspoon never intended the Lectures for publication, and in fact threatened to prosecute a publisher who planned to bring out an unauthorized edition.[22] Thus, the Lectures remained in manuscript form until Green himself edited the first compilation of Witherspoon's *Works* in 1800–1801.

The Lectures on Moral Philosophy are arranged into sixteen numbered lectures and one "Recapitulation," which concludes with a brief bibliographical essay on various writers, including some of "the chief writers upon government and politics."[23] The subject matter of the Lectures moves, as the chapters of this book move, from analyses of what might be called pre-political or sub-political structures to more formal political arrangements. Lecture I introduces the students to moral philosophy, "that branch of Science which treats of the principles and laws of Duty or Morals. It is called *Philosophy*, because it is an inquiry into the nature and grounds of moral obligation by reason, as distinct from revelation" and is "nothing else but the knowledge of human nature."[24] In other words, this was to be no course on systematic theology—there were Lectures on Divinity for that. Still, the pious student need not be alarmed: "If the Scripture is true, the discoveries of reason cannot be contrary to it; and therefore, it has nothing to fear from that quarter. And as we are certain it can do no evil, so there is a probability that it may do much good." After the introduction, Witherspoon divided the remaining Lectures between "Ethics and Politics," the "two great branches" of moral philosophy.[25] Lectures II through V deal with human nature and the relation of virtue to government; Lectures VI through IX deal with ethics; Lectures X through XIII consider politics (individual lectures are titled "Of Politics," "Of Civil Society," and "Of the Law of Nature and Nations"); Lectures XIV through XVI are on jurisprudence ("Jurisprudence" and "Of Oaths and Vows"); and the seventeenth is the "Recapitulation" and abbreviated bibliography.

Jack Scott, editor of the best, and annotated, edition of the *Lectures,* has conclusively demonstrated Witherspoon's indebtedness to Hutcheson's *System of Moral Philosophy* in both structure and content, while noting that Witherspoon did not copy it "slavishly."[26] Of course, the danger in tracing the sources of such intellectual rivers is that the headwaters are almost impossible to find. In the case of Hutcheson's *System,* for example, its own outline is nearly identical to Samuel von Pufendorf's *On the Law of Nature and Nations,*[27] and we can suppose that Pufendorf himself did not conjure up his own moral philosophy out of nothing. For our purposes, more important than tracing precisely who got what philosophical tidbit from whom are the harmonies between the Scottish and American moral philosophies, and Witherspoon's central role in producing what Thomas Jefferson called the "harmonizing sentiments of the day" in America.

Some of the most important sentiments of that day were belief in a "moral sense," a qualified optimism in the new methods of science, a bias toward pragmatism, and a predilection for republican self-government. All of these sentiments were driven home in Witherspoon's Lectures on Moral Philosophy, and in fact Benjamin Rush likely had his friend's Lectures in mind when he suggested a national curriculum to include "the law of nature and nations, the common law of our country, the different systems of government, history, and everything else connected with the advancement of republican knowledge and principles." And well he might have: not only were they the first presidential lectures of their kind in the colonies, but also, more important, through them Witherspoon almost single-handedly gave a philosophy to the embryonic nation and helped transform a generation of young idealists into hardheaded politicians of the first rank.

The Scottish Philosophy

When he stepped onto the Philadelphia wharf in 1768, John Witherspoon brought with him a mind that was almost perfectly suited to the pragmatic, empirical American intellectual and political temper. His philosophical training in Scotland had given him premises and a method that led him to conclusions in moral anthropology identical to those drawn by his American colleagues like Jefferson, who arrived at radically different conclusions in religion. Trained at the University of Edinburgh at a time when the Scottish universities were arguably the best in the English-speaking world (Franklin considered the Edinburgh faculty "a set of as truly great Professors of the several branches of knowledge, as have ever appeared in any age or Country"),[28] Witherspoon had cut his intellectual teeth on the philosophy of the Scottish Enlightenment. That philosophical tradition—committed to the methods of natural science as well as to empirical and experiential theories of knowledge, and distrustful of metaphysical speculations—actually helped fit Witherspoon and his students for productive American careers. His version of the Scottish philosophy, which, as we will see, was an amalgam of the Scottish moral and common sense philosophies, made excellent grounding for an American career in politics. Certain tenets of the Scottish philosophy that Witherspoon held and taught helped transform him from an apolitical cleric and educator into a practical American politician. Those tenets gave him a moral epistemology identical to that of other founders, particularly Jefferson, which in turn opened political doors to him and his students in the infant republic. His unique and powerful position in the colonies allowed Witherspoon to become the principal transatlantic aqueduct of the Scottish Enlightenment philosophy into early America.[29]

Because the term "Scottish Enlightenment" has at times been used in a simplistic way, perhaps a brief tour of that philosophical terrain is called for. In reality, the period of Scottish history that spanned the century and a half beginning about 1725 and crested in the last half of the eighteenth century was a rich and varied intellectual and cultural movement. The Scottish Enlightenment included a wide array of achievements in different fields: the political economy of Adam Smith (1723–1790); the powerful skeptical epistemology of David Hume (1711–1776); the common sense realism of Hume's prime philosophical opponents Thomas Reid (1710–1796) and Dugald Stewart (1753–1828); Hugh Blair's (1718–1800) ubiquitous treatises on rhetoric; the work of James Boswell (1740–1795) and Robert Burns (1759–1796) in belles lettres; and the architecture of Robert Smith (d. 1777), who emigrated to America where he designed Carpenter's Hall in Philadelphia, a house for Benjamin Franklin, and President Witherspoon's home on the Princeton campus.[30] Possibly the crowning achievement of the Scottish Enlightenment as a whole, the *Encyclopaedia Britannica*, appeared in 1768 (the year of Witherspoon's emigration) in three volumes, the first of which began with the words, "Utility ought to be the principal intention of every publication."[31]

The formal philosophy of the Scottish Enlightenment, including its epistemology, was likewise diverse, although there were two distinct schools. The first was the moral sense school of Francis Hutcheson (1694–1746), the second the common sense school of Thomas Reid and his pupil Dugald Stewart. Hume, the towering intellect of the Scottish Enlightenment, does not fit readily into either movement, although he is sometimes referred to as a moral sense philosopher. The common sense school arose as a direct challenge to Hume's epistemological skepticism.

While the Englishman Anthony Cooper (third Earl of Shaftesbury, 1671–1713) was perhaps the originator of the moral sense school, it was Hutcheson who formulated the arguments with the greatest force and whose philosophy was adopted — and adapted — by Witherspoon and channeled to his Princeton students. Hutcheson was a third-generation Presbyterian minister and professor of moral philosophy at the University of Glasgow from 1730 until his death in 1746. His lectures on moral philosophy were brought out posthumously as *A System of Moral Philosophy* (1755), and, as noted earlier, it was upon the foundation of this work that Witherspoon built his own Lectures on Moral Philosophy. Hutcheson taught that all persons are endowed by their Creator with a faculty, the "moral sense," by which they apprehend moral distinctions and discern virtue from vice. The deliverances of this sense are sentiments or feelings, and when we see virtuous acts we experience feelings of pleasure or approval; when we see vicious acts we feel pain or disapproval. Moral judgments are therefore made by consulting these sentiments, although they are not relativistic. Hutcheson was careful to avoid the moral relativism that could follow from a too-close association of morality with individual feelings, by grounding the distinction between good and evil on God's will. Thus, virtuous acts are not virtuous because they please; they please because they are virtuous. And since God in his providence has made us to be pleased by virtue and repulsed by vice, our feelings can be a reliable guide to morality, provided our moral sense does not fail, like our other physical senses sometimes do. And most important for American political thought: proper moral judgments can be made by anyone with a properly functioning moral sense, and they do not require an extraordinary intellect or clever reasoning. In short, the moral sense is a militantly *democratic* one; moral judgments are self-evident and, to the extent that we all share this faculty, we are all created equal.[32]

Roughly a generation after Hutcheson, Thomas Reid founded what is called the common sense school of Scottish philosophy. Reid, like Hutcheson, was a Presbyterian minister and an able philosopher who succeeded Adam Smith as chair of moral philosophy at Glasgow in 1764. While he accepted the notion of a moral sense, Reid stressed the rational component of that sense more heavily than had his predecessor. The primary purpose of Reid's common sense philosophy, particularly as it was expressed in his *Inquiry into the Human Mind on the Principles of Common Sense* (1764), was to vindicate common sense against the skepticism of the "British empiricists" Locke, Berkeley, and Hume. Reid thought that there was a dangerous skepticism that was implicit in John Locke (1632–1704), made explicit by George Berkeley (1685–1753), and taken to its logical conclusion by the unsparing analysis of David Hume. Like Immanuel Kant (1724–1804) after him, Reid was aroused from his intellectual slumbers by reading Hume, with whom he later developed a mutually cordial and respectful correspondence.[33] In Berkeley, and especially in Hume, there is indeed a great deal of skepticism with regard to what the mind can truly know of the external world. This skepticism, so Reid thought, was the result of the theory of *"ideas."* Sometimes called the theory of "representative perception," this theory held that we cannot truly know objects as they are, but must rely on ideas to represent the objects to our minds. Hume even called into question the universality of cause and effect and had, seemingly, reduced the mind to a bundle of ideas. Of Hume, Witherspoon said in Lecture VI:

> great stir has been made by some infidel writers, particularly David
> Hume, who seems to have industriously endeavored to shake the

certainty of our belief upon cause and effect, upon personal identity and the idea of power. It is easy to raise metaphysical subtleties, and confound the understanding on such subjects. In opposition to this, some late writers have advanced with great apparent reason, that there are certain first principles or dictates of common sense, which are either simple perceptions, or seen with intuitive evidence. These are the foundation of all reasoning, and without them, to reason is a word without a meaning. They can no more be proved than you can prove an axiom in mathematical science. These authors of Scotland have lately produced and supported this opinion, to resolve at once all the refinements and metaphysical objections of some infidel writers.[34]

Against Hume's epistemological skepticism, Reid set what he called "common sense." For Reid, its truths were, to use that weightiest of eighteenth-century phrases, "self-evident." Common sense carried with it the notion of an intuitively based common consent and thus presupposed the trustworthiness of ordinary folk, and common sense philosophers such as Reid and Witherspoon were accordingly suspicious of "philosophers." As Reid saw it, only a philosopher could come up with a theory so woefully out of touch with the conclusions of ordinary people as Hume's skeptical theory of ideas. Judgments did not rely, as Locke and Hume held, on hazy, ill-defined "ideas"; many judgments were instead "intuitions," which Reid termed "axioms, first principles, principles of common sense, self-evident truths."[35]

There was a kind of family resemblance between Witherspoon's peers in the Scottish moral sense and common sense schools, as they dissented from Locke's theory of ideas, and as they affirmed that in both moral epistemology (Hutcheson) and natural epistemology (Reid) there can be immediate perception. According to these Scottish philosophers, all persons had been endowed by Providence[36] with a moral sense and with the power of moral judgment, and so it followed naturally that common people were competent judges in moral and political matters. Thus, there was a strong providential strain (Hume excepted) among the Scottish philosophers' moral epistemology. Also, both Scottish schools were committed to the methods of natural science and to empiricism and were therefore skeptical of high-flown metaphysical theories. Like so many of their Enlightenment contemporaries, the Scots had learned to look less to the received authority found in what was habitually termed the "books of men" and to look more carefully into the book of nature, which included not only the physical universe but human nature as well. A preference for nature rather than books was already in place by the time that Thomas Hobbes (1588–1679), who did much himself to further the methods of the new science, published *Leviathan* in 1651. "[T]here is a saying much usurped of late," Hobbes wrote, "that *wisdom is acquired, not by reading of books,* but of *men.*"[37] The so-called scientific method that was developed by Francis Bacon (1561–1626) and Isaac Newton (1642–1727) and that was most closely associated with the epistemology of Locke was understood by all Enlightenment thinkers to be applicable to the entire range of human knowledge, including knowledge of moral philosophy, which, as noted, at that time included politics and jurisprudence in addition to formal philosophy.

Having briefly surveyed the Scottish intellectual terrain, we should return to the American scene, where we recall that Thomas Jefferson had named those very three—Bacon, Locke, and Newton—as "the three greatest men that have ever lived, without any exception . . . having laid the foundation of those superstructures which have been raised in the Physical and Moral sciences."[58] The foundation to which Jefferson referred was one of empirical observation and, above all, of experience. Bacon and Newton's method was based on repeated observations, and Locke's epistemology began with sense experience (and indeed had to be based entirely on experience, since for Locke there were no innate ideas). In the Lectures on Moral Philosophy, Witherspoon followed Locke in saying: "[t]hat our senses are to be trusted in the information they give us seems to me a first principle, because they are the foundation of all our reasonings."[59] But he did not follow blindly: he insisted that there were innate ideas, contradicting Locke on this point by name.

> The opposers of innate ideas, and of the law of nature, are unwilling to admit the reality of a moral sense, yet their objections are wholly frivolous. The necessity of education and information to the production and exercise of the reflex senses or powers of the imagination, is every whit as great as to the application of the moral sense. If therefore any one should say, as is often done by Mr. Locke, if there are any innate principles, what are they? enumerate to me, if they are essential to man they must be in every man; let me take any artless clown and examine him, and see if he can tell me what they are.—I would say, if the principles of taste are natural, they must be universal. Let me try the clown then, and see whether he will agree with us, either in discovering the beauty of a poem or picture, or being able to assign the reasons of his approbation.[40]

It was Jefferson's hero Isaac Newton who had first suggested that the scientific method could be put to use in the moral realm. Newton predicted that if "natural Philosophy in all its Parts, by pursuing this Method, shall at length be perfected, the Bounds of Moral Philosophy will be also enlarged."[41] And Locke, the second person in Jefferson's trinity of heroes, wrote in a similar vein that

> [t]he *Idea* of a supreme Being, infinite in Power, Goodness, and Wisdom, whose Workmanship we are, and on whom we depend; and the *Idea* of our selves, as understanding, rational Beings, being such as are clear in us, would, I suppose, if duly considered, and pursued, afford such Foundations of our Duty and Rules of Action, as might place *Morality amongst the Sciences capable of Demonstration:* wherein I doubt not, but from self-evident Propositions, by necessary Consequences, as incontestable as those in Mathematicks, the measures of right and wrong might be made out, to any one that will apply himself with the same Indifference and Attention to the one, as he does to the other of these Sciences.[42]

Witherspoon shared some of the optimism of Newton, Hutcheson, and Locke and recast their predictions, saying that "at first sight it appears that authors differ much more, and more essentially on the principles of moral than natural philosophy. Yet perhaps a time may come when men, treating moral philosophy as Newton and his successors have done natural, may arrive at greater precision. It is always safer in our reasonings to trace facts upwards than to reason downwards upon metaphysical principles."[43] Hutcheson began his *System of Moral Philosophy* not with reiterations of past authorities — that is, with the books of men — but with an investigation of human nature, and Witherspoon began his Lectures the same way. It was a common Scottish Enlightenment tenet, held by Deists and Christians alike, that the mind of the Creator could be discerned from the order within the creation, including the order in human nature. Thus, Hutcheson could say, "[w]e must search accurately into the constitution of our nature to see what sort of creatures we are; for what purposes nature has formed us; what character God our Creator requires us to maintain."[44]

Reid picked up the language regarding the "constitution of our nature" and put the matter thus: "[i]f there are certain principles, as I think there are, which the constitution of our nature leads us to believe, and which we are under a necessity to take for granted in the common concerns of life, without being able to give a reason for them—these are what we call the principles of common sense; and what is manifestly contrary to them is what is called absurd."[45] It is easy to see how Witherspoon's reasoning followed that of Hutcheson and Reid with respect to moral conclusions that could be drawn from an examination of human nature. "[T]he principles of duty and obligation," he said, "must be drawn from the nature of man. That is to say, if we can discover how his Maker formed him, or for what he intended him, that certainly is what it ought to be."[46] And Witherspoon, like Hutcheson, was convinced that "[j]ustice seems to be founded on the strong and unalterable perception we have of right and wrong, good and evil, and particularly that the one deserves reward, the other punishment. The internal sanction, or the external and providential sanction of natural laws, point out to us the justice of God."[47]

In sum, the Scottish philosophy as a whole contained a strong providential strand and viewed the human mental faculties as designed by God to suit the kind of moral and rational universe in which men lived. The Scottish philosophy was also marked by a general empiricism, a corresponding distrust of "metaphysics" or theorizing at too high a level of abstraction, and a desire to apply the methods of natural philosophy (science) to questions of morality.

Political Pragmatism

The Scottish Enlightenment philosophy that Witherspoon had brought with him to America and passed on to his students may have been an amalgam of the moral sense and common sense schools, but it is best typified by the Reidian phrase (nearly ubiquitous in the late eighteenth century) "common sense." The phrase enjoyed wide circulation during the eighteenth century, and it was put to use by thinkers with the most opposite opinions, particularly concerning religion. That the same words could appear, for instance, in the titles of the freethinking Thomas Paine's *Common Sense* (1776) and the devout James Oswald's *Appeal to Common Sense in Behalf of Religion* (1766–1772) is testimony to both the plasticity and the rhetorical power of the phrase in the eighteenth century. Nor was Paine the only political pamphleteer to employ it. The *Federalist Papers* contain nine references to "common sense," eight of which are from the pen of the half-Scot Hamilton, and all of which align the dictates of common sense on the side of the newly proposed Constitution.[48]

The upshot of Scottish moral sense and common sense thinking was that the deliverances of the human faculties were reliable, and that experience was a key to understanding in the physical and moral worlds. If the metaphysical speculations of some philosopher such as Berkeley or Hume (or Jonathan Edwards) led us to doubt the obvious conclusions drawn from our common experiences of the world; if they led us to doubt the existence of a mind-independent material universe as had Berkeley, or to doubt the reality of cause and effect as had Hume, then so much the worse for those speculations. They were to be rejected as patently absurd. To Reid, Witherspoon, and the other common sense philosophers, such conclusions were the inevitable result of too much "metaphysical" speculation and not enough attention paid to the dictates of what Witherspoon praised as "plain common sense."[49] The word "metaphysical" almost invariably carried a pejorative meaning in Witherspoon's Lectures on Moral Philosophy. Hume's efforts to shake our common sense belief in cause and effect were dismissed as "metaphysical subtleties," and Berkeley's (and Edwards's) immaterial system was labeled a "wild and ridiculous attempt to unsettle the principles of common sense by metaphysical reasoning."[50] Absurd conclusions such as these that followed from the theory of ideas could only come from brains addled by too much "theory"; long on armchair metaphysics, they were woefully short on empirical science.

The Scottish common sense approach led to conclusions that fit seamlessly with the thinking of Witherspoon's colleagues in the New Jersey legislature and the Continental Congress. For example, the similarities are striking between Witherspoon, a product of the Scottish Enlightenment, and Jefferson, a product of the American Enlightenment, despite their deep differences over theological questions such as the inspiration of the Bible. Jefferson held to precisely the same definition of the moral sense as did Witherspoon; in fact, entire sections of the Lectures on Moral Philosophy could be replaced with passages from Jefferson's correspondence without disrupting at all the sense of the Lectures. Jefferson wrote:

> Man was destined for society. His morality therefore was to be formed to this object. He was endowed [by his Maker] with a sense of right and wrong merely relative to this. This sense is as much a part of his nature as the sense of hearing, seeing, feeling; it is the true foundation of morality, and not the το καλον truth, &c., as fanciful writers have imagined. The moral sense, or conscience, is as much a part of man as his leg or arm. It is given to all human beings in a stronger or weaker degree, as

force of members is given them in a greater or less degree. It may be strengthened by exercise, as may any particular limb of the body. This sense is submitted indeed in some degree to the guidance of reason; but it is a small stock which is required for this: even a less one than what we call Common sense. State a moral case to a ploughman and a professor. The former will decide it as well, and often better than the latter, because he has not been led astray by artificial rules.[51]

Jefferson continued to hold to this definition of the moral sense until at least 1814, as evidenced by a letter he wrote to Thomas Law:

> [H]ow necessary was the care of the Creator in making the moral principle so much a part of our constitution as that no errors of reasoning or of speculation might lead us astray from its observance in practice. . . . The Creator would indeed have been a bungling artist, had he intended man for a social animal, without planting in him social dispositions. It is true that they are not planted in every man, because there is no rule without exceptions; but it is false reasoning which converts exceptions into the general rule. Some men are born without the organs of sight, or of hearing, or without hands. Yet it would be wrong to say that man is born without these faculties, and sight, hearing, and hands may with truth enter into the general definition of man.[52]

These words could just as well have been Witherspoon's. "This moral sense," he said, "is precisely the same thing with what, in scripture and common language, we call conscience. It is the law which our Maker has written upon our hearts, and both intimates and enforces duty, previous to all reasoning."[53] Further, "we ought to take the rule of duty from conscience enlightened by reason, experience, and every way by which we can be supposed to learn the will of our Maker, and his intention in creating us such as we are. And we ought to believe that it is as deeply founded as the nature of God himself, being a transcript of his moral excellence, and that it is productive of the greatest good."[54] Thus, when it came time to sign the Declaration of 1776, with its reference to truths that were "self-evident" and confirmed by "all Experience," Witherspoon could subscribe without hesitation.[55] After all, Jefferson and Witherspoon spoke the same moral language and shared a common moral epistemology.

Such close agreement between Witherspoon and Jefferson can be explained by their common debt to the Scottish philosophy. Jefferson in fact found Reid's protégé Dugald Stewart "a great man, and among the most honest living. . . . I consider him and [Destutt de] Tracy as the ablest metaphysicians living; by which I mean investigators of the thinking faculty of man. Stewart seems to have given its natural history from facts and observations; Tracy its modes of action and deduction, which he calls Logic and Ideology." Jefferson had met Stewart in Paris and "became immediately intimate" with him there; they called "mutually on each other and almost daily, during [his] stay at Paris, which was of some months."[56]

Because they shared a moral epistemology that emphasized experience and a common moral faculty, Witherspoon and Jefferson also agreed that ordinary people were trustworthy enough for self-government. Although Witherspoon was a Federalist (as we shall see), and Jefferson had Antifederalist leanings, both had sufficient faith in the ability of common people to reason aright on moral and political questions and therefore to govern themselves. Jefferson's "ploughmen" (he had borrowed the illustration from Thomas Reid)[57] were Witherspoon's more cumbersome "persons of the middle degrees of capacity." Such persons, Witherspoon said, "perhaps generally fill the most useful and important stations in life."[58] Moreover, in a newspaper article defending Paine's *Common Sense,* he came down squarely on the side of the political instincts of the common people, who were behind independence. Paine's arguments for American self-government were, to Witherspoon's mind, irrefutable. *Common Sense* may have "wanted polish" in places, he observed, and "sometimes failed in grammar, but never in perspicuity."[59]

Paine began his pamphlet (whose title was suggested to him by Witherspoon's friend and Princeton-Edinburgh alumnus Benjamin Rush) by assuring his readers that "[i]n the following pages I offer nothing more than simple facts, plain arguments, and common sense,"[60] all of which presumably could be understood by simple, plain, and common folk. Witherspoon chose to defend Paine's pamphlet as "Aristides," a choice of names perhaps not insignificant in itself. Like so many of the founders, Witherspoon looked back to antiquity for his rhetorical inspiration, in this case to Aristides, the rhetorician and philosopher profiled in Plutarch's *Lives of the Noble Grecians and Romans,* a copy of which was in Witherspoon's library, as it was in the library of nearly every literate founder.[61]

Aristides, called "the Just," had argued that "the Many are not to be contemned [*sic*], and their opinion held of no account; but that in them, too, there is a presentiment, an unerring instinct, which, by a kind of divine fatality, seizes darkling on the truth."[62] Plutarch had said of him that "Aristides walked, so to say, alone on his own path in politics, being unwilling, in the first place, to go along with his associates in ill-doing, or to cause them vexation by not gratifying their wishes; and, secondly, observing that many were encouraged by the support they had in their friends to act injuriously, he was cautious; being of opinion that the integrity of his words and actions was the only right security for a good citizen."[63] Aristides was also seen by Sir William Hamilton, himself a Scottish common sense philosopher and the editor of Reid's *Philosophical Works*, as a forerunner of modern common sense thought. Like the ancient Aristides, Witherspoon appreciated the "unerring instinct" of the many to seize upon the truth. Although liberally educated himself, he was no pedant; he believed, as we have already seen, in the good common sense of "persons of the middle degrees of capacity." Speaking in Congress on a proposed meeting with British General John Burgoyne, Witherspoon insisted that on political matters "a person of integrity will pass as sound a judgment . . . by consulting his own heart, as by turning over books and systems."[64] Here again is the Scottish Enlightenment tenet that the most reliable knowledge comes not from the books of men but from observation of the book of nature—in this case, human nature.

Having rehearsed the major tenets of Witherspoon's Scottish philosophy and seen how that philosophy dovetailed with the positions of other founders, chiefly Jefferson, we are now in a position to see a concrete example of one of those tenets in action. Confidence in the "heart," as Witherspoon expressed it, and the common sense of the average sturdy American, helped provide answers to the grave questions that were being asked at the time of the Revolution. For one: How were persons of "integrity" (Witherspoon's word) such as the Americans to know whether they had a natural right to separate themselves from an oppressive mother country? Or another: How, in the words of the Declaration, might one people determine whether the time had come to "dissolve the political bands which [had] connected them with another"? The answer of Witherspoon's Scottish philosophy was, in essence, to consult the self-evident truths written on the hearts of the people by their Creator, rather than arcane theories. "The chief use of books and systems," he said, was "to apply the principle to particular cases and suppositions differently classed, and to point out the practice of nations in several minute and special particulars, which unless ascertained by practice, would be very uncertain and ambiguous."[65] And here is Alexander Hamilton's answer to the same question: "The sacred rights of mankind are not to be rummaged for among old parchments or musty records. They are written, as with a sunbeam, in the whole volume of human nature, by the hand of Divinity itself, and can never be erased or obscured by mortal power."[66] The logic of the American Revolution, as expressed in a representative source such as Hamilton, and supremely in the Declaration of Independence, presumes the moral epistemology of Witherspoon and his Scottish philosophy and thus provides us with an example of its practical application in founding politics.[67] As Michael Novak has written in a similar context, there are political corollaries to metaphysical premises.[68]

Witherspoon as Moral Philosopher

By common consent, Witherspoon was a principal carrier of the Scottish philosophy in early America, and the importance of that role should not be minimized. For one thing, through Witherspoon that Scottish philosophy inoculated Americans of the Revolutionary era against the kind of utopian excesses (to say nothing of the Terror) that infected the French during their own revolution. To be sure, historians of colonial philosophy have always acknowledged Witherspoon's role in transmitting the Scottish philosophy into the colonies, but the more influential among them, I. Woodbridge Riley and Herbert Schneider, for example, have not thought too highly of either Witherspoon or the Scottish philosophy, especially that of common sense associated with Thomas Reid and Dugald Stewart.[69] And yet Schneider himself admits that "the Scottish Enlightenment was probably the most potent single tradition in the American Enlightenment,"[70] and no one did more to see that tradition established in America than John Witherspoon. The merits of the Scottish philosophy may be open to debate, but the fact remains that it was (if we extend Scottish realism into the Pragmatism of the late nineteenth and early twentieth centuries) the dominant philosophical school in America for nearly a century and a half after Witherspoon established it at Princeton. For reasons like this, some historians of philosophy have, contra Riley and Schneider, given Witherspoon higher marks as a moral philosopher. One insists that "Witherspoon must be included among the early American philosophic thinkers."[71] Another, writing in the *William and Mary Quarterly,* names only four "colonial philosophers who deserve the title in its full meaning: Jonathan Edwards, Samuel Johnson, Cadwallader Colden, and John Witherspoon."[72]

Others, too, have viewed the influence of Scottish philosophy in America in a more positive light. The political philosopher Eric Voegelin, for one, felt the power of the Scottish common sense legacy. After seeing the connection between Thomas Reid and Sir William Hamilton and American thought, Voegelin "began to sense that American society had a philosophical background far superior in range and existential substance, though not always in articulation, to anything that I found represented in the methodological environment [in Germany] in which I had grown up."[73] Douglass Adair, for another, saw the mark of the Scottish philosophy on the American founding, particularly in the influence of David Hume on *Federalist* 10.[74] And Frank Balog has noted that "[Adam] Smith's influence on [John] Adams's work was extensive."[75]

A further philosophical legacy of John Witherspoon is the ultimate triumph of Scottish realism over idealism in the colonies. One of the seminal debates in early American philosophy was between the idealism of Jonathan Edwards, who was elected president of the College of New Jersey in 1758, and the realism of Witherspoon, who became president ten years later in 1768. Witherspoon even claimed that before he went to America he had anticipated in print the arguments of Reid, James Beatty (1735–1803), and others against George Berkeley's idealism. Ashbel Green heard Witherspoon maintain "that before Reid and Beatty, or any other author of their views, had published any thing on the ideal system, he wrote against it, and suggested the same train of thought which they adopted, and that he published his essay in a Scotch Magazine."[76]

When Witherspoon arrived in Princeton he found to his consternation that the College was overrun with what Green called the "Berklean system of Metaphysics."[77] (In point of fact, Princeton's idealism probably owed more to Jonathan Edwards and Samuel Johnson, Edwards's tutor at Yale, than to Bishop Berkeley.) The idealists held, in brief, that the universe consists solely of minds and ideas, and that there is no such thing as mind-independent matter. As we saw in an earlier chapter, at the time Witherspoon became president, nearly all of the Princeton tutors (especially Jonathan Edwards, Jr.) held to the ideal system, and Witherspoon, who was no friend to it, quickly laid the ax at the root of the idealist teaching at the College. Indeed, except for agreement on the basic theological tenets of Calvinism, Witherspoon was opposed to Edwards on almost every front. Edwards was a New Light revivalist, Witherspoon an Old Side Presbyterian who may have had grave doubts about the religious enthusiasm that swept the Princeton campus in the early 1770s; Edwards was a philosophical idealist while Witherspoon an uncompromising realist. Edwards found it necessary to attack the moral sense epistemology of Francis Hutcheson, while Witherspoon always remained a firm believer in the moral sense.

By the end of 1769, his first full year at the helm, all of the idealist tutors, including Edwards, Jr., had been replaced with common sense realists.[78] By his own example at Princeton, through his graduates, many of whom later founded academies and colleges, and through the influence of his Lectures on Moral Philosophy, Witherspoon and Scottish realism prevailed over Edwards's idealism, thereby helping to set the long term course of American philosophy. The victory of realism over idealism had far-reaching implications for the life of the mind in America, for it allowed realism to act as "a bridge between the Enlightenment and the pragmatists," as Elizabeth Flower and Murray Murphey put it.[79] This in itself seems reason enough to count Witherspoon among the handful of moral philosophers in colonial America.

A second conflict between the philosophies of Edwards and Witherspoon concerned Hutcheson's moral sense epistemology. In 1755, the year that Hutcheson's *System of Moral Philosophy* (the source of much of Witherspoon's Lectures on Moral Philosophy) was published, Edwards wrote out his own moral philosophy in a brief treatise titled *The Nature of True Virtue*. In this treatise, which was not published until ten years later, Edwards located virtue in the will rather than in a separate moral sense, as had Hutcheson. Thus, Edwards was compelled by the logic of his theory of virtue to argue against Hutcheson, whose views he had actually accepted while a teenager at Yale.[80] Arguing that true virtue was a benevolence rooted in the will toward "Being in general," not toward particulars or individuals, Edwards parted company with Hutcheson and the moral sense philosophers, who thought benevolence to individuals was indeed true virtue.[81] Edwards's assault on the moral sense epistemology simply gave Witherspoon another reason to root out the Edwardsean philosophy at Princeton. Once again, by siding with Hutcheson against Edwards in favor of the moral sense, Witherspoon supported a moral epistemology that ended up dominating American thinking.

Witherspoon was therefore a bona fide moral philosopher of considerable influence in early American thought. Few intellectual historians, however, have seen him in this light. Many have instead trivialized his contribution and his intellectual abilities because his moral philosophy was unoriginal, eclectic, and occasionally naive. Compared to several other supposedly more sophisticated founders, Witherspoon is thought to be second-rank. Although he was not the first to introduce Hutcheson's moral sense epistemology into the colonies, and many other Americans (Jefferson, John Adams, and James Wilson among them) accepted the moral sense, by argu-

ing for it in his Lectures on Moral Philosophy, Witherspoon did a great deal
to disseminate that view. By contrast, Thomas Jefferson, for all his infatuation
with theory, never wrote anything approaching a treatise on a philosophical subject, and he thought that moral philosophy as a discipline was worth-
less. Writing to the young Peter Carr concerning his studies at Williamsburg,
Jefferson recommended avoiding "Moral philosophy. I think it lost time to attend lectures in this branch. He who made us would have been a pitiful bun-
gler if he had made the rules of our moral conduct a matter of science."[82]
Jefferson also wrote to Witherspoon at Princeton, suggesting that an acquaintance who was studying under Witherspoon be exempted from the
study of moral philosophy. "As he [Bennet Taylor of Virginia] has no time to
spare, I have mentioned to him that I thought he might undertake the subject of Moral philosophy in his chamber, at leisure hours, and from books,
without attending lectures or exercises in that branch."[83] We can assume that
in the event, Jefferson's young friend found little or no leisure for such study.
(Witherspoon, by contrast, insisted in his Lectures on Moral Philosophy that
"[t]he languages, and even mathematical and natural knowledge, are but
hand-maids to this superior science [moral philosophy].")[84]

Nor does the fact that Witherspoon borrowed widely from Hutcheson
and others negate his importance as a moral philosopher in America. Jefferson himself was a borrower of legendary proportion, and so, for that matter,
were all the founders. There was not a man among them — not Jefferson,
not Franklin, not even the cerebral Madison, certainly not Washington —
who was a truly original political thinker or profound philosopher in his own
right. The Sage of Monticello, as his biographer Dumas Malone calls him,
contributed nothing original to formal philosophy in America, and was
accused of outright plagiarism of John Locke in the Declaration. Jefferson's
defense, made half a century after the fact, was essentially to admit to a lack
of originality and to deny that the Declaration was meant to be original.
The object of that document, Jefferson said, was precisely to be *unoriginal*
and eclectic: "Neither aiming at originality of principle or sentiment, nor yet
copied from any particular and previous writing, it was intended to be an expression of the American mind, and to give to that expression the proper tone
and spirit called for by the occasion. All its authority rests then on the harmonizing sentiments of the day, whether expressed in conversation, in letters, printed essays, or in the elementary books of public right, as Aristotle,
Cicero, Locke, Sidney, etc."[85] Jefferson was representative of the whole founding generation in this respect. According to Morton White, "we may repeat
what scholars have always known, and what the most candid rebels always

admitted, namely, that they did not invent a single idea that may be called philosophical in the philosopher's sense of the word."[86]

We should not, therefore, be shocked to find that Witherspoon borrowed heavily from other thinkers. In this respect he was a typical founder. We ought not to think less of him just because he was a philosophical borrower, or, if we do, then for the sake of consistency we ought to think less of the famous founders like Jefferson as well. And in at least one respect, Witherspoon seems to have been more philosophically original, or at least more innovative, than many colonial American thinkers. Frederick Mayer notes that "[i]n colonial times the progress of philosophy was hindered by the ecclesiastical tradition. . . . There were two ways of thinking: one severely orthodox, usually Calvinistic; the other scientific and Newtonian and usually exposed to the antagonism of the clergy."[87] If this characterization is accurate (and there is reason to doubt it),[88] then Witherspoon was a happy exception to the rule. By synthesizing Calvinism and Enlightenment science, he was arguably more original than most orthodox thinkers of his day.

Similarly, the charge that Witherspoon's moral philosophy lacked the depth and consistency to make him a genuine philosopher seems rather selective when he is compared to the more revered founders. True enough, Witherspoon was no great philosopher in the technical sense of that word: he seems not to have understood some of Hume's arguments very well, and there are instances in his Lectures where he has gotten Hume and Berkeley confused. Indeed, when weighed against his contemporaries in Britain and Europe such as Adam Smith or Immanuel Kant, Witherspoon looks light.[89] But once again, Jefferson could be as inconsistent—if that is the correct word for it—as any of the other founders, certainly as Witherspoon. For example, it has frequently been remarked that Jefferson's philosophy was thoroughly Lockean, and indeed he did rank Locke as one of "the three greatest men that have ever lived, without any exception."[90] But we must recall that this same Jefferson also called Reid's disciple Dugald Stewart one of the two greatest philosophers of the age, even though Stewart made a career of attacking Locke for his theory of ideas.[91] So it seems that Thomas Jefferson, at least in several instances, was manifestly unoriginal, eclectic, and inconsistent as a moral philosopher.

Although he may not have been a great moral philosopher in the European mold, still Witherspoon was a legitimate *American* moral philosopher. This may be rather faint praise considering how few philosophers there were in colonial America, but it does place Witherspoon above Franklin, Jefferson, and other founders more renowned for their so-called philosophical abilities. For example, there were very few "pure" or formal philosophers among the early members of the American Philosophical Society, the colonies' first learned society, for the simple reason that America had so few pure philosophers anywhere at all. We must repeat that neither Franklin, the founder of the Society, nor David Rittenhouse, nor Jefferson (both early officers in the Society) ever wrote anything approaching Witherspoon's *Lectures on Moral Philosophy*. Franklin, considered by many a sort of American Socrates, made only one detour into metaphysics as a young man, his "Dissertation on Liberty and Necessity, Pleasure and Pain" (1725), and then spent the rest of his life dismissing it as a youthful indiscretion.[92]

In fact, early Americans like the founders were remarkably uninterested in formal philosophy, as Tocqueville was quick to notice. "Less attention, I suppose, is paid to philosophy in the United States than in any other country of the civilized world. The Americans have no school of philosophy peculiar to themselves, and they pay very little attention to the rival European schools. Indeed they hardly know their names." Tocqueville concluded that "of all countries in the world, America is the one in which the precepts of Descartes are least studied and best followed,"[93] by which he meant that Americans preferred to make themselves and their own experiences the starting-point of their thinking, as Descartes had, rather than the theories of others. Surely, Tocqueville was correct in his observation: Americans in general have been, and eighteenth-century American politicians in particular were, rather skeptical of formal philosophy. Americans such as John Adams were more likely to see philosophers as "mad" than as trustworthy guides to truth. (He once wrote Jefferson that "Philosophers antient and modern appear to me as Mad as Hindoos, Mahomitans and Christians.")[94] Even the theoretical Jefferson, we recall, in his advice to Peter Carr, saw little profit in studying moral philosophy because most people could judge for themselves and would only be led astray by "artificial rules" invented by "professors."[95] Jefferson, Witherspoon, and their colleagues were more inclined to rely, at least in the Declaration, on what "all experience" could teach than on theories found in dusty books.

Witherspoon's training in the Scottish philosophy, in moral sense and especially in common sense epistemology, could hardly have been better preparation for his distinguished career in American politics. When he arrived in 1768, just as trouble with England was beginning to boil over in the colonies, Witherspoon brought along a mind naturally inclined toward the pragmatic and stocked with concepts and language — "experience, moral sense, common sense, self-evidence" — that enjoyed the widest currency among his American colleagues. In short, he and the other founders spoke the same language of moral discourse.

His mind also was cast in essentially the same mold as theirs: pragmatic, willing to use formal philosophy, but at root skeptical of too much "metaphysical" theorizing. Witherspoon was intimately acquainted with the common sense philosophy of Reid, whom James Wilson quoted verbatim as Supreme Court justice in *Chisholm v. Georgia* (1793),[96] and with Reid's pupil Dugald Stewart, later Jefferson's friend and philosophical hero; he was also conversant, though to a lesser extent, with David Hume, whose language on experience Hamilton used to close out *The Federalist Papers*. The formal philosophers whom Witherspoon knew and borrowed from were the least metaphysical and the most empirical and pragmatic; they were the most — if it can be put this way — unphilosophical of philosophers. And they were the only ones whom pragmatic Americans were likely to heed. By teaching him to hold high the lamp of experience, the Scottish philosophy ideally prepared Witherspoon for his highly successful political career in America.

As a moral philosopher, and as a formal philosopher more generally, Witherspoon must rank among the few bona fide philosophers in early America. Although his mind was more synthetic than original, this charge does not seem terribly damaging when we reflect that it can be leveled against practically any thinker, including an undisputed philosopher such as John Locke. For example, it has been said that "[i]t is doubtless true that Locke himself brought to articulate expression an already existing movement of thought; but this articulate expression was itself a powerful influence in the consolidation and dissemination of the movement of thought and drift of political life which it expressed."[97] Even less were the founders creative moral philosophers.

The importance of Witherspoon's contribution to American moral philosophy and political thought lies in his promotion of Scottish realism over idealism against Jonathan Edwards and George Berkeley, and his articulation of Scottish moral sense epistemology in his Lectures on Moral Philosophy, through which they were passed on at Princeton to Madison and a host of other future prominent politicians, clergy, and educators. Certainly, Witherspoon was a more influential and sophisticated moral philosopher than either Jefferson or Franklin, who wrote exactly one philosophical treatise between them. In fact, the founding generation was almost entirely devoid of men who could be considered formal philosophers. Witherspoon thus stands out as a founder who made a genuine, though mostly unoriginal, contribution to moral philosophy in America as well as to its political culture. And his Lectures on Moral Philosophy are perhaps the clearest proof of Tocqueville's observation that "[t]here is no country in the world in which the boldest political theories of the eighteenth-century philosophers are put so effectively into practice as in America."[98]

chapter four

"An Animated Son of Liberty"

Revolution

He is the best friend to American liberty who is most sincere and active in promoting . . . religion.

—John Witherspoon, 1776

The Revolution was in the minds and hearts of the people; a change in their religious sentiments of their duties and obligations.

—John Adams, 1818

In 1768, the year of Witherspoon's immigration, the American colonies were in a state of no little agitation. Only weeks after he debarked in August, a flotilla of British warships arrived in Boston Harbor and landed troops who were forcibly billeted in Faneuil Hall and the Massachusetts State House. This show of force was partly a response to John Hancock's refusal to allow his ship, the portentously named *Liberty*, to be searched by British customs officials, and to the subsequent violence by angry Bostonians in support of Hancock. In that same year, John Dickinson's *Letters From a Farmer in Pennsylvania* were published in the *Pennsylvania Chronicle* and elsewhere, and the so-called Massachusetts Circular Letter made its rounds. (Witherspoon, although destined to become Dickinson's opponent in Congress over the question of declaring independence, nevertheless had a high estimate of the value of Dickinson's *Letters:* "Public spirited writers took care that it [the spirit of liberty] should not sleep; and in particular the celebrated Pennsylvania Farmer's Letters were of signal service, by furnishing the lovers of their country with facts, and illustrating the rights and privileges which it was their duty to defend.")[1] Troubles in New England, the middle colonies, and the south, aggravated by the hated Townshend Acts, showed that relations between England and all of its American colonies were becoming dangerously taut.

As we look back from the present, the Revolution and independence can seem inevitable, but at the time the outcome of all that tension was far from certain. Americans in the Revolutionary period were by no means unanimous, despite language to the contrary in the Declaration, in their support for independence. And what was true of the American people as a whole was especially true of the inhabitants of New Jersey. Although that state has been called the "cockpit of the Revolution,"[2] in fact Jerseymen were slow in coming out for independence. This was particularly the case with New Jersey politicians, naturally cautious men such as William Livingston (1723–1790), Richard Stockton (1730–1781), and Elias Boudinot (1740–1821).[3] The one notable exception to this group was the parson-politician from Somerset County, John Witherspoon.[4]

Revolutionary Practice

Recall that John Adams, stopping off in Princeton on his way back to the Continental Congress in Philadelphia in the fall of 1774, recorded in his diary after his second meeting with the president that "Dr. Witherspoon enters with great Spirit into the American Cause. He seems as hearty a Friend as any of the Natives — an animated Son of Liberty."[5] Adams's estimate turned out to be prophetic: in April 1776 Witherspoon became the first man in New Jersey to call publicly for independence.[6]

Witherspoon's revolutionary ardor had been working itself up for years prior to his meeting with Adams in 1774. As early as 1769, his first full year at the College of New Jersey, Witherspoon granted honorary degrees to men who had gained notoriety for their resistance to England. Prior to his arrival at Princeton, honorary degrees were customarily conferred upon clergymen, but in 1769 the three recipients were John Dickinson, Joseph Galloway, and John Hancock, none of whom was known for his piety.[7] Hancock in particular had been made famous by the customs incident of the previous year. During the next academic year, on July 13, 1770, Princeton students who had a letter from New York merchants encouraging their counterparts in

Philadelphia to violate the non-importation agreement, "at the tolling of the College Bell, went in Procession to a Place fronting the College, and burnt the Letter by the Hands of a Hangman, hired for the Purpose, with hearty Wishes, that the Names of all Promoters of such a daring Breach of Faith, may be blasted in the Eyes of every Lover of Liberty, and their Names handed down to Posterity, as Betrayers of their Country."[8]

A young James Madison wrote an account of this incident to his father:

We have no publick news but the base conduct of the Merchants in N. York in breaking through their spirited resolutions not to import, a distinct account of which I suppose will be in the Virginia Gazette before this arrives. Their Letter to the Merchants in Philadelphia requesting their concurrence was lately burnt by the students of this place in the college yard, all of them appearing in their black Gowns & the bell Tolling. The number of Students has increased very much of late, there are about an hundred & fifteen in College & the Grammar School twenty-two commence this Fall all of them in American Cloth.[9]

During Commencement in September 1770, the president's son, James Witherspoon (who was to die in 1777 at the Battle of Germantown),[10] delivered an oration arguing that it was the obligation of subjects to resist a tyrannical king.[11] All of this was done without a word of rebuke from the president.

In 1774, Witherspoon became a founding member of the Committee of Correspondence for Somerset County, and he was appointed to the New Jersey provincial legislature where he consistently urged compliance with the directives of the Continental Congress. That year Witherspoon also worked, according to his own account to John Adams, with William Livingston to prevent the duty on imported tea from being paid in New Jersey.[12] It is worth noting that in the summer of 1774 even George Washington was unsure whether nonpayment of such duties was justified or warranted. "As to the withholding of our remittances, that is another point, in which I own I have my doubts on several accounts, but principally on that of justice; for I think, whilst we are accusing others of injustice, we should be just ourselves; and how this can be whilst we owe a considerable debt, and refuse payment of it to Great Britain, is to me inconceivable. Nothing but the last extremity, I think, can justify it. Whether this is now come, is the question."[13] Apparently, Witherspoon was quicker than Washington to answer it.

In that same year, Witherspoon also wrote "Reflections on the Present State of Public Affairs, and on the Duty and Interest of America in this Important Crisis" and "Thoughts on American Liberty," the latter containing eight resolutions, including a non-importation resolution, to be considered by the Continental Congress.[14] In 1775 he drafted "A Pastoral Letter from the Synod of New-York and Philadelphia," which was read from the Presbyterian pulpits on the general Fast Day of June 29, and which counseled loyalty to the king personally and at the same time adherence to the resolves of the Continental Congress.[15]

Thus, by the spring of 1776, Witherspoon had laid the groundwork for a plea for independence. On April 18 he convened a committee of county delegates to meet at New Brunswick to discuss matters that "greatly concerned the Province" but that he intentionally left unspecified.[16] At that meeting, according to Elias Boudinot,

> Dr. W. rose and in a very able and elegant speech of one hour and an half endeavoured to convince the audience & the Committee of the absurdity of opposing the extravagant demands of Great Brittain, while we were professing a perfect allegiance to her Authority and supporting her courts of Justice — The Character of the speaker, his great Influence among the People, his known attachment to the liberties of the People, and the artful manner in which he represented the whole subject, as worthy their attention, had an effect, on the assembly that astonished me — There appeared a general approbation of the measure, and I strongly suspected an universal acquiescence of both Committee & Audience in approving the Doctor's Scheme — I never felt myself in a more mortifying Situation . . . I was at my wit's end, to know how to extricate myself from so disagreeable a situation, especially as the measure was totally ag's my Judgment.[17]

Boudinot and other moderates were able to turn the tide of the New Brunswick meeting against Witherspoon, but the subject of New Jersey independence was finally out in the open, where it would remain until it was declared on behalf of all the colonies with Witherspoon's help in early July.

On June 21, Witherspoon and other members of the New Jersey provincial legislature had the loyalist Governor William Franklin placed under house arrest and prepared to have him sent to New England.[18] The following day Witherspoon was named a delegate to the Second Continental Congress in Philadelphia. On June 28, Witherspoon's credentials, along with those of the other four delegates from New Jersey (Francis Hopkinson, Richard Stockton, Abraham Clark, and John Hart), were presented to Congress by Hopkinson.[19] It is likely that Witherspoon arrived in Philadelphia on June 28 along with Hopkinson, but in any event he was there by the first of July, in time to argue in favor of declaring independence. A subsequent tradition developed that the conservatives who wanted a declaration postponed were led by John Dickinson, whom Witherspoon argued down. Although the *Journals* of Congress are silent on the matter, there is evidence to support this version of events.[20] Another tradition, that Witherspoon delivered a rousing speech in Congress beginning "there is a tide in the affairs of men, a nick of time," is almost certainly apocryphal. Although the text of the alleged "nick of time" speech is reproduced on the heroic statues of Witherspoon in Philadelphia and Washington, modern scholarship has dismissed it as the work of Presbyterian myth-makers.[21]

Having helped to assure passage of the Resolution for Independence on July 2, Witherspoon entered the debate over Jefferson's draft of the Declaration. He was able, probably with help from James Wilson (another native Scot), to have the word "Scotch" stricken from the phrase "Scotch and foreign mercenaries" in the final wording of the Declaration.[22] Benjamin Rush asserted that Witherspoon objected to calling King George a "tyrant" on the floor of the Continental Congress,[23] and V. L. Collins says that he "protested, as he always did, against calling the King a tyrant, etc., as being false and undignified."[24] (However, Witherspoon was not shy about calling Charles I a tyrant in the "Dominion of Providence": he reminded his hearers that the English civil war ended by "bringing the tyrant to the block.")[25]

Other writings of Witherspoon tend to support this stance, including the "Pastoral Letter" of 1775, which urged Presbyterians to show their "attachment and respect to our sovereign King George, and to the revolution principles by which his august family was seated on the British throne" while obeying the resolutions of the Continental Congress,[26] and "On the Controversy About Independence," probably written between May and April of 1776 for the British press but never published. The latter contained the following avowal: "That you may not pass sentence upon me immediately as an enemy to the royal authority, and a son of sedition, I declare that I esteem his majesty king George the third to have the only rightful and lawful title to the British crown, which was settled upon his family in consequence of the glorious revolution. . . . I not only revere him as the first magistrate of the realm, but I love and honour him as a man, and am persuaded that he wishes the prosperity and happiness of his people in every part of his dominions."[27] (If Witherspoon did indeed object to the word "tyrant," he was in good company. Adams himself resented Jefferson's so labeling the king in his draft of the Declaration: "There were other expressions which I would not have inserted . . . particularly that which called the King tyrant. I thought this too personal; for I never believed George to be a tyrant in disposition and in nature; I always believed him to be deceived by his courtiers on both sides of the Atlantic.")[28]

Unfortunately, we do not know Witherspoon's thoughts on Jefferson's indignant paragraph on slavery in the Declaration, which was stricken from the final version by Congress. It would be especially interesting to know his reaction because, like Thomas Jefferson himself, Witherspoon was a slaveholder. An inventory of his modest estate at the time of his death in 1794 catalogues furniture, china, his library, livestock, and "[t]wo slaves," valued at "a hundred dollars each."[29] Tusculum, Witherspoon's country home, was surrounded by more than 500 acres, which apparently were maintained for a number of years with the aid of slave labor.[30] In his Lectures on Moral Philosophy, Witherspoon admitted that while "there are many unlawful ways of making slaves, . . . [there are] also some that are lawful," and cited the Law of Moses as precedent. And though "it is very doubtful whether any original cause of servitude can be defended, but legal punishment for the commission of crimes," which certainly seemed to rule out the African slave trade, he said "I do not think there lies any necessity on those who found men in a state of slavery, to make them free to their own ruin."[31] Between 1774 and 1776, Witherspoon admitted two free blacks, John Quamine and Bristol Yamma, to the College, where he privately tutored them.[32] And in 1790 he chaired a state committee on abolition, during which time he proposed legislation providing for gradual emancipation and expressed his hope that "from the state of society in America, the privileges of the press, and the progress of the idea of universal liberty," slavery would wither away within a generation or two.[33] But like so many of the founders (and none more than Jefferson), Witherspoon was unwilling to sacrifice his own personal economy to the seemingly universal principles of liberty in the Declaration of Independence. This calls to mind the Englishman Samuel Johnson's pointed question, "How is it that the loudest yelps for liberty come from the drivers of Negroes?"

The most provocative assertion of all concerning Witherspoon and the Declaration—that he urged adoption of the phrase "with a firm reliance on the protection of divine Providence" in Congress—can neither be proved nor disproved. The assertion is part of the oral tradition concerning Witherspoon, and has found its way into the musical *1776* and polemical books such as *Christianity and the Constitution*.[34] There is no contemporary written record of Witherspoon making such a suggestion, either in the notoriously scanty records of the Continental Congress from July 1776 or elsewhere. However, the providential language does not appear in Jefferson's "Original Rough Draft" (which includes the changes made by Jefferson himself and the Committee of Five);[35] that language was, by Jefferson's own account, inserted by someone else from the floor of Congress.[36] Whether it was Witherspoon or another delegate, we cannot say with certainty; but such a suggestion would have been in keeping with Witherspoon's political theology, and, furthermore, "divine Providence" was his preferred way of referring to God's active superintendence over creation.

Between his work in and out of Congress, the year 1776 was the high-water mark of Witherspoon's revolutionary career, as it was of his political career as a whole. That year saw Witherspoon issue the first public call in New Jersey for independence in April; the delivery and publication of the "Dominion of Providence" and the "Address to the Natives of Scotland" in May; his involvement in the deposition of William Franklin on June 21; his appointment to the Second Continental Congress on the following day; his debate in Congress urging independence in the first week in July and his signing of the Declaration in August; and finally, his service on a number of congressional committees through the end of the year. It was precisely this kind of revolutionary practice that got Witherspoon burned in effigy by the British, that prompted one of His Majesty's officers to label him "the political firebrand, who perhaps had not a less share in the Revolution than Washington himself," and that caused Adam Ferguson to tremble when he thought of the cunning and determination of Adams, Franklin, and the 150,000 or so rebels "with Johnny Witherspoon at their head."[37] Though he never shouldered a musket himself, a small army of his Princeton students did: V. L. Collins found it "startling to note that, even if commissions were cheap, among these young graduates of his were eleven captains [in the Continental army], six majors, four colonels, and ten lieutenant-colonels. Four of these officers died in service. Of the eleven army chaplains found among his students of theology seven gave up their lives on the same altar."[38]

Revolutionary Theory

Like most Americans in the 1760s and 1770s, Witherspoon relied on a variety of past theorists when he argued for resistance and ultimately independence. Two groups of thinkers, however, were predominant in their influence on Witherspoon: the liberal Whig theorists and the Protestant Reformers. These groups are examples of what Wilson Carey McWilliams has called two "voices" of the American political tradition, one liberal and the other biblical.[39] McWilliams has laid particular emphasis on the Bible, "the second voice in the grand dialogue of American political culture," and in Witherspoon we have an especially full-throated example of that voice.[40] Still, he was perfectly comfortable using it as harmony, to stretch the metaphor a bit, with the liberal voice. Like many other colonial dissenters, Witherspoon perceived a common threat to civil and religious liberties in revolutionary America, and so rather easily employed liberal and religious arguments to ground resistance to the British government.

Witherspoon was certainly not alone in seeing this connection. One of the best-known cartoons of the Revolutionary era, "An Attempt to Land a Bishop in America," published in the *Political Register* in 1768, conveniently illustrates the rough equation in the minds of American dissenters between civil and religious tyranny as well as their reliance on liberal and Reformed theorists for support. The cartoon depicted New England dissenters driving an Anglican bishop from their shores as they brandished books titled "Locke," "Sydney on Government," and "Barclay's Apology," and threw at him "Calvin's Works," all the while shouting that they will have "no lords spiritual or temporal."[41] That this cartoon was a typical expression of American thinking at the time is supported by John Adams's recollection in 1815:

> the apprehension of Episcopacy contributed fifty years ago, as much as any other cause, to arouse the attention, not only of the inquiring mind, but of the common people, and urge them to close thinking on the constitutional authority of parliament over the colonies[.] This . . . was a fact as certain as any in the history of North America. . . . The reasoning was this . . . if parliament can erect dioceses and appoint bishops, they may introduce the whole hierarchy, establish tithes, forbid marriages and funerals, establish religions, forbid dissenters, make schism heresy, impose penalties extending to life and limb as well as to liberty and property.[42]

Adams again suggested that the War had a religious as well as a civil cause when he claimed that "[t]he Revolution was in the minds and hearts of the people; a change in their religious sentiments of their duties and obligations.... *This radical change in the principles, opinions, sentiments, and affections of the people, was the real American Revolution.*"[43] Subsequent historians including Perry Miller and William G. McLoughlin have made similar assessments of the role of religion in the Revolution. Miller, writing in 1967, said that "we still do not realize how effective were generations of Protestant preaching in evoking patriotic enthusiasm."[44] McLoughlin, in a similar vein, saw the Great Awakening as "really the beginning of America's identity as a nation—the starting point of the Revolution."[45]

In line with Adams and the anonymous cartoonist, Witherspoon drew heavily on those theorists (primarily John Locke and John Calvin) being used by the Americans against the Anglican bishop in 1768. But there is nothing remarkable in this reliance; indeed, it would be remarkable if Americans as a whole had drawn on Locke, Algernon Sydney (both of whom Jefferson mentioned by name as sources of the "harmonizing sentiments of the day" put down in the Declaration),[46] and Calvin to justify their resistance to *religious* tyranny but then proceeded to draw only on Locke and Sydney, for instance, to justify their resistance to *civil* tyranny.

Witherspoon, like other Reformed Americans, saw himself as the inheritor of a sturdy tradition of Protestant resistance to the divine right of kings and civil tyranny that antedated Locke and Sydney by a century. The principle of popular sovereignty (at least in limited form) can, it is true, be traced to the early Middle Ages, and a more radical statement of the doctrine was made by Marsilius of Padua in the late Middle Ages.[47] But of the modern constitutionalists, the English, French, Scottish, and Swiss reformers developed a sophisticated body of literature arguing against the divine right of kings and, more important to Witherspoon, articulating a case for resistance to arbitrary or tyrannical government. The resistance literature that arose during the later stages of the Protestant Reformation built on the work of John Calvin (1509–1564), but went far beyond the limited right of resistance articulated in his *Institutes of the Christian Religion.* Even that arch-predestinarian, who generally emphasized the obligation of individual Christians to obey their earthly rulers in the *Institutes,* had to admit that "[n]othing is more desirable than liberty."[48] Calvin accordingly left the door to resistance slightly ajar by recognizing a right of "magistrates of the people, appointed to restrain the willfulness of kings" to disobey oppressive rulership. These magistrates were to be appointed by the people in extraordinary circumstances to restrain the "fierce licentiousness of kings" who "betray the freedom of the people."[49]

Witherspoon appears to have considered the Continental Congress just such a magistracy, appointed to protect the people's freedom and to restrain a willful British ministry and Parliament. (Like Calvin, he believed that "[a]ll persons, young and old, love liberty.")[50] Especially to Reformed audiences, he repeatedly emphasized that the Revolution was a popular movement and that Congress was composed of the legitimate representatives of the people, and he rejected the notion that a small group of political elites engineered the War over the wishes of the people.[51] In the "Thanksgiving Sermon" of 1782, Witherspoon reminded the congregation that "[t]he truth is, the American Congress owes its existence and its influence to the people at large. I might easily shew, that there has hardly any great or important step been taken, but the public opinion has gone before the resolutions of that body."[52] The "Pastoral Letter" to the Presbyterian ministers of the Synod of New York and Philadelphia in 1775 emphasized that Congress had been appointed under extraordinary circumstances. "In particular, as the Continental Congress, now sitting at Philadelphia, consist of delegates chosen in the most free and unbiased manner, by the body of the people, let them not only be treated with respect, and encouraged in their difficult service . . . but adhere firmly to their resolutions."[53]

Moreover, in a personal letter from 1778, Witherspoon related that "[a]nother mistake, into which the ministry and parliament of England fell, was, that this was a deep-laid scheme of a few artful and designing men, who stirred up the multitude for their own ends; that the sentiments in favour of America, were by no means general; but that the artful leaders imposed upon them. . . . Alas! they know nothing of the matter."[54] Two years later he wrote to a friend in Scotland that "[t]here is no instance in the whole contest, in which the public opinion did not go before their [Congress's] resolutions. To go back to the very beginning—the declaration of independence was forced upon the majority of the then Congress, by the people in general."[55] Finally, even a public document such as "Thoughts on American Liberty" (1774) contained an analysis of Congress that sounded remarkably similar to Calvin's magistracy:

> The Congress is, properly speaking, the representative of the great body of the people of North America. Their election is for a particular purpose, and a particular season only. . . . It is an interruption or suspension of the usual forms, and an appeal to the great law of reason,

the first principles of the social union, and the multitude collectively, for whose benefit all the particular laws and customs of a constituted state, are supposed to have been originally established.[56]

In addition to the writings of Calvin himself, Witherspoon was doubtless familiar with other influential works of late-Reformation resistance theory, including François Hotman's *Franco-Gallia* (1573), Theodore Beza's *Right of Magistrates* (1574), the Huguenot Philippe du Plessis-Mornay's *Vindiciae contra Tyrannos [A Defence of Liberty Against Tyrants]* (1579), George Buchanan's *De jure regni apud Scotos [The Law of Scottish Kingship]* (1579), and Samuel Rutherford's *Lex, Rex [The Law and the Prince]* (1644).[57] We can say this with some certainty because we know that Witherspoon owned, at the time of his death, volumes by Calvin, including the *Institutes of the Christian Religion,* by Calvin's student Beza, and by Buchanan.[58] His personal library also contained Sydney's *Discourses Concerning Government* and the 1713 edition of Locke's *Two Treatises.*[59]

The Reformation treatises from which Witherspoon drew collectively contained what Herbert Foster has called the "five points of political Calvinism," which were "fundamental law, natural rights, contract and consent of people, popular sovereignty, resistance to tyranny through responsible representatives."[60] Foster also claims that these five points were passed along to the American revolutionaries through Locke's *Two Treatises,* which, if true, would help explain how Witherspoon so easily mixed the liberal and biblical arguments. Nor is Foster the only intellectual historian to notice the similarity between the liberal Lockean arguments and those from the late-Reformation period that preceded them. J. N. Figgis, for one, has noticed the remarkable similarity between the *Vindiciae contra Tyrannos* and Locke's "Second Treatise of Government," insisting that "[i]t is hard to overestimate the resemblance between the ideas of Locke and the author of the *Vindiciae.*"[61] (One can also point to an uncanny resemblance between Locke's *Two Treatises,* the first of which was written to refute the divine right of kings theory in Sir Robert Filmer's *Patriarcha: or, The Natural Power of Kings,* and Rutherford's 1644 *Lex, Rex,* written before Locke's work in order, as its lengthy subtitle indicated, to refute John Maxwell's *Sacro-Sancta Regum Majestas, or The Sacred and Royal Prerogative of Christian Kings.*) Harold Laski, for another, writes that the *Vindiciae* was "an essential source of English radicalism" and that "through Locke . . . it supplies the perspective of the American Revolution."[62] Locke's contemporary Pierre Bayle (1647–1706), himself profoundly ambivalent about Protestantism, acknowledged that

"Locke's Civil Government proves that the sovereignty belongs to the people. . . . This is the gospel of the day among Protestants."[63] Montesquieu (1689–1755) thought that "[t]he Genevese should bless the birthday of Calvin,"[64] and even Voltaire (1694–1778) had to admit that "Calvinism conforms to the republican spirit."[65] It seems, therefore, that Locke's contemporaries and modern scholars have perceived a genuine connection between late-Reformation political theory and Locke, and it is possible that Locke read the *Vindiciae* before writing his *Two Treatises*, as it appears among his 1681 "Catalogue of my Books at Oxford."[66]

Yet none of the foregoing means that Reformed Puritan political theory held an exclusive, or even necessarily preeminent, place in John Locke's political thought. It does, however, suggest that the influence of Puritan resistance theory upon Locke was not merely trivial; that Locke was in some sense, as Winthrop Hudson has put it, an "heir of Puritan political theorists,"[67] just as he was the fleshly heir of Puritan parents.[68] That he may have sought to secularize Puritan political theory is perhaps beside the point. Locke adopted the categories of Puritan resistance theory, although he filled in those categories with more secular content. Like Nathaniel Hawthorne in America,[69] Locke's writing was haunted by the Puritan ideas of his forebears even though he was not a Puritan himself. Religious Americans—even the highly literate such as Witherspoon—could and probably did see Locke in the long Reformed tradition begun by Calvin and carried on by his English, Scottish, and Huguenot followers. That a reasonably sophisticated moral philosopher such as Witherspoon was able to harmonize the basic tenets of Reformation political theory with those of an English liberal such as Locke suggests that the latter may indeed have been a carrier of Puritan political theory. Even so clever an unbeliever as Edward Gibbon, a contemporary of the American founders, saw Locke in Christian terms: "Nor can it be deemed incredible that the mind of an unlettered soldier [Constantine] should have yielded to the weight of evidence [for Christianity] which, in a more enlightened age, has satisfied or subdued the reason of a Grotius, a Pascal, or a Locke."[70] But even if the modest connection between Locke and Reformation thought is weaker than I have suggested, it would have required very little effort—or no effort at all—for Witherspoon to view Locke as an heir of the Puritans. As Herbert Foster notes, "Locke cites authorities sparingly; but in his *Two Treatises on Government*, his citations are almost entirely Calvinistic: . . . seven Calvinists (Hooker, Bilson, James I., Milton, Hunton, Ainsworth, Selden); one ex-Calvinist, the Dutch Remonstrant Grotius; and only one reference uninfected by Calvinism, the Scottish Catholic Barclay."[71]

This Puritan infection in Locke may account for the apparent ease with which Americans in general, and Witherspoon in particular, could rely simultaneously on Locke, Sydney, and Calvin for support in resisting perceived British religious and civil tyranny.[72] Witherspoon could speak with equal eloquence, to return to Carey McWilliams's metaphor, in at least those two voices of English liberalism (Locke and Sydney) and Reformed Christianity (Calvin). Nowhere is this better illustrated than in his celebrated political sermon, "The Dominion of Providence Over the Passions of Men."[73]

The sermon is interesting as a near-perfect exemplar of the melding of Christian and liberal political theory. This melding is apparent in the text of the sermon itself, and it becomes even more apparent when the published version, including the appended "Address," is examined. The "Address to the Natives of Scotland Residing in America" argued for independence much as the "Dominion of Providence" had, but in more secular-sounding, liberal language. The published sermon containing both pieces is therefore a noteworthy example of a larger religio-political mindset present in the colonies around the time of the Revolution.[74] Witherspoon's contemporaries—many of them hostile to the American cause—recognized it as such. The critical editor of the 1777 Glasgow edition of the sermon noted that Witherspoon had "the audacity to affirm, that not only the temporal but eternal happiness of the revolted colonists depends upon persevering in their independence, and undauntedly opposing the arms of their lawful sovereign," and that his sermon combined "the most rebellious sentiments with the most sacred and important truths."[75] Just as the Glasgow editor recognized, Witherspoon's arguments for independence in the "Dominion of Providence" can conveniently be grouped under two heads, overtly religious arguments and liberal arguments, although Witherspoon moved back and forth between the two with little difficulty.

Witherspoon prefaced his religious arguments with an appropriate allusion to David and the Philistine Goliath, suggesting, of course, that the United States were playing David to Great Britain's Goliath. (Biblical images such as these were standard fare in Reformed sermons of the period: George Duffield, minister of the Third Presbyterian Church in Philadelphia, preached a sermon the same day with John Adams in attendance, in which he drew a parallel between Pharaoh and George III.) Just as God favored the righteous David and the rest of his chosen people over Goliath and the Philistines, so he was siding with the Americans against the British.

The first religious argument in the sermon was thus an implicit endorsement of America's status as God's favored nation, and of Americans as his almost-chosen people, to borrow a phrase from Lincoln. Although he presented it "as a matter rather of conjecture than certainty" and disclaimed any intention to speak "prophetically," Witherspoon pointed out that "[s]ome have observed that true religion and in her train dominion, riches, literature, and arts have taken their course in a slow and gradual manner from east to west since the earth was settled after the flood, and from thence forebode the future glory of America."[76] (Recall that five years earlier, Philip Freneau and Hugh Henry Brackenridge wrote Princeton's 1771 Commencement address, which they titled "The Rising Glory of America" and published in 1772.) The belief that America was somehow uniquely singled out by God was shared by several of the counselors who had urged Witherspoon to emigrate. Not least of these was George Whitefield, who, along with Jonathan Edwards, had sparked the First Great Awakening. Witherspoon later recalled how Whitefield had told him, "[y]ou will be greatly mortified to see the difference between a small country society in America, and a large city congregation in Scotland; but if you be instrumental in sending out ministers of the New Testament, it will be a still more important station, for every gownsman [clergyman] is a legion."[77]

Even more pointedly, the Reverend Thomas Randall, a Scottish minister and Witherspoon's confidant, wrote to his friend that "[w]hen I heard, some time ago, of your being called to the Presidency of N. Jersey College, I judged it a matter of thankfulness to GOD; as I have long thought it the intention of Providence (after our abuse of our great mercies, & our dreadful degeneracy from real religion) to fix the great seat of truth and righteousness in America; and that N. Jersey seemed to promise fair for being the *nursery* of the most approved instruments, for carrying on that great design, in that wide continent."[78] By the time Randall's letter arrived, Witherspoon had already made up his mind to sail for America, since "[f]rom the Persuasion of you & other friends at Edinbr & what Mr Stockton has said of the State of Religion in America I find a pretty favourable Inclination in my own Mind to the Proposal though many Difficulties ly [*sic*] in the Way."[79] To minds like these, independence was seen as the next step in the divinely ordained glorification of America.

A second religious argument for independence used by Witherspoon in the "Dominion of Providence" was the intertwining of civil and religious rights. To reiterate a point made earlier, for Witherspoon resistance and ultimately independence were necessary because both religious and civil liberties were at stake. "I am satisfied," he said, "that the confederacy of the colonies has not been the effect of pride, resentment, or sedition, but of a deep and general conviction that our civil and religious liberties, and consequently in a great measure the temporal and eternal happiness of us and our posterity, depended on the issue." History teaches that true religion has been spread almost exclusively in those parts of the world that experienced political liberty and justice. Lose your civil liberty, and religious liberty will go with it. "If therefore we yield up our temporal property, we at the same time deliver the conscience into bondage."[80]

Witherspoon was implying that religious liberty or freedom of conscience was the end, and civil liberty the means to that end. Since the two liberties were interdependent, the struggle for civil liberty became a struggle for religious liberty. As Witherspoon saw it, the Revolution was, in Marvin Olasky's language, a matter of "fighting for liberty and virtue," or, in Perry Miller's, "a protest of native piety against foreign impiety."[81] As early as 1771, Witherspoon was arguing that American Christianity and morality had surpassed those of the decadent British. Speaking of the New England Congregationalists, he wrote in a letter to the Scottish press, "[n]or do I think that any part of the British empire is at this day equal to them for real religion and sound morals."[82] Thus, Witherspoon could claim that "[t]he cause [independence] is sacred, and the champions for it ought to be holy."[83] Two years later he was more convinced than ever that "[a]s to the public cause, I look upon the separation of America from Britain to be the visible intention of Providence."[84] This belief was reiterated in 1782 in the "Thanksgiving Sermon." "Upon the whole," Witherspoon explained, "nothing appears to me more manifest, than that the separation of this country from Britain has been of God; for every step the British took to prevent [it], served to accelerate it, which has generally been the case when men have undertaken to go in opposition to the course of Providence, and to make war with the nature of things."[85] Note that an equation is made between "the course of Providence" and "the nature of things," or, in slightly different but more famous terms, between the laws of nature and of nature's God.

But no sooner had he used the prophetic biblical voice than Witherspoon added the more secular-sounding liberal voice as a complement. This voice spoke the language of necessity, of fixed laws of government like those in the Newtonian physical universe, and of natural laws. "I do not refuse submission," Witherspoon argued,

> because they [the British] are corrupt or profligate, although probably many of them are so, but because they are men, and therefore liable to all the selfish bias inseparable from human nature. I call this claim

unjust, of making laws to bind us in all cases whatsoever, because they are separated from us, independent of us, and have an interest in opposing us. Would any man who could prevent it give up his estate, person, and family to the disposal of his neighbor, although he had liberty to choose the wisest and the best master? Surely not. *This is the true and proper hinge of the controversy between Great Britain and America.* It is however to be added that such is their distance from us that a wise and prudent administration of our affairs is as impossible as the claim of authority is unjust.[86]

The British were not merely trying to do what was unjust; they were also trying to do what was unnatural and impossible. "I mention these things, my brethren, not only as grounds of confidence in God . . . but as decisive proofs of the impossibility of these great and growing states" remaining dependent on Great Britain. Due to their distance and ignorance, the British were no longer competent to "give direction and vigor to every department of our civil constitutions from age to age." There are "fixed bounds" to such things: just as when "the branches of a tree grow very large and weighty, they fall off from the trunk," so "there is a certain distance from the seat of government where an attempt to rule will either produce tyranny and helpless subjection, or provoke resistance and effect a separation."[87] Not only was the separation of the colonies from Great Britain according to God's will, but it was also as natural as any terrestrial motion described by Isaac Newton.

In contrast to the pietism and moral Newtonianism of the "Dominion of Providence," the arguments set out in the "Address to the Natives of Scotland Residing in America" were presented exclusively in McWilliams's first "voice," that voice of British liberalism. Aimed at Witherspoon's "countrymen and friends" in the colonies, the "Address" was an attempt to convince expatriate Scots that American opposition was based on the most "rational and liberal principles."[88] There was, to be sure, an allusion to America's uniqueness, but what had been its unique covenanted status in the "Dominion of Providence" was transmuted into exceptionalism in the "Address." That is, the argument based on a national covenant in the sermon was primarily about God singling out America, just as he had chosen the children of Israel, to be the repository of true religion. The other benefits—"riches, literature, and arts"—were by-products of God's blessing, icing on the religious cake. However, in the "Address," America, instead of being a partner in a solemn covenant with the Lord God, became a unique combination of agricultural and economic success. "In America we see a rich and valuable soil, and an extensive country, taken possession of by the power, the learning, and the wealth of Europe. For this reason it is now exhibiting to the world a scene which was never seen before."[89]

America was indeed unique, as Witherspoon suggested in the sermon, but not because it was the repository of true religion and virtue, as he said before, but because it was rich and cultivated, a sort of western European Promised Land. The idea of a national covenant in the "Dominion of Providence" had been subtly changed into American exceptionalism in the "Address," while the language of religion and virtue had been replaced by language about interest and industry. On the subject of industry, Witherspoon even footnoted the Scottish infidel David Hume's "Essay on the Jealousy of Trade."[90] Summing up the arguments for independence, Witherspoon hoped to show: "1. That it was necessary. 2. That it will be honourable and profitable. And, 3. That in all probability it will be no injury, but a real advantage to the island of Great Britain."[91] Here we have a clear example of Witherspoon calibrating the pitch of his religious language to the ears of his audience.

Much the same pattern had been used by Witherspoon in "On Conducting the American Controversy" (1773) from the *Scots Magazine,* and in the fragmentary "Reflections on the Present State of Public Affairs" (1774). Without relying on pious arguments, he nevertheless said in 1773 that he looked "upon the cause of America at present to be a matter of truly inexpressible moment. The state of the human race through a great part of the globe, for ages to come, depends upon it."[92] In his "Reflections," also written for the press but apparently never published, Witherspoon hinted that America was a virtuous and chosen nation, but he once again cast that argument in more liberal, economic terms. Instead of the frank language in the "Dominion of Providence" about "true religion" moving westward to America, Witherspoon suggested that American improvements in population and cultivation offered the world a sight "differing in many respects from what it ever beheld" that is "next to miraculous."[93] Note that there was an acknowledgment of America's uniqueness and talk of progress that was "*next to* miraculous," without the forthright claim that America was in fact God's chosen nation.[94] Instead of comparisons between American and British Christianity, Witherspoon portrayed British commercial virtue degenerating into greed and laziness, which in turn resulted in British exploitation of the colonies.[95] In place of the Bible's David, with which he began the

"Dominion of Providence," Witherspoon transformed America in the "Reflections" into Locke's industrious yeoman.

Another pertinent Witherspoon document from the Revolutionary era is the "Memorial and Manifesto of the United States of North-America, to the Mediating Powers in the Conferences for Peace, to the Other Powers in Europe, and in General to All Who Shall See the Same" (1781).[96] The "Memorial" is especially interesting because its purposes run parallel to those of the Declaration of Independence: to rehearse the events leading to the declaration of American independence, to argue the case for independence, and to enlist the aid of foreign nations. Writing with the empress of Russia and the emperor of Germany in mind, Witherspoon intended to give "a brief detail of the steps by which they [the states] have been brought into their present interesting and critical situation," much as the Declaration had rehearsed "the causes which impel[led] them to the separation."

Once more, Witherspoon used both secular and religious arguments to justify American independence. The original settlers of the colonies came for a variety of reasons: some were "actuated by the spirit of curiosity and enterprise," some by "the hope of riches," and others "were driven from their native country by the iron rod of sacerdotal tyranny." Although their governments were founded on various principles, all agreed "that they considered themselves as bringing their liberty with them, and as entitled to all the rights and privileges of freemen under the British constitution. . . . With respect, indeed to the whole of their internal government, they considered themselves as not directly subject to the British parliament, but as separate *independent* dominions under the same sovereign, and with similar co-ordinate jurisdiction."[97]

A recitation of the abuses of the British government, along much the same lines as the bill of particulars in the Declaration, followed. The various oppressive acts of Parliament—the Stamp Act, Declaratory Act, Boston Port Bill—all had the potential effect of reducing the Americans to "beggary" and "unconditional submission."[98] Then, after reciting the British violations of natural law, Witherspoon slipped into the second "voice," claiming that "we found it absolutely necessary to declare ourselves independent of that prince who had thrown us out of his protection. This great step was taken with the full approbation, and indeed at the ardent desire of the public at large. . . . The thing indeed seems to have been the purpose of God Almighty; for every measure of the court of Great Britain had the most direct tendency to hasten, and render it unavoidable."[99]

Declaring Independence

The close parallels between Witherspoon's "Memorial and Manifesto" and the Declaration of Independence, both in form and content, together with his unique position as the lone clerical signatory of the Declaration raise the question of how he might have viewed that controversial document. (I do not mean that the Declaration was controversial in its day — it was not particularly — but that since the Civil War, and especially since the twentieth century, there has been significant controversy about the meaning of the Declaration and its place in the American political tradition.)[100]

In the first place, Witherspoon doubtless found much that was familiar in the Declaration. In fact, almost all of the political theory therein is present in Witherspoon's writing, especially in the Lectures on Moral Philosophy, composed half a dozen years before the Declaration. In Lecture XII on "civil society," he discussed the legitimate circumstances of resistance, and he anticipated Jefferson's argument regarding "light and transient causes" in the Declaration. There is an "exception" to the authority of the "supreme power" in any government, Witherspoon said, if that power "come[s] to be exercised in a manifestly tyrannical manner." Under such tyranny "the subjects may certainly if in their power, resist and overthrow it." However, the meaning of "[t]his doctrine of resistance . . . is not, that any little mistake of the rulers of any society will justify resistance. We must obey and submit to them always, till the corruption becomes intolerable; for to say that we might resist legal authority every time we judged it to be wrong, would be inconsistent with a state of society, and to the very first idea of subjection."[101] This anticipation of the Declaration's language by Witherspoon should come as no surprise if, as Jefferson himself claimed, the document was a sort of compendium of the political theory of the day, derived from "Aristotle, Cicero, Locke, Sidney, etc." — all of whose works were in Witherspoon's library. (One figure conspicuously absent from Jefferson's list is Calvin, but I have suggested that Calvin was present, if only in spectral fashion, in Locke.) In addition to anticipating portions of the Declaration in his Lectures, Witherspoon reiterated many of its arguments — although somewhat less elegantly than had Jefferson and Congress — in his "Memorial and Manifesto" of 1781 (without the high-flown language of the Declaration's second paragraph).

Certainly, Witherspoon would have had no objections to the Declaration's four references to "Nature's God," the "Creator," the "Supreme Judge of the World," and the "[protection of] divine Providence." Each of those phrases (or at least a variant of each) appears in the quintessential Reformed statement, the Westminster Confession of Faith of 1647, and in fact three of the four appear in that document's first sentence.[102] The Westminster Confession, which Witherspoon knew virtually by rote, began: "the light of nature, and the works of creation and providence, do so far manifest the goodness, wisdom, and power of God, as to leave men inexcusable."[103] All good Calvinists of that day believed that God was the creator, endower of inalienable rights, giver of the laws of nature, and supreme judge, and that he acted in the world through his providence.[104] The "Supreme Judge," to whom the revolutionaries appeal for the "rectitude of our intentions," has an especially Reformed ring to it. The Westminster Confession states that "[t]he Supreme Judge, by which all controversies . . . and private spirits, are to be examined, and in whose sentence we are to rest, can be no other but the Holy Spirit."[105] Closer to home, and to the writing of the Declaration, Jonathan Edwards used the precise phrase, "Supreme Judge of the world," to refer to God in his sermon "The Final Judgment."[106] (It is revealing to contrast this theistic background of the American Declaration with the ground of the French Revolution, represented by Simon Linguet. During his disbarral hearing in 1775, Linguet made the following appeal: "I will place between you and me this Supreme Judge to which the most absolute tribunals are subordinated: *public opinion*.")[107]

Witherspoon himself referred to God as "the Author of nature" in a section of the Lectures on Moral Philosophy dealing with natural religion and virtue.[108] The term "Providence" in particular, although it has been pointed to as evidence of deistic influences at the founding,[109] was Witherspoon's favorite name for the biblical God's activity in the world. (One need simply recall the title of his famous "Dominion of Providence Over the Passions of Men" sermon, and the fact that he was a strict believer in God's sovereignty, to realize what an active God such language would have conjured up in his mind.) Even the Declaration's "protection of divine Providence" is set in the context of God's intervention on behalf of the righteous colonies. Jefferson himself used "Providence" to refer to a personal god's intervention during the Revolution. In a now-famous letter to Maria Cosway in 1786, he described "the ways of Providence, whose precept is to do always what is right, and leave the issue to *him*."[110] As to the "Laws of Nature" in the Declaration, Witherspoon would not have understood them to be hostile in any way to the notion of the biblical God: they are merely those laws that have been written by God on the hearts of men and are discoverable by the *natural* means of reason and conscience. In the Lectures on Moral Philosophy, Witherspoon differentiated between the light of nature and the law of nature, defining the latter as that which, when discovered "by our own powers, without revelation or tradition . . . appear[s] to be agreeable to reason and nature."[111] He again seems to have taken his arguments and general phrasing from the Westminster Confession, which continues: "the light of nature, and the works of creation and providence . . . [are] not sufficient to give that knowledge of God, and of his will, which is necessary unto salvation; therefore it pleased the Lord, at sundry times, and in divers manners, to reveal himself . . . [u]nder the name of holy Scripture."[112]

Because he was a prominent religious and political leader in the colonies, not to mention one of the boldest patriots in both practice and theory, an understanding of Witherspoon's thought on resistance and independence is of no small importance in interpreting the American mindset of that day. Using a metaphor of two "voices" of liberalism and biblical Christianity in the American political tradition (and Tocqueville's understanding of the harmony of religion and politics in early America) as a guide, we have heard the ease with which Witherspoon could speak in both of those voices.[113] Although he could be uncompromising in church settings, in the political arena he did not allow himself to be hamstrung by his own orthodoxy. He was a careful student of language, and he knew how to modulate the religious fervor in his addresses according to his audience. Always sensitive to their situation, Witherspoon calibrated his remarks to his hearers, toning down the religious rhetoric in more secular settings and emphasizing the Reformed, biblical language when he spoke or wrote in a religious setting. At those times, Witherspoon took his verbal cues from Calvin and later Reformed theorists by stressing what have been called the "five points of political Calvinism." When the audience was not known to be sympathetic, as in the case of the "Address to the Natives of Scotland Residing in America," Witherspoon tended to speak in the first voice of liberalism and moral Newtonianism. In some cases, including the "Dominion of Providence" and the "Memorial and Manifesto of the United States of North-America," which he knew would be read by colonists of all religious persuasions, Witherspoon harmonized both voices, apparently without seeing any contradiction between the two. In fact the Lockean liberal theory might have been seen by Witherspoon and the many Reformed Americans as a complement to, and even carrier of, the Calvinist doctrine of resistance.

Seeing himself as an heir of a Protestant tradition of resistance that went back more than two hundred years, Witherspoon viewed the American struggle as a supremely conservative movement—a revolution prevented, not made, to borrow Edmund Burke's phrase about the English revolution. (Witherspoon later recalled that until the spring of 1776, Americans "were contending for the restoration of certain privileges under the government of Great Britain, and we were praying for re-union with her.")[114] However, even if the connection between Locke and the Calvinists is rejected, Witherspoon remains an especially interesting example of a theologico-political ethos present during the Revolutionary period.

chapter five

"An Equal Republican Constitution"

Confederation, Union, and Nationhood

Nothing is of so much consequence to us at present as union; and nothing is so much the desire of all unprejudiced, public-spirited and virtuous men. The federal constitution is but new. It is, we hope, taking place; but cannot yet be said to have taken root. It will from the nature of things, take some time before it can acquire the respect and veneration necessary in every government from the body of the people.
— John Witherspoon, "On the Federal City"

In the next place, it may be considered as an objection inherent in the principle, that as every appeal to the people would carry an implication of some defect in the government, frequent appeals would in great measure deprive the government of that veneration, which time bestows on every thing, and without which perhaps the wisest and freest governments would not possess the requisite stability.
— James Madison, *Federalist* 49

Having played a significant part in severing the political ties that bound the colonies to Great Britain, Witherspoon, along with the rest of Congress, turned his attention to ordering what the Declaration of Independence had called "free and independent states." That is precisely how Witherspoon viewed the states after independence had been declared. To him the Declaration merely created, as Willmoore Kendall liked to put it, a "baker's dozen" of independent states,[1] but it did not create any political order among those states.[2] This was certainly the view of Luther Martin of Maryland, who argued in the Federal Convention that "the separation from G.B. [Great Britain] placed the 13 states in a state of nature towards each other."[3] Witherspoon, worried that they might remain "independent states, *separate and disunited,* after this war,"[4] speculated on how best to form them into a permanent union. Like Martin, Witherspoon understood the Revolution as a kind of political revolving that had spun the states back into their original, natural posture toward one another while it broke them free of the king. "With respect, indeed to the whole of their internal government, they [the states] considered themselves as not directly subject to the British parliament, but as separate *independent* dominions under the same sovereign, and with similar co-ordinate jurisdiction."[5]

The states had always considered themselves, so he claimed, as independent of Parliament even while they were subject to the same king. The Revolution simply returned them to that state of nature in which all independent nations exist: separate and independent of any power save the law of nature, which Witherspoon equated with the "law of nations."[6] "[S]eparate and independent states are, with regard to one another," he said in the Lectures on Moral Philosophy, "in a state of natural liberty, or as man to man before the commencement of civil society."[7] Since independence had been declared, and the Articles of Confederation were then being debated, it seemed to Witherspoon that the states were "entering into a new compact, and therefore stand on original ground."[8] How solid that ground would be remained for the Congress to determine.

Confederation and the Articles

From the moment of his entry into the Continental Congress in the summer of 1776, Witherspoon advocated a strong, permanent union of the states. One of the best examples of this advocacy, and the most thorough statement of his views of the Confederacy, is to be found in a speech he made in Congress on July 30, 1776.[9] That speech, delivered when the issue of an enduring confederacy was in serious doubt (as we now know it should have been), was a plea for a "lasting confederacy"—a permanent league that would outlive the war for independence. (The full title of the Articles was the "Articles of Confederation and perpetual Union between the States.")[10] The benefits of such a league were several. To begin with, a permanent confederacy would strengthen the resolve of Americans to fight. If the public were to learn that Congress considered a lasting union impracticable, it would "greatly derange the minds of the people, and weaken their hands in defence of their country." Such knowledge would "greatly diminish the glory and importance of the struggle, whether considered as for the rights of mankind in general, or for the prosperity and happiness of this continent in future times."[11]

Moreover, a lasting confederacy would secure all the states — and especially the smaller ones such as New Jersey — against the danger of civil war once the fight with Britain was over. What difference would it make whether Americans won their independence from the British if they "must, in the end, be subjected, the greatest part of [them], to the power of one or more of the strongest or largest of the American states?"[12] There was in fact a sectional rivalry at the time between the three geographic regions (northern or "eastern," middle, and southern), to which Publius alluded in *Federalist* 1 and 13.[13] A permanent confederation would also guard against foreign wars better than a monarchy or a single consolidated state. And finally, in language that anticipated the Articles of Confederation, Witherspoon suggested that a "firm confederacy" would promote general order and happiness.[14]

There was no denying the "absolute necessity of union" for securing independence; what Witherspoon wished to see was "the colonies settled upon a lasting and equitable footing" once the War was over.[15] (Although he slipped momentarily back into the language of "colonies" rather than "states," he apparently never doubted that independence would be won.) Sufficient power would have to be given the Confederation to make it lasting, and fair principles of representation were necessary to make it equitable. Equity would in turn contribute to its longevity.

The power that Witherspoon envisioned for the Confederation was to derive primarily from money and land. A truly continental or national revenue was required, and on February 3, 1781, he offered a motion granting Congress unprecedented powers to tax and oversee the commercial regulations of each state. It was, he said, "indispensably necessary that the United States in Congress assembled, should be vested with a right of superintending the commercial regulations of every State, that none may take place that shall be partial or contrary to the common interest; and that they should be vested with the exclusive right of laying duties upon all imported articles, no restriction to be valid, and no such duty to be laid, but with the consent of nine states."[16] Although the power to levy import duties was to be limited to a specific period and specific circumstances, Witherspoon's motion was defeated, five states to four. In retrospect, had that motion been adopted, the greatest weakness of the Confederation—its inability to compel the states to pay—would have been avoided. As it was, Congress's continuing financial impotence became an impetus for the Federal Convention six years later.

National land was equally important to a reliable national revenue. Ever since his appointment to the congressional committee for the oversight of the western territories, Witherspoon had a keen interest in those lands and the part they would play in strengthening the nation as a whole.[17] Again in 1781, during debate over ownership of the vacant western lands, which prior to independence had been thought the property of Britain, Witherspoon insisted that title to those territories should be reserved to the Confederation, not to any individual states. (Recall that at this time the western boundary of Virginia reached, in theory, to the Pacific Ocean.) He stubbornly saw the issue as a matter of national interest and refused to view it in terms of states' rights. Witherspoon's position prompted heated responses, especially from Richard Henry Lee of Virginia, but eventually a majority of states came around to the nationalist position. Edward Corwin has noted that after 1781, the year under discussion, the tide of opinion in Congress concerning the western lands turned from narrow provincialism to nationalism, and "the interest of all States in seeing the American title established became what it originally had been," namely, continental in scope.[18] V. L. Collins has correctly pointed out that Witherspoon, no less than any other member of Congress, was responsible for this move toward nationalism.[19]

Witherspoon thus argued in Congress that national revenue and lands were necessary to a strong and lasting confederation. But a strong confederacy was not enough: equity had to accompany strength, in taxation and particularly in representation, that thorniest of issues in the Federal Convention of 1787. In fairness to the states, monies they were to pay into the national treasury had to be determined on the basis of the value of land and houses, not on population. Jefferson recorded that "Dr. Witherspoon was of opinion that the value of lands & houses was the best estimate of the wealth of a nation, and that it was practicable to obtain such a valuation. . . . [T]his is the true barometer of wealth."[20] Despite having shown strong national sensibilities regarding revenue and the western lands, Witherspoon here thought and acted like the small-state delegate that he was. And he had the same perspective on representation: each state, from smallest to largest, was to have one vote in Congress. Against opposition from John Adams, the loudest voice from the large state of Massachusetts, Witherspoon clung to his position of one state, one vote.[21] Congress, of course, finally settled on equal representation and decided that in "determining questions in the United States, in Congress assembled, each State shall have one vote."[22] A strong confederation that was also fair in apportioning taxes and representation was, according to Witherspoon, the best formula for a "lasting and equitable" league of American states. Although many of his proposals were not adopted, Witherspoon nevertheless thought that a confederated union was better than none at all, and he signed the Articles of Confederation and Perpetual Union on November 26, 1778.

The ten years that followed the signing of the Articles were the great decade of constitution-making in America, but Witherspoon did not participate directly in drafting either the New Jersey document or the federal Constitution. This was perhaps a source of disappointment to Witherspoon, who noted approvingly that after independence, "[w]e shall have the opportunity of forming plans of government upon the most rational, just, and equal principles. I confess I have always looked upon this with a kind of enthusiastic satisfaction. The case never happened before since the world began."[23] Although it "has always been understood that the Rev. John Witherspoon . . . took an active part in preparing it (the constitution of New Jersey, adopted July 2, 1776),"[24] a careful examination of the records shows that he took no part, active or otherwise. True, he was elected a delegate to the New Jersey constitutional convention and was present when it convened, but Witherspoon was off to Philadelphia and the Continental Congress before a word of the New Jersey constitution had been drafted. The only one he participated in writing was the Presbyterian constitution, a document with its own political significance, as I shall be arguing.

Witherspoon's importance to the federal Constitution derives from several of his subsidiary roles. He was a leader in the New Jersey convention that ratified the Constitution in 1787; the college president and professor of moral philosophy to fourteen members of their own state ratifying conventions; the former mentor of James Madison at Princeton and continuing adviser to both Madison and Alexander Hamilton, the principal authors of *The Federalist Papers;* and the author of the *Essay on Money,* an implicitly pro-Constitution economic treatise. He also contributed by way of indirection to an increased sense of American nationhood by nationalizing the Presbyterian church and drafting its ecclesiastical constitution.

Ratifying the Federal Constitution

There is a heightened interest today in the original understanding of the ratifiers of the Constitution among constitutional scholars, some of whom take the opinions of the ratifiers to be more important even than those of the framers in determining the meaning of that document. Henry Paul Monaghan, for one, has insisted that "[t]he relevant inquiry must focus on the *public* understanding of the language when the Constitution was adopted."[25] Among the framers themselves, James Madison and Alexander Hamilton both implied that what really counted were the intentions of the delegates to the ratifying conventions. Madison focused on the importance of the ratifiers' understanding when he argued that "[w]ith a view to this last object [a just construction of the Constitution], I entirely concur in the propriety of resorting to the sense in which the Constitution was accepted and ratified by the nation. In that sense alone it is the legitimate Constitution."[26] (This belief of Madison's helps explain why he was never in a hurry to publish his authoritative notes of the Convention debates.) Hamilton went so far as to downplay altogether the intentions of the Philadelphia Convention when he wrote, "whatever may have been the intention of the framers of a constitution, or of a law, that intention is to be sought for in the instrument itself, according to the usual & established rules of construction. . . . [A]rguments drawn from extrinsic circumstances, regarding the intention of the [Federal] convention, must be rejected."[27] So we have it on rather good authority, both present and past, that the ratifiers' understanding of the federal union should be examined with some care. And since Witherspoon was arguably the leading figure in New Jersey politics and religion during the founding era, his views on the new Constitution and his role as a Federalist take on added importance.

Discussion of Witherspoon's views of the union under the Constitution should begin by piecing them together from the various sources. Unfortunately, the record of the New Jersey ratifying convention is a bare outline of proceedings when compared with the record of the Virginia convention, for example. Nor do the activities of Witherspoon's Princeton students at the Federal Convention provide much of a clue to his own views of the Constitution. Of the five Witherspoon graduates at Philadelphia, three (James Madison, Gunning Bedford, and Jonathan Dayton) were signers, while two (William Churchill Houston and William Richardson Davie) were not. Madison, who was close to President Witherspoon (despite disagreements when they were both in the Continental Congress),[28] was the strongest pro-constitutionalist among his graduates, while Houston, who as master of the Princeton grammar school and the College's first chair of natural philosophy (1771–1783) was even closer, was a non-signer. (Illness forced Houston to leave the Convention after only a week.)[29] Madison, from the large state of Virginia, fought Bedford, his 1771 classmate and a small-state champion from Delaware, throughout the Convention; yet Bedford ended up signing. Thus, there is no discernable pattern among Witherspoon's students at the Philadelphia Convention as a whole.

Among those students, we might expect Madison, the so-called Father of the Constitution,[30] to bear the strongest marks of Witherspoon's intellectual patrimony, but even in his case we must take care not to claim undue credit for Witherspoon's influence. Still, there was enough apparent influence to prompt Douglass Adair to conclude that "since James Madison became one of the chief architects of our political democracy . . . his sojourn at Nassau Hall under the tutelage of the learned Dr. John Witherspoon was of incalculable importance to the destiny of the United States."[31] As noted, Witherspoon did reinforce certain religious presuppositions in the young Madison that remained in his mature political thought, and to these presuppositions we can add Madison's nationalistic mindset. He stopped off to consult with Witherspoon on August 9, 1786, just prior to the Annapolis Convention, and the two conversed about national and international affairs.[32] Yet the real importance of that meeting lies in the fact that Madison still respected his old mentor sufficiently in the summer of 1786—less than a year before the Constitutional Convention—to consult with Witherspoon prior to his first efforts at strengthening the union in Annapolis. And there are too many provocative similarities between Witherspoon's works and Madison's *Federalist* essays to dismiss the former's influence out of hand.

Fortunately, we do not have to rely on the actions of Madison or on any of Witherspoon's students at the Philadelphia Convention to draw a portrait of him as a Federalist. Witherspoon's views on the union can be reconstructed accurately from various records left by other contemporaries, the findings of subsequent scholarship, and, not least, from his own political speeches and writings. These sources yield a substantial body of evidence that Witherspoon not only favored the Constitution but also was an active proponent of it.

Witherspoon, along with all of the other state delegates (the vote was unanimous), signed the New Jersey Form of Ratification on behalf of Somerset County on December 18, 1787. Beyond this, there is strong corroborating evidence that he was a consistent and vocal Federalist during the period

December 11–20 when the New Jersey convention met. This evidence can be found in contemporary testimony from the *Pennsylvania Packet* newspaper, and in correspondence from Henry Knox and Madison. The *Pennsylvania Packet* of January 14, 1788, reported that "[t]he same characters who took the lead in each of the states in the struggle for liberty in the glorious years 1775 and 1776, now take the lead in their exertions to establish the federal government, viz Sullivan and Langdon in New-Hampshire . . . [and] Stevens and Witherspoon in New-Jersey."[33] Knox claimed that all of New Jersey was "warmly for it [the Constitution] excepting Mr A[braham] Clark who now & then gives it a kick."[34]

Madison wrote in a similar vein to Edmund Randolph that "I discovered no evidence on my journey through N. Jersey that any opposition whatever would be made in that State," and it is impossible that he would have failed to record Witherspoon's disapproval had the old Doctor been unhappy with the Constitution.[35] Finally, Ashbel Green, another of Witherspoon's students and his first systematic biographer, recorded that "[a]s he supported the necessity of a well organized system of union, so he opposed and lamented, in the subsequent formation of the original confederation, the jealousy and ambition of the individual states, which were unwilling to intrust the general government with adequate powers to promote the common interest." When it came time to ratify the Constitution, Witherspoon

> greatly rejoiced in the adoption of the present Federal government, as embracing principles, and carrying into effect measures, which he had long advocated, as essential to the preservation of the liberties, and the promotion of the peace and prosperity of the country. His anticipations of the rapid improvements of every description, which were in futurity to be witnessed in the United States, were of the most sanguine kind. The present writer, having mentioned to him the completion of the Turnpike Road between Philadelphia and Lancaster, he said—"You are not to be surprised, if you live to see a Turnpike road that shall extend from Philadelphia to the Pacific Ocean."[36]

His support of the Constitution in New Jersey was an outgrowth of his political opinions in the years and months leading up to September 1787 when that document was finalized. A number of secondary writers have noted Witherspoon's consistent support of nationalization. His best biographer, V. L. Collins, echoes Green's judgment, noting that a "broad national view had marked his attitude toward all questions of policy from the very beginning of his presence in Congress; it was a view he had never lost an opportunity to emphasize."[37] The editors of the James Madison papers likewise note that since Witherspoon deplored "the petty spirit of the individual states, he wished to see a strong central government established, and he envisioned the development of the country's vast resources and its growth from coast to coast. . . . Thus Witherspoon concurred with the southern states in believing that the free navigation of the Mississippi was a territorial right of the U.S. not to be relinquished under any terms."[38]

Virtually all of Witherspoon's published pieces, including the speeches in Congress, favored a stronger national union, and, as we have seen, he even suggested giving Congress greater taxing powers under the Articles of Confederation than it ended up receiving. At the outbreak of the Revolution, Witherspoon chastised a faction of the New York legislature who tried, "to their eternal infamy," to break the union of the colonies.[39] Mention has already been made of Witherspoon's support for national revenue and title to the western territories under the Confederation. Further, during the Confederation's negotiations with foreign nations, he quickly realized the value of centralizing American diplomatic powers and frequently sought to unify those powers under Benjamin Franklin. "Careful scrutiny of the votes in the *Journal*," Collins observes, "shows that Dr. Witherspoon carried into the young republic's diplomacy his adherence to the idea of centralized authority, advocating a system with one central diplomatic executive, while other members of the committee continually strove for individual envoys responsible directly to Congress under a de-centralized system."[40] And Francis Wharton, editor of the *Revolutionary Diplomatic Correspondence of the United States* (1889), notes that Witherspoon "at once saw the necessity of a strong executive, both in the military and civil side of the government, and he uniformly gave his support to whatever measures were calculated to strengthen Washington and to sustain Franklin, and afterward Livingston and Morris."[41]

Witherspoon and *The Federalist Papers*

There are a number of specific similarities between Witherspoon's various writings and passages in *The Federalist Papers* by Hamilton and Madison. Witherspoon shared with their Publius, and indeed helped bequeath to founding-era Americans, belief in a distinctively Scottish "faculty psychology" concerning human mental faculties and what the mind can know.[42]

But beyond this shared commitment to an early school of psychology, there are many specific similarities in thought and phrasing between Witherspoon and Publius.

Witherspoon, as noted, continually harped upon the connection between religion and civil liberty. There is his prayer, for example, in the "Dominion of Providence" that God would grant that true religion and civil liberty would continue to be preserved and inseparable.[45] Madison, in a familiar section from *Federalist* 51, argued that "[i]n a free government, the security for civil rights must be the same as that for religious rights. It consists in the one case in the multiplicity of interests, and in the other, in the multiplicity of sects."[44] Witherspoon and Madison also agreed that free government depends upon the veneration of the people over time, as the epigrams that begin this chapter illustrate. Madison was concerned that "frequent appeals [to the people] would in great measure deprive the government of that veneration, which time bestows on every thing, and without which perhaps the wisest and freest governments would not possess the requisite stability."[45] Witherspoon, writing just a few years later, saw a constitution that was "taking place; but cannot yet be said to have taken root. It will from the nature of things, take some time before it can acquire the respect and veneration necessary in every government from the body of the people, who are always guided by feeling and habit, more than by a train of reasoning, however conclusive."[46]

A more arresting similarity exists between language from Witherspoon's "Address to the Natives of Scotland Residing in America," first published along with his "Dominion of Providence" sermon in 1776, and Hamilton's first *Federalist* essay. In 1776, Witherspoon exulted in the fact that "[a]ll the governments we have read of in former ages were settled by caprice or accident, by the influence of prevailing parties or particular persons, or prescribed by a conqueror. . . . But to see government in large and populous countries settled from its foundation by deliberate counsel, and directed immediately to the public good . . . is certainly altogether new."[47] Hamilton, in a passage from *Federalist* 1 that is highly reminiscent of Witherspoon's "Address," reminded Americans that they were "called upon to deliberate on a new Constitution for the United States of America. . . . It has been frequently remarked, that it seems to have been reserved to the people of this country . . . to decide the important question, whether societies of men are really capable or not, of establishing good government from reflection and choice, or whether they are forever destined to depend, for their political constitutions, on accident and force."[48] Because their language is so similar, and because we know of Hamilton's respect for Witherspoon and familiarity with his other writings, it is hard to resist the conclusion that Witherspoon was one of those who had so "frequently remarked" that it was up to the Americans to form a government based on reflection and choice.

The suggestion was made earlier that Witherspoon strengthened a Calvinistic strain in Madison by repeatedly emphasizing the depravity and fallen state of man. (The clearest instance of this tendency of Madison's is found in *Federalist* 55, in which he says bluntly that "there is a degree of depravity in mankind which requires a certain degree of circumspection and distrust.")[49] Perhaps the best known example is the well-worn passage from *Federalist* 51 in which he reminds his readers (as if they needed reminding) that men are not angels, but imperfect beings whose baser motives must always be accounted for when framing a government.[50] And we could point with equal justice to a lesser-known line of Hamilton's from *Federalist* 6, in which Publius concludes "that men are ambitious, vindictive, and rapacious."[51]

Witherspoon always stared the fact of human imperfection full in the face, but it never led him into political hopelessness. When arguing in Congress in favor of the Articles of Confederation, he denied that mankind's depravity prevented them from forming decent governments:

> There is one thing that has been thrown out, by which some seem to persuade themselves of, and others to be more indifferent about the success of a confederacy—that from the nature of men, it is to be expected, that a time must come when it will be dissolved and broken in pieces. I am none of those who either deny or conceal the depravity of human nature, till it is purified by the light of truth, and renewed by the Spirit of the living God. Yet I apprehend there is no force in that reasoning at all. Shall we establish nothing good, because we know it cannot be eternal? Shall we live without government, because every constitution has its old age, and its period [end]? Because we know that we shall die, shall we take no pains to preserve or lengthen out life? Far from it, Sir: it only requires the more watchful attention, to settle government upon the best principles, and in the wisest manner, that it may last as long as the nature of things will admit.[52]

This same guarded optimism can be found in Madison's *Federalist* 38. "It is a matter both of wonder and regret," he wrote, "that those who raise so many objections against the new Constitution, should never call to mind the defects of that which is to be exchanged for it. It is not necessary that the former should be perfect: it is sufficient that the latter is more imperfect."[53] In *Federalist* 85, Hamilton advanced a similar line of reasoning: "I should esteem it the extreme of imprudence to prolong the precarious state of our national affairs, and to expose the union to the jeopardy of successive experiments, in the chimerical pursuit of a perfect plan. I never expect to see a perfect work from imperfect man."[54]

Witherspoon deplored the "local jealousies and prejudices" that kept Americans from thinking and acting like one people. Arguing that a delay in establishing a confederacy would be tantamount to madness, he demanded to know whether the same difficulties, or worse, would not be present in the future. "Will they [the states] not have the same jealousies of each other, the same attachment to local prejudices, and particular interest? So certain is this, that I look upon it as on the repentance of a sinner — Every day's delay, though it adds to the necessity, yet augments the difficulty, and takes from the inclination."[55] For his part, Publius used the phrase "local prejudices" seven times and "local jealousies" once, though he claimed to have found a way to neutralize them by enlarging the sphere of the republic.

Witherspoon himself seems to have anticipated the extended republic theory of *The Federalist Papers* back in 1781. In one of the most prescient passages to be found in the *Works*, he envisioned a sort of forerunner to the European Union while addressing Congress on the virtues of confederation.

There have been great improvements . . . the progress of which can be easily traced in history. Every body is able to look back to the time in Europe, when the liberal sentiments that now prevail upon the rights of conscience, would have been looked upon as absurd. It is but little above two hundred years since that enlarged system called the balance of power, took place; and I maintain, that it is a greater step from the former disunited and hostile situation of kingdoms and states, to their present condition, than it would be from their present condition to a state of more perfect and lasting union. It is not impossible, that in future times all the states on one quarter of the globe, may see it proper by some plan of union, to perpetuate security and peace; and sure I am, a well planned confederacy among the states of America, may hand down the blessings of peace and public order to many generations.[56]

The extended republic, spelled out with the most clarity by Publius in *Federalist* 14, is a variation on the national level of Witherspoon's "balance of power" and on the international level of his "more perfect and lasting union."

Of course, none of these ideas was original with Witherspoon, and Publius was drawing on Montesquieu (Witherspoon's favorite French writer)[57] and Hume when he articulated the theory of the extended republic. The same can be said of all of these similarities: the ideas and the language were in the air, so to speak. In some cases — that of Hamilton's *Federalist* 1 and Witherspoon's "Address to the Natives of Scotland Residing in America," for example — the similarities are startling. But the importance of the parallels is that they show how Witherspoon and Publius were thinking along parallel Federalist lines. The parallels illustrate just how representative Witherspoon was of the prevailing American political theory during the founding and how he contributed to the political atmospherics of the day.

The *Essay on Money*

In 1786, after his retirement from the Confederation Congress and at the behest of his former colleagues, Witherspoon collected and edited his congressional speeches on finance and brought them out as *An Essay on Money as a Medium of Commerce, with Remarks on the Advantages and Disadvantages of Paper Admitted into General Circulation*. Recall that he republished the *Essay* in 1787 and again in 1788, which suggests that it was used as a Federalist tract supporting the hard-money clause in Article I, Section 10 of the proposed Constitution.[58] The 1787 edition was published at New York by S. and J. Loudon at the same time the *Federalist* essays of Publius were running in the New York newspapers, and the 1787–1788 dates of publication coincided with the debates in the various state ratifying conventions. The *Essay on Money* is an ambitious piece, adding to the "controversial discussion of the subject in pamphlets and periodical publications" while trying to be thorough and dispassionate.[59] It was thorough, indeed: Witherspoon ranged over the rise and use of money through history, the nature and meaning of signs, and the ends of commerce, and in general outlined one of the first free-market, hard-money treatises produced in North America.

According to Witherspoon, paper money was not, properly speaking, money at all.[60] The only real advantage of paper was that of giving credit, while there were several evils that attended its circulation. The worst of these was inflating the cost of "industry and its fruits," or goods and services. But Witherspoon was realistic enough to acknowledge that the rage for paper might well result in its being issued, and to recommend that "[i]f therefore paper is to be employed in circulation," then there are "principles on which it ought to be conducted . . . ends that ought to be aimed at, and . . . evils that ought to be avoided."[61] Significantly (in light of his relationship with Hamilton and the national bank), Witherspoon included a section on American banking practices, arguing that there was no reason in theory why a bank should destroy credit instead of extending it. Descending momentarily from the theoretical to the practical, he also touched on a banking controversy in Pennsylvania and Benjamin Franklin's role in it.[62]

Witherspoon closed the *Essay* with a hard-money plea that would have pleased any supporter of the proposed Constitution, which forbade states from making "any Thing but gold and silver Coin a Tender in Payment of Debts." Professing to derive his opinions on money "from the best civilians of this and the last age, and from the history of all ages, joined with a pretty considerable experience and attention to the effects of *political* causes within the sphere of my own observation," Witherspoon believed that he had dealt with one of "the great objects of national interest."[63] The practical upshot of the piece was that "[t]hose who refuse doubtful paper, and thereby disgrace it, or prevent its circulation, are not enemies, but friends to their country."[64]

The Presbyterian Constitution of 1787

Witherspoon's energetic role in the nationalization of the Presbyterian Church in the United States—he drafted the Introduction to its national constitution and was elected the first Moderator (the ecclesiastical equivalent of president) of the newly created General Assembly—provides an interesting corollary to his pro-federal Constitution stand and is an indicator of his desire for the formation of a new nation. Witherspoon understood that the mere formal arrangements of government were not enough to hold together a body politic. Habits of thinking, speaking,[65]—like Noah Webster, Witherspoon was fascinated by the effect of language on national character—and even worship had to be cultivated. In effect, a national conscience needed to be developed, and the strengthening of the Presbyterian church could be an essential factor in that development. During the War, Witherspoon lamented that while the fact of independence seemed imminent, "we have not yet acquired the whole *ideas and habits* of independence."[66] If, as some histo-

rians insist, "[r]eligion was one of the more potent factors in the making of
the United States of America," and not merely in the creation of certain
political documents but also in the unifying of a "free people held together
by ties such as . . . language, religion, manners and customs,"[67] then Witherspoon's role in the nationalization of the Presbyterian church is worth
emphasizing. Examining the form of government outlined in the Presbyterian constitution also provides evidence of his position in the New Jersey
ratifying convention.

The unification of the Presbyterian Church in the United States and
the subsequent drafting of its constitution were events of no small significance in the nationalization of America. Edward Humphrey has written
that "[w]e cannot but repeat that the centralized governing body of the
Presbyterian Church in America during the colonial period, the Synod of
New York and Philadelphia, was the most influential of all colonial institutions towards the development of a centralized national conscience."[68] The
activities of the Synod of New York and Philadelphia, which culminated
in the writing of the Presbyterian constitution in 1787, not only helped
heal the breach between two rival groups within the denomination (Old
Side and New Light), but they also created a constitution that was curiously
similar, as we will see, to the one produced at the same time by the Federal
Convention.[69]

When they set about to affirm a confession of faith as the first document
within their constitution, the Synod quite naturally turned to the Westminster Confession of Faith of 1647. On the whole they reaffirmed the Westminster Confession verbatim, yet with one notable exception. Article III of
Chapter XXIII of the 1647 Confession dealt with the rights and responsi-
bilities of the civil magistrate concerning the proper worship of God by the
churches. The Americans made substantial changes to this article, severely
limiting the magistrate's power to interfere in church government to reflect
their greater degree of distinctness between church and state. The original
article from 1647 read as follows:

III. The civil magistrate may not assume to himself the administration
of the Word and Sacraments, or the power of the keys of the kingdom
of heaven: yet he hath authority, and it is his duty to take order, that
unity and peace be preserved in the Church, that the truth of God be
kept pure and entire, that all blasphemies and heresies be suppressed,
all corruptions and abuses in worship and discipline prevented or reformed, and all the ordinances of God duly settled, administered, and

observed. For the better effecting whereof he hath power to call synods, to be present at them, and to provide that whatsoever is transacted in them be according to the mind of God.[70]

The Americans proceeded to reword Article III, removing the language about the magistrate's authority to suppress all blasphemies and heresies, and denying the state any power to interfere with matters of religious faith.

> III. Civil Magistrates may not assume to themselves the administration of the word and sacraments; or the power of the keys of the kingdom of Heaven; or, in the least, interfere in matters of faith. Yet, as nursing fathers, it is the duty of civil magistrates to protect the church of our common Lord, without giving the preference to any denomination of christians above the rest, in such a manner, that all ecclesiastical persons whatever shall enjoy the full, free, and unquestioned liberty of discharging, every part of their sacred functions, without violence or danger. And, as Jesus Christ hath appointed a regular government and discipline in his church, no law of any Commonwealth, should interfere with, let, or hinder, the due exercise thereof, among the voluntary members of *any* denomination of christians, according to their own profession and belief. It is the duty of civil magistrates to protect the person and good name of all their people, in such an effectual manner as that no person be suffered, either upon pretence of religion or infidelity, to offer any indignity, violence, abuse, or injury to any other person whatsoever; and to take order, that all religious and ecclesiastical assemblies be held without molestation or disturbance.[71]

While civil magistrates were denied any interference in matters of *faith*, we should note that there was no explicit mention of their role in enforcing religious *practice* beyond protecting the churches as "nursing fathers." The state in America could protect and nurture the church, but it could never interfere with it.

Because there is no transcript of the actual debates in the Synod, we do not know what role, if any, Witherspoon played in having the language regarding the magistrate's ecclesiastical powers stricken. We do know that on an earlier occasion he suggested that local magistrates could punish profaneness and obscenity in the press. In 1776, Witherspoon suggested that "[w]hether we are to suppose it was pay or profaneness, that introduced into the paper printed by the infamous R——, pieces containing the grossest obscenity," the printer "ought to have been punished by the magistrates of the Place, as a public nuisance[.]"[72] But the thrust of the American change seems to have been to limit the state's power over matters of faith and practice in the "internal government" of the churches, as Witherspoon's Introduction to the Presbyterian constitution read,[73] rather than to make a more general prohibition against the civil government ever punishing offenses that may, like obscenity, have a moral component. Still, the members of the Synod of New York and Philadelphia were more scrupulous than their English counterparts at Westminster in restraining the state from interfering with the church, and it is reasonable to assume that Witherspoon had a part to play in that restraint.

That Witherspoon had a part to play in the Introduction rests on more than mere assumption: all scholars agree that he was its sole author and that it was adopted by the Synod without any substantive changes to his original draft. The Introduction laid out eight political first principles of the fledgling American church, including several on church-state relations that were wholly compatible with the proposed federal Constitution. The Introduction provided for broad religious liberty and protection of the Presbyterian churches (and those of all Christian denominations) from government control of any kind. Beginning with familiar language from the Westminster Confession to the effect that "God alone is Lord of the conscience," the Presbyterians concluded that "they consider the rights of private judgement, in all matters that respect religion, as universal and alienable [*sic*]: They do not even wish to see any religious constitution aided by the civil power, further than may be necessary for protection and security, and, at the same time, equal and common to all others." The final article of Witherspoon's Introduction insisted that "ecclesiastical discipline must be purely moral or spiritual in its object, and not attended with any civil effects."[74] This protection of the church from the state in the Presbyterian constitution foreshadowed the general protection of the church in the unamended federal Constitution (as evidenced by its silence on religious matters) and, to a certain extent, the Free Exercise clause of the First Amendment.

The Introduction to the Presbyterian constitution, with its protection of the internal governments of religious bodies, and with its changes to Chapter XXIII of the Westminster Confession forbidding civil magistrates from meddling in matters of faith, approached matters of religion and civil government in much the same way as the Philadelphia Constitution. Witherspoon surely found much that was familiar in a federal constitution that forbade religious tests for officeholders in particular and protected religion from the federal government in general. He had, after all, helped create a constitution for the new Presbyterian Church in the United States just six months prior with the same protections for religion. Witherspoon must have thought like Edmund Randolph of Virginia, who remarked in his own ratifying convention that "[i]t has been said, that if the exclusion of the religious test were an exception from the general power of Congress, the power over religion would remain. I inform those who are of this opinion, that no power is given expressly to congress over religion."[75]

Even more, Witherspoon must have felt comfortable with a civil constitution that shared many other features with the Presbyterian constitution hammered out that May. Indeed, the two constitutions of 1787, one sacred and the other secular, turned out to be remarkably similar. Both documents, for example, were finalized in 1787, ratified in 1788, and went into effect in 1789. Each created an innovative national (or at least "partly national") government:[76] the federal government on the one hand, and the Presbyterian General Assembly on the other.[77] And beyond the historical curiosity of these coincidences, the governments produced by the two conventions had a number of common features, and this commonality strongly suggests that Witherspoon found the Philadelphia Constitution to his liking. The Presbyterian Form of Government shared the following elements with the federal Constitution: religious liberty, federalism, proportional representation, an innovative national legislature, a single chief executive, and, overall, a limited government whose power was derived ultimately from the people.

Power in the Presbyterian Church under its constitution of 1787 was shared, just as in the federal government, between several layers of government from the very local (congregations alone had the power to call their own pastors) to the national.[78] The Presbyterian Church was organized from lowest to highest into sessions (congregations), presbyteries, synods, and finally into a national General Assembly. These levels corresponded, in a rough way, to the local, county, state, and national levels of the federal government that grew up under the Constitution. Furthermore, representation in the national General Assembly, like that in the national Congress, was proportional by presbytery and indirectly by population. The Presbyterian constitution provided that the "General Assembly shall consist of an equal delegation of Bishops and Elders, from each Presbytery, in the following proportion: viz. each Presbytery, consisting of not more than six Ministers, shall send one Minister and one Elder; each Presbytery, consisting of more than six Ministers and not more than twelve, shall send two Ministers and two Elders," and so on.[79] Finally, the General Assembly was headed by a single chief executive, analogous to the president of the United States, who was elected by its delegates rather than directly by the people, just as the president was to be decided by the Electoral College. Witherspoon himself, although he served only on an interim basis, was elected first Moderator of the national General Assembly.

The Nature of the Federal Government

To Witherspoon the federal Constitution that he ratified had created a confederated union, not a consolidated union. (The charge that the proposed government was a consolidated one became a principal Antifederalist argument against ratification.) "If the American empire *come to be one consolidated government,*" Witherspoon wrote for the public press on the proposed federal city, "I grant it would be of some consequence that the seat of that government and source of authority should not be too distant from the extremities, for reasons which I need not here mention. But if the particular states are to be preserved and supported in their constitutional government, it seems of very little consequence where the Congress, consisting of representatives from these states, shall hold their sessions."[80] Witherspoon actually opposed, at least during the early years of the republic, a federal city and wished that the matter "may be suffered to sleep in its present situation at least for a considerable time, and till some other business of greater and more confessed importance shall be completely finished."[81]

He also understood that the federal government created by the Constitution, while much stronger than the league under the Articles of Confederation, was strictly limited in its powers. The federal government had by no means been granted plenary powers. Witherspoon favored brief annual sessions for Congress, implying that the legislature not be allowed to entrench or exceed its authority unnecessarily.[82] One could also argue that by opposing the building of a federal city (at least for a time), Witherspoon saw the task of the federal government as rather limited, or at least so limited that it did not merit permanent structures for transacting government business. The federal government furthermore had no power to interfere with religion, that great prop of moral, theological, and civic virtues. Since during the ratification debates in the state conventions Witherspoon came out in the public press mocking a provision of the revised Georgia constitution

forbidding clergymen from holding civic office, it is difficult indeed to imagine that he would have allowed any similar exclusion under the federal Constitution of the religious from public life.

Still, Witherspoon seemed to have a slightly more expansive view of
civil government in general than certain other founders. For example, he disagreed with Jefferson, who held that "persons and property make the sum of
the objects of government."[83] To Witherspoon, the legitimate ends of civil
government reached beyond the physical to touch moral qualities such as
virtue. A "constitution is excellent," Witherspoon taught his Princeton students, "when the spirit of the civil laws is such as to have a tendency to prevent offences and make men good, as much as to punish them when they
do evil. . . . But how shall the magistrate manage this matter, or what can
be done by law to make the people of any state virtuous?"[84] Laws were not
meant to be entirely amoral or merely to protect life and property, as Jefferson asserted; good laws had a role to play in the formation of virtuous citizens.[85] Witherspoon also believed, as noted, that civil government had the
right (at least at the local level) to prosecute obscenity and profanity as public nuisances. Thus, he believed in a confederated union of states under the
new Constitution overseen by an energetic but limited federal government:
a government that was, to paraphrase Publius, enabled to control the governed while obliged to control itself.[86] These, in short, were the features of
what Witherspoon had called in 1782 "an equal republican constitution."[87]

John Witherspoon consistently backed a strong union of American states,
during the Revolution, under the Articles of Confederation, and finally under
the federal Constitution that he ratified in 1787. In the years immediately
prior to 1787, he supported a number of features of civil and church polity —
federalism, national revenue and landholdings, religious liberty, an energetic
single executive, and hard money — that were built into the Philadelphia
Constitution. Further, there are not a few similarities between Witherspoon's
writings and the *Federalist* essays of Hamilton and Madison, both of whom
sought out Witherspoon as a counselor during their public careers. All of
these factors, in addition to the contemporary accounts that document his
pro-Constitution sentiments and activities, provide ample proof that Witherspoon was a vigorous Federalist both in and out of the New Jersey ratifying convention. We could also add that Witherspoon's position as one of the
most prominent Americans in church and state, coupled with the fact that
New Jersey ratified quickly and early, surely lent credibility to Federalist arguments in the other states.

chapter six

John Witherspoon and
Early American Political Thought

> *A very great genius is often like a very fine flower, to be wondered*
> *at, but of little service either for food or medicine.*
> —John Witherspoon, *Lectures on Eloquence*

> *[Americans] prefer the good sense which creates fortunes to the*
> *genius which often dissipates them; their minds, accustomed to*
> *definite calculations, are frightened by general ideas; and they*
> *hold practice in greater honor than theory.*
> —Tocqueville, *Democracy in America*

The American founding was a complex business, if the secondary literature on the subject is to be trusted. There was apparently a variety of forces at work in America during the last half of the eighteenth century. The vast number of books and articles that have been devoted to explaining the founding, and their sometimes strident disagreement with one another, ought to convince us of that. It thus seems appropriate in a study of an important, if neglected, founder to take stock of his contributions to American political thought and to locate him among those various forces. What follows is an attempt to put Witherspoon on the intellectual map of the founding.

Political Theory at the Founding

Americans have ever been a pragmatic people. This is no less true of those political thinkers to whom genius has customarily been ascribed: Madison, Hamilton, even Thomas Jefferson, author of the soaring rhetoric of the Declaration. Habitually distrustful of "general ideas," as Tocqueville put it in the nineteenth century, or of unserviceable "genius," as John Witherspoon and his eighteenth-century colleagues put it, Americans have on balance gone for experience over experiment. The fact that the new government created at Philadelphia was called by its framers, and by nearly all students of American politics since, the American "experiment," should not blind us to its nature as more an experiment in practice than in theory. The political theories that lie back of the Constitution were already in existence when the framers pieced them together from Montesquieu and Hume (the extended republic), from Hutcheson and Calvin (the right of resistance), from Locke (the social contract), and from the existing state constitutions. What the American people got as a result of the Constitutional Convention was thus a cobbled-together affair: stronger, perhaps, for the cobbling, but highly derivative of European and earlier American thought. The American political talent has always been, and was especially in the eighteenth century, for the practical application of theory to unique American circumstances.[1]

Madison's record of the Constitutional Convention debates is filled with admonitions by the delegates to adapt existing political theory to the fixed habits and spirit of the American people. On June 1, 1787, Edmund Randolph of Virginia admitted that he personally admired the British system of government, and "[i]f we were in a situation to copy it he did not know that he should be opposed to it; but the fixt genius of the people of America required a different form of Government."[2] And George Mason had referred in the Convention to "experience, the best of all tests."[3] The framers at Philadelphia may have wanted, as Publius insisted they did, to construct the first government in the history of the world based on reason and reflection, but they were not about to foist a novel system on a people unprepared to handle it. In *Federalist* 1, Publius (Hamilton) acknowledged that it was up to the Americans to decide whether good government could be established from "reflection and choice" rather than from accident and force;[4] however, Hamilton closed the *Federalist* essays with a quotation from David Hume in which the latter emphasized that "no human genius . . . by the mere dint of reason and reflection" is able to establish good government: "The judgments of many must unite in the work; EXPERIENCE must guide their labour; TIME must bring it to perfection; and the FEELING of inconveniences must correct the mistakes which they *inevitably* fall into in their first trials and experiments."[5]

The framers were not anxious to reach into the heavens and bring down an imaginary scheme that would run counter to the lived experience and habits of the American people—habits that had been ingraining themselves, in Virginia and Massachusetts, for example, for the better part of two hundred years. This spirit of acquiescence to practical concerns, and of resistance to merely theoretical schemes, is reflected in *Federalist* 34, in which Publius (Hamilton again) warned that "to argue upon abstract principles . . . would be to set up theory and supposition against fact and reality."[6]

The word that the founders most often used to describe such untried theory and supposition was "metaphysical." James Wilson implied in the Philadelphia Convention that there was something positively dishonest about "metaphysical distinctions" that the American people would be all too quick to see through. On June 30, 1787, he asked, "[c]an we forget for whom we are forming a Government? Is it for *men,* or for the imaginary beings called *States?* Will our honest constituents be satisfied with metaphysical distinctions?"[7] (The Convention had to endure only one metaphysical lecture during the entire assembly, a two-day "harangue," as one delegate called it, by the combustible Luther Martin of Maryland on June 27–28. Martin actually read passages from Locke, Joseph Priestley, and other pertinent theorists, and was derided for his efforts by other delegates such as Oliver Ellsworth, who wrote abusive newspaper articles about Martin afterward.)[8] Ben Franklin once chided himself for making naive errors of the "metaphysical" sort. Upon reexamination, an argument from a pamphlet he had written and published in London "appeared now not so clever a performance as I once thought it; and I doubted whether some error had not insinuated itself unperceived into my argument, so as to infect all that followed, as is common in metaphysical reasonings."[9] In *Federalist* 37, Publius (Madison) used the word "metaphysical" for the first and last time in those eighty-five essays, scoffing at the inability of even "the most acute and metaphysical philosophers" to describe adequately the human mental faculties.[10] Such hard-headed realism can also be seen in Madison's remark in *Federalist* 49 that "a nation of philosophers is as little to be expected as the philosophical race of kings wished for by Plato."[11]

As a matter of fact, Plato stood, in the minds of many of the key founders, for utopian philosophy at its worst. He was cited as an authority rarely, if ever, in the speeches and literature of the founding period.[12] Instead, Plato was frequently used as an example of a political philosopher whose work is so heavenly minded that it is no earthly good, as the old saying goes. John Adams once wrote that he learned only two things from Plato, one of which was that sneezing cured his hiccups.[13] Just recalling his attempt thirty years earlier to read through Plato's works was enough to send Adams off on an epistolary tirade. He found Plato's political works, the *Republic* and the *Laws,* especially disappointing. In a protracted passage in a letter to Jefferson, Adams complained that "[m]y disappointment was very great, my Astonishment was greater and my disgust was shocking."

> Some Parts of some of his Dialogues are entertaining, like the Writings of Rousseau: but his Laws and his Republick from which I expected most, disappointed me most. . . . In a late letter to the learned and ingenious Mr. Taylor of Hazelwood, I suggested to him the Project of writing a Novel in which The Hero should be sent upon his travels through Plato's Republick, and all his Adventures, with his Observations on the principles and Opinions, the Arts and Sciences, the manners Customs and habits of the Citizens should be recorded. Nothing can be conceived more destructive of human happiness; more infallibly contrived to transform Men and Women into Brutes, Yahoos, or Daemons than a Community of Wives and Property.

Recalling Plato's *Republic* set Adams to thinking about Rousseau, and ultimately about all utopian philosophers. "Yet, in what, are the Writings of Rousseau and Helvetius wiser than those of Plato? 'The Man who first fenced a Tobacco Yard, and said this is mine ought instantly to have been put to death' says Rousseau. 'The Man who first pronounced the barbarous Word "Dieu," ought to have been immediately destroyed,' says Diderot. In short," as noted earlier, Adams wrote "Philosophers antient and modern appear to me as Mad as Hindoos, Mahomitans and Christians."[14]

Nor did Thomas Jefferson have anything good to say about Plato or his *Republic.* He labeled Plato a dealer in "mysticisms incomprehensible to the human mind," who used Socrates as a cover for his own "whimsies" and who had been deified by certain sects of Christians "because, in his foggy conceptions, they found a basis of impenetrable darkness whereon to rear fabrications as delirious, of their own invention." Jefferson further considered him the perfect prototype of that "diffuse, vapid" philosopher Epicurus.[15] Regarding Plato's *Republic,* Jefferson wrote to Adams that "[w]hile wading thro' the whimsies, the puerilities, and unintelligible jargon of this work, I laid it down often to ask myself how it could have been that the world should have so long consented to give reputation to such nonsense as this?" Jefferson then went on at length, wondering how Cicero, of all people, "practised in the business of the world" as he was, could have been duped by "the dreams of Plato."[16]

Founders such as Adams and Jefferson seem to have objected above all to Plato's rationalistic method, which emphasized the power of *a priori* reason (that is, reason prior to experience) to apprehend truths about the world. Rationalism of the Platonic type was thought to begin with a principle or general theory and then work "down" to particulars, often suggesting that real-world conditions be conformed to that theory. Perhaps the clearest statement of this method is found in Chapter XXII of the *Republic,* where Socrates suggests that if the philosopher-king "should find himself compelled to mold other characters besides his own and shape the pattern of public and private life into conformity with his vision of the ideal, he will not lack the skill to produce such counterparts of temperance, justice, and all the virtues as can exist in the ordinary man."[17] A common criticism of rationalists, no less today than in the eighteenth century, is that they often arrive at their general theories simply by reasoning about the world, which can be performed from an armchair in a study; they need not examine the myriad particulars of the "real" world to confirm their theories.

The founders contrasted this philosophical method with what we today call empiricism, which relies on *a posteriori* experience and begins its work by observing and collecting information and only then proceeds to reason "upward" and formulate general theories. This method, as opposed to the top-down one of rationalism, was what John Witherspoon had in mind when he suggested that "[i]t is always safer in our reasonings to trace facts upwards than to reason downwards upon metaphysical principles."[18] This was also the method employed by Aristotle (the sole Greek philosopher mentioned by Jefferson as an inspiration for the Declaration), the greatest observer and classifier of the ancient Greeks and the forefather of modern empiricism in this sense. It is no coincidence, for example, that Aristotle begins his *Politics* with observation, and it is for this reason that he has been seen as the first common sense philosopher.[19] Nor perhaps is it a coincidence that Witherspoon's personal library contained volumes by Aristotle and Cicero, but none by Plato.[20]

Using these simple philosophical categories of rationalism and empiricism to sort the founders, we may conclude that they were on balance empiricists rather than rationalists. That is, to the extent that they were philosophers at all, the founders were Aristoteleans rather than Platonists:

natural-born observers and practitioners rather than pure theorists. The rhetorical evidence — the lack of positive allusions to Plato and the hostile references to him — seems to corroborate what has been suggested about the character of the early American political mind. The founding generation had a strong empirical and scientific bent together with a healthy distrust of metaphysical speculations divorced from the hurly-burly of real-world American political life.

The pragmatic orientation of the American political mind is further illustrated by the fact that membership in our first scientific association, the American Philosophical Society, founded in 1743, comprised nearly all of the leading political figures in the colonies, including its founder, Benjamin Franklin, and John Witherspoon. The Society's scientific character accounts for the ease with which it was able to merge with the American Society for Promoting Useful Knowledge during its reorganization in 1769. Even in the names of those societies we see the practical bent of the American mind: only philosophy or knowledge that was *useful* was thought worth pursuing by the members of our first learned society. The early members of the American Philosophical Society were nearly all amateur scientists ("natural philosophers," in the language of the day) in addition to being leading politicians.

Most of them, in fact, were natural historians rather than "scientists" in the modern sense of that term. Jefferson, to take a prime example, wrote only one book during his long life, the *Notes on the State of Virginia*, which was one of the first important American natural histories; it consisted, as the title implies, of a series of notes and observations on Virginia and America. Jefferson was primarily concerned with answering a set of queries put to him by the Frenchman François Barbé de Marbois on such topics as "Rivers," "Sea-ports," and "Productions Mineral, Vegetable and Animal," and not with laying out any comprehensive scientific theories. (We have already seen that Marbois made a similar request of Witherspoon and received in return "A Description of the State of New Jersey.")[21] Of the four councillors of the Society elected to two-year terms in 1781, for example, three of the four — Witherspoon, Jefferson, and William Livingston — were Continental Congressmen, and two of those three — Jefferson of Virginia and Livingston of New Jersey — were governors of their respective states. Witherspoon himself was too busy presiding over Princeton and with his pastoral duties during the War to hold any political office other than congressman.

It appears that this practical and experiential strain in the founders' political thinking has been present in the American mind from the very beginning, or at least since the English settlements in New England. The Pu-

ritans, who left such an indelible mark not only on New England but also
on the American consciousness, came to the New World for no other reason
than to put their version of a biblical ethic into practice. The theology of
the New England Puritans differed in no substantial way from that of their
Old English Puritan cousins. What the New Englanders wanted was to make
a fresh start at building a political community around the principles of God's
Word as they understood them. As Daniel Boorstin has pointed out, New
England, for all its theology-mindedness, did not produce a single work of
speculative theology until that of Jonathan Edwards in the middle of the
eighteenth century,[22] nearly 150 years after the landing at Plymouth. The differences with the Church of England that compelled the Puritans to leave
the mother country were all differences of practice, not those of subtle theology. The hairs that the Puritans were willing to split concerned matters of
church practice — whether wedding rings should be used in marriage ceremonies, or whether clerics should wear surplices — not theoretical matters of
faith.[23] Neither did the New England Puritans have time for questions of abstract political theory. They were too busy working out whether the franchise
should be extended to non-church members and laying out townships — in
short, with putting their biblical ethic into practice — to bother much with
political theorizing.

All of this is not to say, of course, that political theory has never mattered in America. Particularly during the last third of the eighteenth century, it mattered a great deal indeed. Americans were willing to fight a revolutionary war, in part at least, over political theory. They fought that war
for political ideas — for liberty, for self-government, for "rights."[24] But we
must not forget that those universal ideas and rights were instantiated in
concrete and particular circumstances. Americans saw their own property,
their own virtue, and perhaps their very own lives as threatened, and this as
much as anything moved them to resist, even at the risk of their own "extermination," as Witherspoon put it.[25] No patriot, least of all an American
patriot, has ever fought for a mere theory.[26]

It is true that political theory was studied more seriously in the late
eighteenth century than perhaps at any other time in our history, and almost
certainly the work of political philosophers (Aristotle and Locke and Sidney,
to name a few whom Jefferson credited) was more familiar to the founders
than to any American politicians since. But as soon as this familiarity is acknowledged, we ought to recall that philosophical ideas, although taken
seriously during the founding period, were primarily valued for how they
could be put into practice. Americans were interested in whether Hume's

and Montesquieu's theory of the extended republic was applicable to the their own political situation; they were not terribly interested in formal philosophy per se. After all, surely it is a mark of American political informality that our greatest work of political theory, *The Federalist Papers*, appeared initially in newspapers.

This political pragmatism has probably been all to the good, and we are perhaps fortunate that America's political thinkers, especially her founders from Tidewater Virginia to Massachusetts Bay to Philadelphia, were so disinclined from utopian scheming. Ours is a regime founded, not by philosophers, but by men of affairs and lawyers.[27] Above all, the founders were men like Patrick Henry, who knew of only one lamp by which his feet were to be guided, and that was the lamp of "experience."[28] (The idealistic Jefferson may be the one outlier among these pragmatic politicians, though even he knew when to subordinate ideals to practice, such as approving the Louisiana Purchase despite his constitutional misgivings.)

Witherspoon's Contributions

It was to this culture of political pragmatism, empiricism, and trust in experience that John Witherspoon was introduced when he arrived in the colonies prior to the Revolution. He himself had precisely this kind of inclination toward the useful and practical, and disinclination from abstract metaphysics. (Questioned by a neighbor woman about the lack of flowers in his garden, Witherspoon replied that gardens were like discourses: neither should be cluttered up with useless flowers, and his grew only vegetables.) He was as familiar with political philosophy as any of the founders, including Madison, whom he had introduced to the great political theorists, but he was more concerned with establishing an independent nation than with working out a perfectly consistent political theory.

His contributions to the founding are best seen under two headings: the foundations of the American republic, and the founding of the republic proper. Witherspoon was keenly interested in what could be called the foundations of political society, particularly in religion and morality, and in education. (Indeed, as noted earlier, his Lectures on Moral Philosophy first consider the foundational or pre-political aspects of civil society—human nature in Lectures I to V, and ethics in Lectures VI to IX—before they address politics and jurisprudence.) To Witherspoon, just as to all the founders, religion and the morality it produced was an indispensable support of republican government. He was therefore concerned with the health of the church and wished to see the civil government prohibited from meddling in the internal government of the churches. Healthy churches not only prepared souls for eternity, they also produced "the more regular citizens, and the more useful members of society."[29]

As an educator Witherspoon was devoted to preparing young men who, he correctly predicted, would one day fill the highest stations in the land. Although he was a scholar of some ability (he wrote pioneering works in moral philosophy, rhetoric, and political economy), he was no ivory-tower professor: he was interested in what ideas could do, in what kinds of people and institutions they would produce. Princeton under Witherspoon was unmatched among American colleges in production of political leaders and was known, as we have seen, as the "nursery of statesmen." He was especially concerned that his students receive regular instruction in moral philosophy, including the moral and common sense philosophies of the Scottish Enlightenment, and this concern led to his seminal Lectures on Moral Philosophy. Indeed, his command of the ideas of the Scottish Enlightenment, and his role in their transmission into the colonies as a professor of moral philosophy and president of the College of New Jersey, made Witherspoon one of only a handful of bona fide moral philosophers in early America.

In addition to his contributions in education, Witherspoon from the beginning played an active role in the founding of his adopted country. His entire American career was spent working either directly (on politics) or indirectly (on religion and education) on that founding. He took time from his duties as an educator and clergyman to serve in the provincial government of New Jersey, in the Continental Congress, and in the New Jersey ratifying convention of 1787. And we should not forget that Witherspoon helped pass three of the four Organic Laws of the United States: the Declaration of Independence, the Articles of Confederation, and the Constitution.

Founding Historiography

Scholarship on the American founding has almost invariably arranged itself under several distinct headings.[30] Prior to the Second World War a consensus formed around the notion that the founding could be understood as an exclusively liberal, Lockean movement.[31] After the War, however, the consensus view came under increasing scrutiny, and a number of revisionist histories were written that focused on intellectual influences on the founding other than liberalism as expressed by John Locke. Among the first revisionists was Caroline Robbins, who saw an English libertarian or Whig tradition that had previously been overlooked.[32] By the early 1960s, scholars led by Bernard Bailyn were coming to emphasize a republican strain from classical antiquity in American founding thought.[33] Since then, dissenting commentators have emphasized the priority of the Scottish Enlightenment and Reformed Protestant Christianity.[34] Disciples of each of these schools of interpretation almost invariably emphasize one influence to the exclusion of, or at least at the expense of, the others. Now, at the beginning of the twenty-first century, a consensus has formed that the thought of the founders can be subsumed under one of three broad headings: classical republicanism, British liberalism, or Protestant Christianity.[35] The foregoing is a necessary simplification of an unwieldy literature, and certainly there are intellectual historians who integrate the lines of influence. But on the whole scholarship has arranged itself into fairly distinct schools, each of which argues the priority of its own chosen influence — or its own "learned anachronism," as David Hackett Fischer has put it — on the political thought of the founding.[36]

Perhaps a more representative (and historically faithful) way of conceiving the intellectual character of the founding is to regard it as a chorus of many voices and many parts — some louder, some more subdued, but all contributing. Yet regardless of how one views the founding, the secondary literature has identified several distinct lines of intellectual patrimony, each of which may be related briefly to Witherspoon and his legacy. The first of these lines is the British (including Scottish) liberalism that came through John Locke.

There can be little doubt that Witherspoon was influenced by Locke, both directly and as Locke was mediated through Francis Hutcheson. We have seen that Witherspoon was sufficiently independent not to swallow the Lockean philosophy whole; he disagreed profoundly with Locke's rejection of innate ideas, for example. He did, however, follow Locke very closely on questions of social theory and in fact repeated the latter's formulation of the social compact almost verbatim. In Section 136 of his "Second Treatise of Government," Locke wrote that "[t]o avoid these Inconveniencies which disorder Mens Properties in the state of Nature, Men unite into Societies, that they may have the united strength of the whole Society to secure and defend their Properties, and may have *standing Rules* to bound it, by which every one may know what is his."[37] In his tenth lecture on moral philosophy, "Of Politics," Witherspoon said: "Society, I would define to be an association or compact of any number of persons, to deliver up or abridge some part of their natural rights, in order to have the strength of the united body, to protect the remaining, and to bestow others. . . . The inconveniences of the natural state are very many."[38]

Witherspoon accepted Locke's definition of the state of nature, although he added to it. "The first thing to be considered, in order to see upon what principles society is formed," Witherspoon wrote in the Lectures on Moral Philosophy,

> is the state immediately previous to the social state. This is called the state of nature —Violent and unnecessary controversies have been made on that subject. Some have denied that any such thing ever existed, that since there were men, they have always been in a social state. And to be sure, this is so far true, that in no example or fact could it ever last long. Yet it is impossible to consider society as a voluntary union of particular persons, without supposing those persons in a state somewhat different, before this union took place —There are rights therefore belonging to a state of nature, different from those of a social state. And distinct societies or states independent, are at this moment in a state of nature, or natural liberty, with regard to each other.[39]

He repeated this formulation in the second of his "Druid" essays from 1776. "Wherever society exists founded upon clearly established laws, this obliges us to form an idea of a state previous to the formation of society . . . [t]his is called a state of nature."[40] One could scarcely find a more clear rephrasing of Locke's state of nature.

But Witherspoon also used a more explicitly Christian formulation for the state of nature than had Locke. In an earlier lecture, Witherspoon referred to "[man's] state with regard to God, or natural relation to him."[41] In this context all men were made by God and "live by his providence." And in the "Dominion of Providence" sermon of May 1776, he reminded his hearers of their "lost state by nature" and exhorted all who were "yet in a state of nature" to be born again.[42] So while he was willing to use concepts from Locke's social contract theory, including the state of nature and the "law of nature and nations,"[43] Witherspoon felt obliged to add a more explicitly Christian, even Reformed, definition of the state of nature to his own moral philosophy.

Moreover, on the other key concepts of social contract theory —natural rights and the law of nature —Witherspoon used the same modes of expression as Locke and Hutcheson. Witherspoon spoke of "natural rights" that were "essential to man" in his Lectures.[44] Two of those "perfect rights"—a "right to life" and a "right to personal liberty," along with an implied right to "happiness"—were to appear in the famous list of inalienable rights in the Declaration of Independence.[45] Quotations such as these could be multiplied many times over. Thus, on the seminal concepts of the state of nature, the law of nature or natural law, and natural rights, Witherspoon followed Locke in most respects. However, as suggested earlier, there was plenty in Locke that called to mind Reformation resistance theory for Witherspoon. This is not meant to imply that Locke was an orthodox Christian; he was a materialist who embraced heterodox positions. The important point here is that for Witherspoon these "Lockean" concepts were either themselves outgrowths of earlier Christian thought (such as the late Reformation resistance literature) or were harmonizable with Christian and especially Reformed expressions (such as the four references to God in the Declaration of Independence, variants of which all appear in the Westminster Confession of Faith).

This suggests that Witherspoon, like the other founders, picked and chose from Locke and earlier political theorists. He accepted those elements of Locke's social theory with which he was comfortable and rejected those from Locke's epistemology with which he was not. He seems to have viewed Locke as within the Christian tradition broadly understood; and in those instances where he thought a more explicitly Christian formulation was needed, he added his own. As to any connection between Locke and Thomas Hobbes, which many political theorists are inclined to see, Witherspoon saw none. There is no question of Witherspoon following Hobbes, at least in any conscious way, regarding the social contract. "Hobbes and some other writers of the former age, treat with great contempt," Witherspoon wrote, "this which is generally called the social compact.—He insists that monarchy is the law of nature."[46] Witherspoon does grant that Hobbes was perhaps half right when he called the state of nature a state of war, but so were those who called it a state of peace.

> Another famous question has been, Is the state of nature a state of war or peace? Hobbes, an author of considerable note, but of very illiberal sentiments in politics, is a strenuous advocate for a state of nature being a state of war. Hutchinson [sic] and Shaftsbury plead strongly, that a state of nature is a state of society. However opposite and hostile their opinions seem to be with regard to each other, it seems no hard matter to reconcile them. That the principles of our nature lead to society—

that our happiness and the improvement of our powers are only to be had in society, is of the most undoubted certainty — and that in our nature, as it is the work of God, there is a real good-will and benevolence to others: but on the other hand, that our nature as it is now, when free and independent, is prone to injury, and consequently to war, is equally manifest, and that in a state of natural liberty, there is no other way but force, for preserving security and repelling injury.[47]

So, then, was Witherspoon a Lockean? Yes, in certain respects; and no, in others. That he was familiar with Locke's *Two Treatises of Government* and that he was indebted to the "Second Treatise" in particular cannot be doubted.[48] Yet on other issues he clearly differed with the Englishman: Witherspoon believed, as Locke did not, in innate ideas; and Witherspoon believed in an incorporeal soul, which Locke seems to have denied. Still, many elements of Locke's political thought were harmonizable with prior Reformed and Christian thought, or at least Witherspoon tried to harmonize them in his own moral philosophy.

Compared to the Lockean British Liberal influence so clearly detectable in Witherspoon, the classical republican strain seems, of all the major influences said to be present at the founding, to have been the weakest in his thought. References to classical thinkers are remarkably absent from his Lectures on Moral Philosophy: there are no citations of Plato or Aristotle (although there is one mention of "Platonists") and only one quotation from Cicero. No classical author appears in Witherspoon's bibliography of "chief writers upon government and politics," and indeed, none of those writers was born before 1500.[49] In fact, he went so far as to denigrate the contributions of the ancients to moral philosophy in his Princeton lectures on divinity.

Moral Philosophy. . . . It is a very pleasant and improving study in itself, or a good handmaid to the Christian morality; and the controversies upon that subject, which are all modern, stand in immediate connection with the deistical controversies, which it is necessary for a divine to make himself master of. There are few of the ancient writers of much value upon that subject, excepting Plato among the Greeks, and Cicero among the Latins, especially the latter. The remains of Socrates, (to be collected from the writers of his country, but chiefly from Xenophon) the works of Epictetus, Marcus Antonius, and Seneca, contain many moral sentiments, but little or nothing of the principles of morals. I think the most beautiful moral writer of the ancients, is the author of the Tablature of Cebes. As to any thing contained in the ancients relative to the truth of theology, it will be found almost universally collected in Cudworth's Intellectual System.[50]

Witherspoon did have an empirical orientation that took its inspiration ultimately from Aristotle, and he repeatedly talked about virtue and occasionally about the magistrate's proper role in encouraging it and "mak[ing] men good."[51] Admittedly, in his concern about virtue, he appears to sound a clear note from the ancient political theorists, who, as Rousseau reminded us, "spoke incessantly about mores and virtue; ours speak only of commerce and money."[52] But, as we have seen, Witherspoon had plenty to say about commerce and money as well.

Utterances such as these seem to be the exception rather than the rule in Witherspoon's political thought. His classicism looks to have been mostly rhetorical, a veneer on a solidly modern structure. The name of his country home, Tusculum, he borrowed from Cicero's rural estate,[53] in much the same way that Joseph Warren delivered an oration on the Boston Massacre in a "Ciceronian toga."[54] Like so many of the founders, Witherspoon chose classical pseudonyms—"Aristides" and "Epaminondas"[55]—to go along with others such as the "Jersey Farmer" and the oddly pagan "Druid." These, however, apparently reflect the conventions of early American political culture more than any deep indebtedness to Greek or Roman political thought. Further, we find no suggestion by Witherspoon that ancient constitutions were to be used as models for modern statesmen, only the admission that in ancient Rome the dominant public spirit was the desire for glory while in Greece it was the preservation of liberty.[56]

Not so with the Scottish philosophy. Through his Lectures on Moral Philosophy and his manifold labors as president of the College of New Jersey, Witherspoon deliberately diverted certain ideas from the Scottish Enlightenment into the mainstream of American political thought. Through Witherspoon they passed to Madison, and to a lesser extent to Alexander Hamilton, the two primary authors of *The Federalist Papers*. They passed as well to four other members of the Constitutional Convention, to three Supreme Court Justices, to members of state constitutional conventions and state ratifying conventions, and on and on. Of course, students at Princeton learned far more than the Scottish philosophy from Witherspoon, but this contribution did set him apart from his contemporaries and helps mark him as the greatest educator of his age, or perhaps any American age. During the quarter century he was at Princeton, Witherspoon provided concepts and modes of expression that helped to create a common moral language during the founding—a language that was shared by the strictly orthodox such as himself, the heterodox such as Jefferson, and everyone in between. No other founder (not even James Wilson) did more to channel the Scottish philosophy into the colonies and thus into American political thought.

This is perhaps natural in light of Witherspoon's Scottish ancestry. Similarly, one would expect, given his uncompromising religious orthodoxy, that he would have been an especially noteworthy example of Reformed Christianity in the founding and that he himself would have been greatly influenced by that tradition. Indeed, Witherspoon was an especially full-throated example of the biblical voice in American political thought, especially when dilating on the indispensable role of "true religion" in public life. But we must guard against reading Reformed Protestantism back into Witherspoon's definition of true religion, which seems to have covered any genuine example of Christianity—Reformed, Protestant, Catholic, or otherwise. With this caveat in mind, we can say that Witherspoon's political thought bore the deep impress of the Reformation, with its rejection of the divine right of kings and affirmation of religious liberty for dissenters. That said, we should be mindful that there was a uniquely American Calvinism, evidenced by the changes to the Westminster Confession made by Witherspoon and the American Presbyterians, that differed from Calvinism in Geneva. But all Reformed denominations, both American and European, followed John Calvin in presuming the depravity of man and the need for law to prevent liberty from turning to license, and these presumptions can be found underlying Witherspoon's thought as well as Madison's. Certainly, Witherspoon, one of the preeminent Reformed pastors in America and the most visible cleric in the Continental Congress, best represented the Reformed presence at the founding. James Hutson has rightly called him the "prototype of the political parson during the Revolutionary War."[57]

Perhaps more than any other single founder, Witherspoon embodied all of the major intellectual and social elements behind the American founding. This was partly circumstantial: Witherspoon was literally peerless among his founding brothers when it came to combining religion, education, and politics, and seldom in American history have so many key vocations been joined in one man. Witherspoon therefore offers us a chance that is genuinely incomparable, to trace the outlines of the American mind at the founding, or, if I may once more employ a useful metaphor, to hear a new recording of the many voices of the founding chorus. If we can successfully reconstruct John Witherspoon's political thought, as I have tried to do here, then we will have a new and perhaps unique transcript of early American intellectual history and political thought. What we find in that transcript are elements of every major intellectual tradition present at the founding—Lockean liberalism, the Scottish Enlightenment, Reformed Protestantism, and, to a lesser extent, classical republican thought. Witherspoon's mind was in one respect like a prism: all of those traditions passed through it and were refracted—some, like the Scottish Enlightenment, brightly, others muted—and passed to a generation of political leaders as remarkable as any ever produced in America. The fact that he embodied all of these traditions to a greater or lesser degree, and, more important, that he was able to combine them in a distinctly American way, suggests that Witherspoon is best seen as a synthesizer and as an eminently representative founder.

But we must take care not to pass him off as merely passive, like some uncritical eighteenth-century conduit. Some of the terms I have used to describe him—an "aqueduct," a "carrier" of a strain of the Scottish Enlightenment—can connote passivity, but Witherspoon had a keen, active intelligence that often left its impress on those traditions even as he passed them along. Instead of looking like a Scotsman transplanted in foreign soil, as some writers have portrayed him, it is striking how very *American* Witherspoon appears. He took root in the soil of the New World remarkably quickly, and his political thought, even in its eclecticism, was typically American. (Writing in the British press in 1773 he himself claimed that "[a] man will become an American by residing in the country three months.")[58] In his political thought and career we can discern, if we have eyes to see it, a miniature of the founding, and in this respect John Witherspoon was a quintessential American founder.

Witherspoon and the Debate in Congress on Independence, July 1776

The supposition that Witherspoon argued down John Dickinson and other congressional conservatives has the ring of authenticity about it. Witherspoon's account of the incident, related to Ashbel Green, is as follows:

> The substance of a statement, made by himself in the hearing of the writer [Green], was, to the best of his recollection, to the following effect — That the principal argument relied on, for those who wished to postpone for a time the declaration of Independence[,] was, that a number of new members had recently entered Congress, who had not heard the whole of the previous discussions; and who could not therefore judge correctly of the reasons for, and against, an immediate declaration which had been so ably advocated and urged before they took their seats; and that the country at large needed more time for reflection, and was not yet ripe for so important and decisive a measure. To this the Doctor [Witherspoon] took an opportunity to reply; that although there were some members who had but recently come into Congress, it did by no means follow that they had not examined this important subject in all its bearings, and weighed the arguments fully, for prompt

action on the one side, and for delay on the other. That this certainly had been done by himself, and he doubted not by others, to whom the objection applied: nor had they wanted ample means of information on the merits of the question, although they had not been favoured with hearing all the debates of that house. As to the country at large, it had been for some time past, loud in its demand for the proposed declaration, and in his judgement it was not only ripe for the measure, but in danger of becoming rotten for the want of it.[1]

Dickinson himself acknowledged the argument as Witherspoon recalled it. In a "Vindication" published years afterward, Dickinson admitted that in Congress he "opposed the making the declaration of independence *at the time when it was made,*"[2] although he was not against independence per se.

Unfortunately, the debates over independence during the week from Friday, June 28, through Thursday, July 4, 1776, recorded in the *Journals of the Continental Congress, 1774–1789,* are sketchy at best.[3] The *Journals* report that on Monday, July 1, after hearing the Resolution for Independence read, "the determination thereof was postponed, at the request of a colony, till to morrow." On July 2 the Resolution was "agreed to," and consideration of the Declaration was put off until the following day because of time. After more "consideration" the Declaration was finally "agreed to" on July 4.[4] Witherspoon's name appears only twice during that period— once on June 28, along with the credentials of the other New Jersey delegates, presented that day by Francis Hopkinson; and then on the list of signatories of the Declaration, inserted in the *Journals* under the records for July 4.[5] Circumstantial evidence supporting Witherspoon's claim, however, does come from the more substantive accounts by Thomas Jefferson and John Adams of the debates.

Jefferson recorded in his "Notes of Proceedings in the Continental Congress" two occasions on which delay was urged because New Jersey and other colonies were not ripe for independence. In the previous month, on June 8, Jefferson has "Dickinson and others" arguing that "the people of the middle colonies (Maryland, Delaware, Pennsylva., the Jersies & N. York) were not yet ripe for bidding adieu to British connection."[6] Sometime between June 8 and June 28 (Jefferson's "Notes" are not precise) he again records an argument that since "the colonies of N. York, New Jersey, Pennsylvania, Delaware[,] Maryland & South Carolina were not yet matured for falling from the parent stem . . . it was thought most prudent to wait a while for them, and to postpone the final decision [on the Resolution for Independence] to July 1."[7]

On June 28 (the day the New Jersey delegation's credentials were presented), Jefferson delivered a draft of the Declaration of Independence to the house, whereupon "it was read and ordered to lie on the table. [O]n Monday the 1st. of July the house resolved itself into a commee. of the whole & resumed the consideration of the original motion made by the delegates of Virginia, which being again debated through the day, was carried in the affirmative by the votes of N. Hampshire, [C]onnecticut, Massachusetts, Rhode island, N. Jersey, Maryland, Virginia, N. Carolina, & Georgia. S. Carolina and Pennsylvania voted against it."[8] Most likely the exchange between Witherspoon and Dickinson took place on July 1, during the debate, which Jefferson says occurred "through the day," over the Resolution for Independence.

John Adams linked Dickinson and Witherspoon when he recounted the congressional debates in a letter to Thomas McKean in 1815. "The most essential . . . debates & deliberations in Congress," Adams wrote, "are now lost forever. Mr[.] Dickinson printed a speech which he said he made in Congress against the declaration of Independence; but it appeared to me very different from that which you and I heard. Dr[.] Witherspoon has published speeches, which he wrote before hand, and delivered Memoriter [by memory], as he did his sermons."[9] (Adams, like Jefferson, kept notes of the debates in Congress, although his were far less detailed than the Virginian's.)[10] Mention of Dickinson and the most "essential" congressional debates seemed to trigger recollection of Witherspoon's part in those exchanges in Adams's mind.

Furthermore, "ripe" and "rotten" were staples of Witherspoon's political vocabulary, and it was his practice to juxtapose them for emphasis. In the "Dominion of Providence" sermon (1776), he remarked that "[n]othing is more certain than that a general profligacy and corruption of manners make a people ripe for destruction. A good form of government may hold the rotten materials together for some time, but beyond a certain pitch, even the best constitution will be ineffectual, and slavery must ensue."[11] Compare this passage with the nearly identical language in the "Sermon Delivered at a Public Thanksgiving After Peace" (1782): "[w]hen the body of a people are altogether corrupt in their manners, the government is ripe for dissolution. Good laws may hold the rotten bark some longer together, but in a little time all laws must give way to the tide of popular opinion, and be laid prostrate under universal practice."[12] Finally, in the "Memorial and Manifesto," written in 1781 to enlist support from Russia and Germany to end the War on terms favorable to the Americans, Witherspoon insisted that "[u]pon the whole, since the American colonies were, from their extent and situation, ripe for a separation from Great-Britain, and the nature of things seemed to demand it . . . it is to be hoped that the revolution which they have effected, will meet with universal approbation."[15] Thus, the accounts of the debates by Jefferson, Adams, and Dickinson, along with Witherspoon's own claim and his practice of using the words in question, tend to authenticate the remark in Congress.

Dating the "Sermon Delivered at a Public Thanksgiving After Peace," November 1782

Since the first edition of Witherspoon's *Works* in 1800–1801, it has been assumed that this sermon was preached in the spring of 1783, "after peace," as the title suggests.[1] V. L. Collins in 1925 put down the exact date as April 19, 1783.[2] However, internal and external evidence points to November 28, 1782, declared by Congress a day of fasting and thanksgiving in a proclamation written by Witherspoon himself, as the date of delivery.

The sermon's title was supplied by Ashbel Green, editor of the 1800 and 1802 editions of Witherspoon's *Works,* which are almost entirely devoid of editorial comment and were prepared in less than careful fashion by today's editorial standards. (Green originally planned for only three volumes of *Works* but added a fourth in 1801.) There is therefore nothing authoritative about Green's title, which puts the time of delivery after peace was declared in 1783.

The most compelling evidence for the earlier date is internal evidence from the text of the sermon. First, in the opening paragraph, Witherspoon speaks of "the course of a war, *which has now lasted* seven years" and "the campaign which is *now drawing to a close,*" and later of the "course of the *present* war."[3] According to Witherspoon the War was still ongoing when he was preaching (and seven years from 1775 would be 1782), so it is immediately doubtful that it could have been delivered after peace had been declared, as Green thought. Second, Witherspoon claims to be preaching "in obedience to public authority,"[4] and the most likely reference is to the congressional Thanksgiving Day Proclamation of October 11, 1782, which set Thursday, November 28, as the day of observance. (Congress issued only one Thanksgiving Day Proclamation in 1783, on October 18,[5] six months after the April 19 date assigned to the Witherspoon sermon by Collins; the other congressional proclamation of 1782 was the Fast Day Proclamation of March 19,[6] which set the last Thursday in April as a day of "fasting, humiliation and prayer.") Witherspoon himself was the author of the Proclamation of October 11, 1782, and there are several identical phrases between the Proclamation and the sermon, including discussions of the conflict in which the states had been "so long engaged," and the year and campaign "now drawing to a close."[7] Thus, Witherspoon appears to have had the Proclamation of October 11 before him when composing the Thanksgiving Day sermon, which again points toward November 28, 1782, as the correct date. Third, Witherspoon refers to a sermon he preached "six years ago on a public fast day" during which he turned the "attention of the hearers to events of a public nature,"[8] an unmistakable reference to the "Dominion of Providence Over the Passions of Men," delivered on May 17, 1776. Six years from the preaching of the "Dominion of Providence" would put the date of the Thanksgiving Day sermon at 1782, not 1783. Fourth, Witherspoon says that he chose the sermon's biblical text, Psalm 3:8, because it was supposedly written by David "before the war with Absalom, his unnatural son, was wholly finished; but when he had such presages of success as made him speak the language of faith and confidence."[9]

Finally, there is external evidence, in the form of a contemporary newspaper account of the ceremonies of April 19, 1783, in Princeton. The *New-Jersey Gazette* of April 23 contains an account, datelined "Princeton, April 21, 1783," which describes how "[t]he gentlemen of this town and neighbourhood having fixed on the *19th of April* (as being the memorable AEra of the commencement of hostilities in America in 1775) to celebrate the *peace* so happily concluded [original emphasis]" gathered. At 1 o'clock "the company met in the College Hall, where an excellent discourse, suitable to the occassion [*sic*], was delivered by the Rev. Dr. Witherspoon, to a very numerous audience." Thus, Witherspoon did not preach a sermon, he delivered a "discourse" (although it was not unheard of in those days to call a sermon a discourse); and the date was chosen by the citizens of Princeton, not set by congressional proclamation.

The "Sermon Delivered at a Public Thanksgiving After Peace" is therefore the Thanksgiving Day sermon preached on November 28, 1782, in obedience to the congressional Thanksgiving Day Proclamation of October 11, 1782. Written by Witherspoon himself on behalf of Congress, it was not a sermon delivered after peace as previously thought.

notes

Preface

1. A third statue of Witherspoon (a good one) was erected on the campus of Princeton University in 2001. As a librarian at Firestone Library pointed out to me, Witherspoon has his front to the campus chapel and his backside to the theater, which he thought corrupted morals.

2. *The Evening Star,* May 20, 1909.

3. The statue "on a granite pedestal" was a gift of the Witherspoon Memorial Association. An act of Congress of May 29, 1908 (35 Stat. 579), appropriated $4,000 "toward [a] pedestal," and the statue was dedicated on May 20, 1909. See *Sculpture in the Parks: Statues, Monuments and Memorials Located in the Parks of the Nation's Capital* (Washington, DC: U.S. Department of the Interior, 1985), 50.

4. S.2996, introduced February 19, 1976, and sponsored by Senator Jackson and cosponsored by Senator Stennis, authorized "the Secretary of the Interior to permit the removal of the statue of John Witherspoon which is presently located on National Park Service lands in the District of Columbia to the National Presbyterian Center, Washington, District of Columbia, and to transfer title to such statue to the National Presbyterian Church Incorporated without compensation."

5. Richard B. Sher, "Introduction: Scottish-American Cultural Studies, Past and Present," in Richard B. Sher and Jeffrey R. Smitten, eds., *Scotland and America in the Age of the Enlightenment* (Princeton: Princeton University Press, 1990), 16.

6. See Ashbel Green, *Life of the Revd. John Witherspoon,* ed. Henry Lyttleton Savage (Princeton: Princeton University Press, 1973); and David Walker Woods, Jr., *John Witherspoon* (New York: Fleming H. Revell, 1906).

7. See L. Gordon Tait, *The Piety of John Witherspoon: Pew, Pulpit, and Public Forum* (Louisville, KY: Geneva Press, 2001); at p. x, Tait claims that his "volume should find its place within the category of theology rather than history."

8. See note 5; and Mark A. Noll, *Princeton and the Republic, 1768–1822: The Search for a Christian Enlightenment in the Era of Samuel Stanhope Smith* (Princeton: Princeton University Press, 1989).

9. More than anything, Witherspoon has merited unpublished doctoral dissertations. See, for example, David D. Bartley, "John Witherspoon and the Right of Resistance," Ph.D. dissertation, Ball State University, 1989; Marvin Bergman, "Public Religion in Revolutionary America: Ezra Stiles, Devereux Jarratt, and John Witherspoon," Ph.D. dissertation, University of Chicago Divinity School, 1990; William Oliver Brackett, "John Witherspoon, His Scottish Ministry," Ph.D. dissertation, New College of Divinity, Edinburgh, 1948; Roger J. Fechner, "The Moral Philosophy of John Witherspoon and the Scottish-American Enlightenment," Ph.D. dissertation: University of Iowa, 1974; George Rich, "John Witherspoon: His Scottish Intellectual Background," Ph.D. dissertation, Syracuse University, 1964; Wayne W. Witte, "John Witherspoon: Servant of Liberty—A Study in Doctrinal History and Political Calvinism," Th. D. dissertation, Princeton Theological Seminary, 1954; and Lawrence G. Wrenn, "John Witherspoon and Church Law," Dissertation, Pontificia Universitas Lateranensis, Rome, 1979.

10. See Benjamin Rush to John Adams, February 17, 1812: "I rejoice in the correspondence which has taken place between you and your old friend Mr. Jefferson. I consider you and him as the North and South Poles of the American Revolution. Some talked, some wrote, and some fought to promote and establish it, but you and Mr. Jefferson *thought* for us all. I never take a retrospect of the years 1775 and 1776 without associating your opinions and speeches and conversations with all the great political, moral, and intellectual achievements of the Congresses of those memorable years." In *Letters of Benjamin Rush*, ed. L. H. Butterfield, 2 vols. (Princeton: Princeton University Press, 1951), 2:1127 [original emphasis].

Chapter One.   Forgotten Founder

1. For Rush's self-evaluation, see Benjamin Rush to John Adams, May 12, 1807, in *Letters of Benjamin Rush*, 2:944; and generally, John A. Schutz and Douglass Adair, eds., *The Spur of Fame: Dialogues of John Adams and Benjamin Rush, 1805–1813* (San Marino, CA: Huntington Library, 1966). Rush himself decided to propose to his future wife, Miss Julia Stockton, partly because of her high opinion of Witherspoon. Rush wrote that his already favorable impression of her "was much strengthened by an opinion I heard her give of Dr. Witherspoon's preaching the next day after I saw her. She said he was the best preacher she had ever heard. . . . From this moment I determined to offer her my hand." See *The Autobiography of Benjamin Rush*, ed. George W. Corner (Princeton: Princeton University Press, 1948), 51, 116.

2. John Adams, diary entry of August 27, 1774, in *The Diary and Autobiography of John Adams*, ed. L. H. Butterfield, 4 vols. (Cambridge, MA: Harvard University Press, 1961), 2:112.

3. Benjamin Rush to John Adams, May 5, 1812, in Schutz and Adair, *The Spur of Fame*, 215; John Adams to Benjamin Rush, May 14, 1812, in ibid., 216.

4. See, for example, Charles S. Hyneman and Donald S. Lutz, eds., *American Political Writing during the Founding Era, 1760–1805*, 2 vols. (Indianapolis: Liberty Press, 1983).

5. Witherspoon earned an M.A. and studied divinity at Edinburgh, and was awarded an honorary Doctor in Divinity from St. Andrews and an honorary Doctor of Laws from Yale College. (Both St. Andrews and Yale conferred honorary degrees on another patriot, Benjamin Franklin.)

6. For the story of how Rush helped woo Witherspoon to New Jersey and the presidency of his alma mater, see Lyman Henry Butterfield, ed., *John Witherspoon Comes to America: A Documentary Account Based Largely on New Materials* (Princeton: Princeton University Library, 1953). For the part played by Whitefield, see Varnum Lansing Collins, *President Witherspoon: A Biography*, 2 vols. (Princeton: Princeton University Press, 1925; reprint ed., New York: Arno Press, 1969), 1:98; and Iain H. Murray, *Revival and Revivalism* (Edinburgh: Banner of Truth Trust, 1994), 41–42.

7. The *Journals of the Continental Congress* record Witherspoon as a member of a "grand committee" on January 7, 1783, although his final congressional term had expired in November 1782; his name does not appear in the *Journals* as an active participant after that date. See *Journals of the Continental Congress, 1774–1789*, ed. Worthington C. Ford et al., 34 vols. (Washington, DC: U.S. Government Printing Office, 1904–37), 24:38–39 [hereinafter *Journals of the Continental Congress*]. For stylistic reasons I have used the term "Continental Congress" to designate the Congress from 1781–82, even though the Second Continental Congress technically became the Confederation Congress after the adoption of the Articles of Confederation in 1781.

8. Witherspoon's *Works*, first published in 1800–1801, quickly went through a number of editions but have not been reprinted since 1815. In his own day, various pieces of Witherspoon's were translated into French, Dutch, and German. The best biography of Witherspoon remains V. L. Collins's *President Witherspoon* (1925).

9. Signer Lyman Hall of Georgia had once been a clergyman though by 1776 he had been defrocked. See Garry Wills, *Inventing America: Jefferson's Declaration of Independence* (New York: Random House, 1979), 46–47. There were at least two other practicing clergymen who were members of Congress along with Witherspoon, Revs. John Joachim Zubly and Jesse Root, though neither was a member in 1776. See Green, *Life of the Revd. John Witherspoon*, 161n.

10. Simon Schama, *Citizens: A Chronicle of the French Revolution* (New York: Alfred A. Knopf, 1989), 44.

11. For example, Joseph J. Ellis's Pulitzer Prize-winning *Founding Brothers: The Revolutionary Generation* (New York: Alfred A. Knopf, 2000) profiles the six founders above (Washington, Adams, Jefferson, Madison, Hamilton, Franklin) and only adds Aaron Burr because of the drama of his duel with Hamilton.

12. The Organic Laws of the United States, as they appear in the first volume of the United States Code, are the Declaration of Independence (1776), the Articles of Confederation (1777), the Northwest Ordinance (1787), and the Constitution (1787). See "The Organic Laws of the United States of America," in *United States Code: Containing the General and Permanent Laws of the United States, in Force on January 4, 1995,* 35 vols. (Washington, DC: U.S. Government Printing Office, 1995), 1:xxxix–lxix [hereinafter *United States Code*].

13. See Kenneth E. Harris and Steven D. Tilley, eds., *Index, Journals of the Continental Congress, 1774–1789* (Washington, DC: General Services Administration, National Archives and Records Service, 1976), 421–22. As noted above, the correct number of committees is probably 125; but either way, it was a herculean effort on Witherspoon's part.

14. Green, *Life of the Revd. John Witherspoon,* 159–60. For verification of Witherspoon's reply to Dickinson and the conservatives, a matter which has been debated by historians, see appendix A, this volume.

15. Edward S. Corwin, *French Policy and the American Alliance of 1778* (New York: Burt Franklin, 1970 [1916]), 301. Corwin is critical of the alliance between France and America; to him, Witherspoon and the Americans were incautious in ceding diplomatic power to France in "the one entangling alliance to which the United States has been party."

16. In David McCullough, *John Adams* (New York: Simon and Schuster, 2001), 261.

17. For Witherspoon as a pamphleteer, see Moses Coit Tyler, "President Witherspoon in the American Revolution," *American Historical Review* 1 (1896): 671–79.

18. Witherspoon, *The Works of John Witherspoon,* 9 vols. (Edinburgh: Ogle and Aikman et al., 1804–5), 9:66–98, 224–91 [hereinafter *Works*].

19. See, generally, James McLachlan et al., eds., *Princetonians: A Biographical Dictionary,* 5 vols. (Princeton: Princeton University Press, 1976–91). These volumes, the most accurate and comprehensive on Princeton alumni produced to date, contain "Appendices of Occupational Listings" including "Holders of Major Public Offices" for each graduating class, which I have used to arrive at the totals given. (I have counted an individual who was elected to both the U.S. Congress and Senate, for example, separately as a congressman and senator.) Past scholarship has invariably given inaccurate (usually undercounted) numbers of major officeholders who graduated under Witherspoon.

The delegates to the Constitutional Convention schooled by Witherspoon were William Churchill Houston of New Jersey (B.A. 1768), Gunning Bedford, Jr., of Delaware (B.A. 1771), James Madison of Virginia (B.A. 1771), William Richardson

Davie of North Carolina (B.A. 1776), and Jonathan Dayton of New Jersey (B.A. 1776). (Of these five, Madison, Bedford, and Dayton signed.) The Supreme Court justices taught by Witherspoon were Henry Brockholst Livingston (B.A. 1774, associate justice 1806–1823), Smith Thompson (B.A. 1788, associate justice 1823–1843), and William Johnson, Jr. (B.A. 1790, associate justice 1804–1834).

20. See correspondence between Madison and Smith in the late 1770s, in Ralph L. Ketcham, "James Madison and Religion—A New Hypothesis," in *James Madison on Religious Liberty*, ed. Robert S. Alley (Buffalo, NY: Prometheus Books, 1985), 182–83.

21. Collins, *President Witherspoon*, 1:139. Cooperation between Presbyterians and Congregationalists came easily since they held nearly identical theologies, both being Calvinists and covenant theologians, and only differed slightly over church polity.

22. Collins, *President Witherspoon*, 1:138. After Witherspoon attended the Yale commencement in the fall of 1773, Stiles recorded in his journal that of all American college presidents, President Locke of Harvard was the most learned, excepting Witherspoon in theology. See ibid., 1:155.

23. Collins, *President Witherspoon*, 2:145.

24. Edward Frank Humphrey calls Witherspoon "the premier of American Presbyterianism" in *Nationalism and Religion in America, 1774–1789* (New York: Russell and Russell, 1965), 441.

25. See Roger Finke and Rodney Stark, *The Churching of America, 1776–1990: Winners and Losers in Our Religious Economy* (New Brunswick, NJ: Rutgers University Press, 1992), 25, noting that Presbyterians had 588 congregations in 1776. See also Edwin Scott Gaustad and Philip L. Barlow, *New Historical Atlas of Religion in America* (New York: Oxford University Press, 2001), 38; and James H. Smylie, "Introduction," in *Presbyterians and the American Revolution: A Documentary Account, Journal of Presbyterian History*, 52, no. 4, special edition (Winter 1974): 304.

26. Fred J. Hood, *Reformed America: The Middle and Southern States, 1783–1837* (University, AL: University of Alabama Press, 1980), 2.

27. Tyler, "President Witherspoon in the American Revolution," 676.

28. See Collins, *President Witherspoon*, 2:251–52. For the text and commentaries on the sermon, see William Safire, ed., *Lend Me Your Ears: Great Speeches in History* (New York: W. W. Norton and Co., 1992), 425–30 (abridged); Ellis Sandoz, ed., *Political Sermons of the American Founding Era, 1730–1805* (Indianapolis: Liberty Press, 1991), 529–58; *The Selected Writings of John Witherspoon*, ed. Thomas P. Miller (Carbondale: Southern Illinois University Press, 1990), 126–47 [hereinafter *Selected Writings*]; and *Works*, 5:176–236.

29. "George III was not far wrong either when he called the Revolution 'a Presbyterian Rebellion.'" Paul Johnson, *A History of the American People* (New York: HarperCollins, 1997), 173.

30. In Smylie, "Introduction," 303.

31. Another interesting example is the "Sermon Delivered at a Public Fast Day After Peace" (1782), in *Works*, 5:237–70. See chapter 4 and appendix B, this volume.

32. Witherspoon was the author of the following proclamations: the Fast Day Proclamation of December 11, 1776; the Thanksgiving Day Proclamation of October 26, 1781; and the Thanksgiving Day Proclamation of October 11, 1782. See *Journals of the Continental Congress*, 6:1022; 21:1074–76; 23:647.

33. No previous writer on Witherspoon mentions his membership in the Society. For records of his membership, see *Early Proceedings of the American Philosophical Society for the Promotion of Useful Knowledge* (Philadelphia: McCalla and Stavely, 1884), 35; *Proceedings of the American Philosophical Society* (Philadelphia: American Philosophical Society, 1934), 73:384; and American Philosophical Society to Thomas Jefferson, February 7, 1781, in *The Papers of Thomas Jefferson*, ed. Julian P. Boyd et al., 30 vols. to date (Princeton: Princeton University Press, 1950–), 4:544–45 [hereinafter *Papers of Thomas Jefferson*].

34. Although Ashbel Green, the editor of Witherspoon's *Works*, did not recognize it as such, the fragmentary "Observations on the Improvement of America" is obviously an address to the American Philosophical Society. Witherspoon was a member of the Committee on Husbandry and American Improvements and in the "Observations" calls his audience the "Philadelphia Society." See *Works*, 9:178–79.

35. An exchange on Newtonian theory took place in the *Pennsylvania Magazine* from April through June 1776. Witherspoon titled his piece, which appeared in the May 1776 issue, "A Few Thoughts on Space, Dimension, and the Divisibility of Matter in Infinitum"; in the following issue (June 1776), Witherspoon was taken to task for misunderstanding Newton by his fellow Society member David Rittenhouse. See Brooke Hindle, "Witherspoon, Rittenhouse, and Sir Isaac Newton," *William and Mary Quarterly*, 3d ser., 15 (1958): 365–72.

36. See "Introduction," in *Selected Writings*, vii.

37. Martin Diamond, *The Founding of the Democratic Republic* (Itasca, IL: F. E. Peacock, 1981), 2. For Witherspoon's coinage, see *The Oxford English Dictionary*, 2d ed. (Oxford: Clarendon Press, 1989), 1:398. See also Witherspoon, "Druid V" (1781), in *Works*, 9:269–70, where he discusses "Americanisms, or ways of speaking peculiar to this country." By the word "Americanism, which I have coined for the purpose," Witherspoon understood a "use of phrases or terms, or a construction of sentences, even among persons of rank and education, different from the use of the same terms or phrases, or the construction of similar sentences, in Great Britain."

38. *Oxford English Dictionary*, 2:815, notes that the word had a U.S. origin and was "[f]irst used at Princeton, New Jersey" in 1774.

39. Hamilton wrote to Witherspoon on October 20, 1789, asking, as Witherspoon said in his reply, for suggestions on "a proper provision for the public Debt." See John Witherspoon to Alexander Hamilton, October 26, 1789, in *The Papers of Alexander Hamilton*, ed. Harold C. Syrett, 27 vols. (New York: Columbia University Press, 1961–87), 5:464–65. Hamilton's letter does not survive. The editor's footnote

to Witherspoon's letter reads: "Letter not found. H presumably wrote to Witherspoon for information on financial matters to use in preparation of his 'Report Relative to a Provision for the Support of Public Credit,' January 9, 1790." Hamilton's first Report was submitted to Congress on January 14, 1790.

40. Editor's note, *Papers of Alexander Hamilton,* 6:56n.

41. Ibid.

42. See John Witherspoon, "On the Proposed Market in General Washington's Camp, To His Excellency General Washington, and the Officers of the American Army," in *Works,* 9:148–53 [abridged].

43. See editor's note, *Papers of Alexander Hamilton,* 7:242n, 244n. For further discussions of the *Essay on Money,* see Collins, *President Witherspoon,* 2:22–31, 256–58; and Tyler, "President Witherspoon in the American Revolution," 676–78. For the essay's text, see John Witherspoon, *Essay on Money as a Medium of Commerce, with Remarks on the Advantages and Disadvantages of Paper Admitted into General Circulation* (Philadelphia: Young, Stewart, and McCulloch, 1786); also *Works,* 9:9–65.

44. See Varnum Lansing Collins, ed., "Introduction," *Lectures on Moral Philosophy by John Witherspoon* (Princeton: Princeton University Press, 1912), xxi.

45. See, generally, *An Annotated Edition of Lectures on Moral Philosophy by John Witherspoon,* ed. Jack Scott (Newark, DE: University of Delaware Press, 1982) [hereinafter *Lectures on Moral Philosophy*].

46. See Hood, *Reformed America,* 17: "Although Witherspoon's Lectures did not appear in print until the first edition of his works in 1800, they were widely circulated prior to that time and their influence on Washington's Farewell Address is immediately apparent."

47. In Scott, *Lectures on Moral Philosophy,* 52.

48. Collins, *President Witherspoon,* 1:126. See also Green in Tyler, "President Witherspoon in the American Revolution," 673; and Witherspoon in *Selected Writings,* 136.

49. Green, *Life of the Revd. John Witherspoon,* 258–59.

50. See Collins, *President Witherspoon,* 2:169–70.

51. See Adams, diary entry of September 3, 1774, in *Diary and Autobiography of John Adams,* 2:121.

52. John Adams to Benjamin Rush, September 1, 1809, in Schutz and Adair, *The Spur of Fame,* 153.

53. See Collins, *President Witherspoon,* 2:181; and McCullough, *John Adams,* 648. MacWhorter, in Newark, New Jersey, was also a Presbyterian clergyman and patriot.

54. Adams to Benjamin Rush, September 1, 1809, in Schutz and Adair, *The Spur of Fame,* 153; see also Adams to Rush, August 14, 1812, in ibid., 185.

55. "Dr. John Witherspoon, jr., who was surgeon of the *De Graaf* letter of marque, taken at St. Eustatius, is sent to England in the *Alcmena* man-of-war, and

very hardly treated, on account of his father being a member of Congress, as is supposed." See James Lovell to Benjamin Franklin, May 9, 1781, in Francis Wharton, ed., *The Revolutionary Diplomatic Correspondence of the United States,* 6 vols. (Washington, DC: U.S. Government Printing Office, 1889), 4:405. Franklin helped secure the release of the younger Witherspoon (1757–1795?) through diplomatic correspondence conducted from Paris in November 1781. See Green, *Life of the Revd. John Witherspoon,* 206–7n.

56. Franklin to Witherspoon, April 5, 1784, in *Benjamin Franklin's Autobiographical Writings,* ed. Carl Van Doren (New York: Viking Press, 1945), 600.

57. Jay to Witherspoon, April 6, 1784, in Green, *Life of the Revd. John Witherspoon,* 206. One wonders whether Jay was referring to spiritual or political fields worked with Witherspoon; "harvest home" was a phrase much used by evangelical Protestants, especially in the eighteenth and nineteenth centuries, in an obvious reference to the harvest fields of salvation spoken of by Christ.

58. See Thomas Jefferson to Benjamin Rush, September 23, 1800, in *The Writings of Thomas Jefferson,* ed. Andrew A. Lipscomb and Albert Ellery Bergh et al., 20 vols. (Washington, DC: Thomas Jefferson Memorial Association of the United States, 1903–4), 10:174; Jefferson to Jeremiah Moore, August 14, 1800, in *The Works of Thomas Jefferson,* ed. Paul Leicester Ford, 12 vols. New York: G. P. Putnam's Sons, 1904–5), 9:143.

59. In Marvin Olasky, *The American Leadership Tradition* (New York: The Free Press, 1999), 36.

60. Fithian to John Peck, August 12, 1774, in *Journal & Letters of Philip Vickers Fithian, 1773–1774: A Plantation Tutor of the Old Dominion,* ed. Hunter Dickinson Farish (Williamsburg, VA: Colonial Williamsburg, 1943), 215.

61. Jefferson to Wilson Cary Nicholas, December 31, 1783, in *Papers of Thomas Jefferson,* 6:432–33.

62. See James A. Bear, Jr., and Lucia C. Stanton, eds., *Jefferson's Memorandum Books: Accounts, with Legal Records and Miscellany, 1767–1826,* 2 vols. (Princeton: Princeton University Press, 1997), 2:1014, 1016; see also E. Millicent Sowerby, ed., *Catalogue of the Library of Thomas Jefferson,* 5 vols. (Charlottesville: University Press of Virginia, 1983), 5:439.

63. Mary Louise Montague, *John Witherspoon, Signer of the Declaration of Independence, George Washington's Closest Friend and Sponsor* (Washington, DC: McQueen, 1932).

64. Washington's financial records for 1773 contain the following entry: "By Doctr Wetherspoon for Mr [William] Ramsay 48.16.0." See Washington, "Cash Accounts," May 1773, in *The Papers of George Washington,* Colonial Series, ed. W. W. Abbot et al. (Charlottesville: University Press of Virginia, 1983–98), 9:227. The editors note that "GW was himself paying £25 a year toward young Ramsay's support at the college." See ibid., 9:228n.

65. George Washington to John Witherspoon, March 10, 1784, in *The Writings of George Washington, From the Original Manuscript Sources, 1745–1799*, ed. John C. Fitzpatrick, 39 vols. (Washington, DC: U.S. Government Printing Office, 1931–44), 27:348–52 [emphasis added]. Witherspoon had been a member of the Committee on Western Lands while he was in the Continental Congress; see *Journals of the Continental Congress*, 19:100.

66. Ibid., 27:352 [emphasis added].

67. "While at Trenton [April 20 or 21, 1789] GW was given a dinner and a public reception in the evening at Samuel Henry's City Tavern. He probably stayed the night in Trenton . . . rather than going on to Princeton, a suggestion reinforced by the newspaper accounts. Tradition, however, has it that he moved on to Princeton after the reception at the City Tavern and spent the night with the Rev. John Witherspoon, the former [*sic*] president of Princeton College . . . . It is uncertain whether he received the address from the president and faculty of Princeton on the evening of 21 April or on the morning of 22 April." Editor's note, *Papers of George Washington*, Presidential Series, 2:109n. However, the fact that the editors of the *Papers* were unaware that Witherspoon was still president of Princeton at the time of Washington's first inauguration, and that Witherspoon himself had delivered the address to Washington, coupled with the appropriateness of the general staying with the college president (who was an acquaintance and correspondent), add up to the possibility that Washington did indeed stay with the Witherspoons on the way to New York.

68. Ferguson to Alexander Carlyle, in Collins, *President Witherspoon*, 2:35.

69. In Green, *Life of the Revd. John Witherspoon*, 2 [emphasis in original] (citing Sir Guy Carleton Papers, Colonial Williamsburg, Vol. 83, Paper 9294); see also Collins, *President Witherspoon*, 2:133.

70. See Collins, *President Witherspoon*, 1:222.

71. Ibid., 2:94.

72. "Sermon Delivered at a Public Thanksgiving After Peace" (1782), in *Works*, 5:261.

73. Horace Walpole to Lady Ossory, August 3, 1775, in *Horace Walpole's Correspondence*, ed. W. S. Lewis et al., 48 vols. (New Haven: Yale University Press, 1937–83), 32:245. Walpole's mistake was understandable. A British newspaper on June 2, 1775, suggested that the "provincials who attacked General Gage's convoy of provisions, were headed and commanded by a dissenting clergyman. . . . HW seems to have thought Joseph Warren leader of the Boston patriots, was a clergyman: 'Dr Warren, a minister, was killed in the Provincial army' (*Last Journals* i.471)." See editor's note, ibid., 32:245n. (Warren was in reality a physician.) All writers on Witherspoon have repeated the error made by Loraine Boettner, supposing it was Witherspoon instead of Dr. Joseph Warren to whom Walpole was referring. See Loraine Boettner, *The Reformed Doctrine of Predestination* (Philadelphia: Presbyterian

and Reformed Publishing Co., 1971 [1932]), 383; more recently, see Marci A. Hamilton, "The Reverend John Witherspoon and the Constitutional Convention," in *Law and Religion: A Critical Anthology*, ed. Stephen M. Feldman (New York: New York University Press, 2000), 54.

74. "[T]he foreigner of distinction to whom they [*Notes on the State of Virginia*] were addressed was Mons. Barbé De Marbois, the secretary of the French Legation in the United States." Editor's note, in *The Works of Thomas Jefferson*, ed. Paul Leicester Ford, 12 vols. (New York: G. P. Putnam's Sons, 1904–5), 3:338–39n.

75. See Witherspoon, "A Description of the State of New Jersey: Answers in Part to Mr[.] Marbois's Questions Respecting New Jersey" [1781?], in *Works*, 9:199–211.

76. Arthur Herman, *How the Scots Invented the Modern World* (New York: Crown Publishers, 2001), 370.

77. Hamilton, "The Reverend John Witherspoon and the Constitutional Convention," 54. See also Hamilton, "The Calvinist Paradox of Distrust and Hope at the Constitutional Convention," in *Christian Perspectives on Legal Thought*, ed. Michael W. McConnell, Robert F. Cochran, Jr., and Angela C. Carmella (New Haven: Yale University Press, 2001), 293–306.

78. James H. Hutson, *Religion and the Founding of the American Republic* (Washington, DC: Library of Congress, 1998), 47.

79. Safire, *Lend Me Your Ears*, 425–30.

80. Garry Wills, *Explaining America: The Federalist* (Garden City, NY: Doubleday and Co., 1981), 18.

81. See Adair, *Fame and the Founding Fathers*, ed. Trevor Colbourn (New York: W. W. Norton, 1974), 124.

82. Savage, ed., in Green, *Life of the Revd. John Witherspoon*, 3.

83. Butterfield, *John Witherspoon Comes to America*, 9.

84. Ketcham, "James Madison and Religion," 179.

85. Almost invariably Witherspoon's *Works*, last published in 1815, are either in noncirculating special collections or on microfilm or microcard in university libraries.

86. See "Description of the State of New Jersey," in *Works*, 9:203.

87. "Old Weatherspoon has not escap'd their ["free booters"] fury. They have burnt his Library. It grieves him much that he has lost his controversial Tracts. He would lay aside the Cloth to take revenge of them. I believe he would send them to the Devil if he could, I am sure I would." Thomas Nelson to Thomas Jefferson, January 2, 1777, in *Papers of Thomas Jefferson*, 2:4. "Free booters" were vandals who took advantage of lawless situations and helped themselves to free "booty"—hence, "free booters." See *Oxford English Dictionary*, 6:164; and Noah Webster, *An American Dictionary of the English Language*, 2 vols. (New York: S. Converse, 1828), 1:n.p.

88. Ashbel Green, ed., "Advertisement to the Second American Edition," in *The Works of the Rev. John Witherspoon*, 2d ed., 4 vols. (Philadelphia: William W. Woodward, 1802), 1:n.p.

89. See Woods, *John Witherspoon*, 6.

90. Humphrey, *Nationalism and Religion in America*, 275. On May 28, 1787, the Synod of New York and Philadelphia ordered 1,000 copies of the final draft of the Presbyterian constitution printed. See Collins, *President Witherspoon*, 2:256; see also *A Draught of the Form of the Government and Discipline of the Presbyterian Church in the United States of America* (New York: S. and J. Loudon, 1787).

91. See, generally, *Records of the Presbyterian Church in the United States of America, Embracing the Minutes of the General Presbytery and General Synod, 1706–1788* (Philadelphia: Presbyterian Board of Publication, 1904) [hereinafter *Records of the Presbyterian Church*], for the years 1758 through 1787. In 1786 the Synod met from Wednesday, May 17, to Wednesday, May 24; in 1785 from Wednesday, May 18, to Tuesday, May 24. See ibid., 505–14, 514.–26. The Synod of 1787 was therefore unusually long.

92. "May 18th, nine o'clock, A.M. . . . Dr. Witherspoon is now come, and his reasons for not coming sooner were sustained." See *Records of the Presbyterian Church*, 532–33.

93. James Madison, *Notes of Debates in the Federal Convention of 1787*, ed. Adrienne Koch (New York: W.W. Norton, 1987 [1966]), 23.

94. See Max Farrand, ed., *The Records of the Federal Convention of 1787*, rev. ed., 4 vols. (New Haven: Yale University Press, 1966), 1:1. The Synod of New York and Philadelphia met from Wednesday, May 16, to Monday, May 28, of 1787, working out their new constitution. See *Records of the Presbyterian Church*, 527–41.

95. *Pennsylvania Packet*, May 31, 1787, in Catherine Drinker Bowen, *Miracle at Philadelphia: The Story of the Constitutional Convention, May to September 1787* (Boston: Little, Brown and Co., 1966), 19–20.

96. As it turned out, only Roger Sherman of Connecticut and Robert Morris of Pennsylvania signed all three documents.

97. "Address to the Inhabitants of Jamaica, and other West-India Islands, in Behalf of the College of New-Jersey" (1772), in *Works*, 8:309.

98. For an account of the meeting between Hamilton and Witherspoon, see Broadus Mitchell, *Alexander Hamilton: Youth to Maturity, 1755–1788* (New York: Macmillan, 1957), 50–52.

99. See Howard Swiggett, *The Forgotten Leaders of the Revolution* (New York: Doubleday, 1955).

100. One exception to this trend was Martha Lou Lemmon Stohlman's hagiographic *John Witherspoon: Parson, Politician, Patriot* (Philadelphia: Westminster Press, 1976), although it shed no new light on his thought or career.

101. This tired line seems to have originated with the historian of philosophy I. Woodbridge Riley, who had an animus against the Scottish common sense philosophers and thus against Witherspoon. See his *American Philosophy: The Early Schools* (New York: Russell and Russell, 1958 [1907]), 483–96.

102. See Smith, diary entry of December 23, 1777, in *Historical Memoirs of William Smith*, ed. William H. W. Sabine, 2 vols. (New York: Colburn and Tegg, 1956–58), 2:277.

103. The assertions that Witherspoon favored a Protestant establishment, and his actual preference for non-establishment, are discussed in chapter 2, this volume.

104. In Bowen, *Miracle at Philadelphia*, 109.

105. A substantial list of neglected founders, including John Dickinson, Oliver Ellsworth, George Mason, and Benjamin Rush, could easily be compiled. One thinks immediately in this context of James Wilson, second only to Madison in influence at the Philadelphia Convention, about whom remarkably few books have been written. See Mark David Hall, *The Political and Legal Philosophy of James Wilson, 1742–1798* (Columbia: University of Missouri Press, 1997), 1.

Chapter Two.   "The Public Interest of Religion": Virtue, Religion, and the Republic

Portions of chapter 2 have appeared as "John Witherspoon and 'The Public Interest of Religion,'" in *Journal of Church and State* 41 (1999): 551–73; and "John Witherspoon's Revolutionary Religion," in *The Founders on God and Government*, ed. Daniel L. Dreisbach, Mark D. Hall, and Jeffry H. Morrison (Lanham, MD: Rowman and Littlefield, 2004), 117–46.

1. Edward Gibbon, *The History of the Decline and Fall of the Roman Empire*, 3 vols. (New York: Modern Library, n.d.), Chap. III, 1:52–53.

2. Ibid., 1:53n.

3. An example of a fighting parson of the "Black Regiment" was Rev. John Peter Gabriel Muhlenberg, who eventually rose to the rank of major general in the Continental army. See Humphrey, *Nationalism and Religion in America*, 114–15; and Hutson, *Religion and the Founding of the American Republic*, 44–45.

4. Ashbel Green records that Witherspoon would never "consent, as some other clerical members of Congress did, to change, in any particular, the dress which distinguished his order." See Green, *Life of the Revd. John Witherspoon*, 161.

5. Article I, Section 18 of the Georgia constitution of 1789 stated that "[n]o clergyman of any denomination shall be a member of the general assembly." See William F. Swindler, ed., *Sources and Documents of United States Constitutions*, 10 vols. (Dobbs Ferry, NY: Oceana Publications, 1973–79), 2:453.

6. See *McDaniel v. Paty et al.*, 435 U.S. 618, 624–25. At p. 624, Chief Justice Burger, writing for the Court, noted that "Madison was not the only opponent of clergy disqualification. When proposals were made earlier to prevent clergymen from holding public office, John Witherspoon, a Presbyterian minister, president of Princeton University, and the only clergyman to sign the Declaration of Independence, made a cogent protest and, with tongue in cheek, offered an amendment to a provision much like that challenged here[.]"

7. Hutson, *Religion and the Founding of the American Republic*, 46.

8. Derek H. Davis, *Religion and the Continental Congress, 1774–1789: Contributions to Original Intent* (New York: Oxford University Press, 2000), xiii.

9. John Adams to Abigail Adams, May 17, 1776, in Julian P. Boyd, "The Drafting of the Declaration of Independence," in *The Declaration of Independence: The Evolution of the Text*, rev. ed. (Washington, DC: Library of Congress, 1999 [1943]), 18. On May 15 the Continental Congress had adopted Adams's resolution that the colonies assume all functions of government independent of Great Britain.

10. "The Dominion of Providence Over the Passions of Men," in *Selected Writings*, 128.

11. *Journals of the Continental Congress*, 6:1022.

12. Hutson, *Religion and the Founding of the American Republic*, 53.

13. Fast Day Proclamation of December 11, 1776, in *Journals of the Continental Congress*, 6:1022 [emphasis added].

14. Thanksgiving Day Proclamation of October 26, 1781, in ibid., 21:1076.

15. Recall that Aitken (1734–1802), a Presbyterian elder, had published Witherspoon's "Dominion of Providence" in the spring of 1776.

16. *Journals of the Continental Congress*, 19:118. A copy of the draft of the resolution in Witherspoon's handwriting is part of the Witherspoon Collection, Manuscripts Division, Department of Rare Books & Special Collections, Princeton University Library.

17. Hutson, *Religion and the Founding of the American Republic*, 57.

18. Fast Day Proclamation of March 19, 1782, in *Journals of the Continental Congress*, 22:138. This proclamation was not written by Witherspoon.

19. *Works*, 5:237–70. This sermon was preached in late 1782, and not on April 19, 1783, as Ashbel Green, V. L. Collins, and others have thought. Internal and external evidence points to November 28, 1782, declared by Congress a day of fasting and thanksgiving in a proclamation written by Witherspoon himself, as the date of delivery. For a discussion of the proper dating of the sermon, see appendix B, "Dating the 'Sermon Delivered at a Public Thanksgiving After Peace,' November 1792," this volume.

20. Thanksgiving Day Proclamation of October 11, 1782, in *Journals of the Continental Congress*, 23:647.

21. "Sermon Delivered at a Public Thanksgiving After Peace," *Works*, 5:237, 265 [emphasis added].

22. In *The Works of John Adams*, ed. Charles Francis Adams, 10 vols. (Boston: Little, Brown and Co., 1850–56), 9:229.

23. "Thanksgiving Sermon," in *Works*, 5:265. Note the similarities between these remarks and those in the "Dominion of Providence" regarding the relationship of religion to society, specifically under a republican form of government.

24. See "On the Georgia Constitution" (1789), in *Works*, 9:223 [emphasis in original].

25. Since the phrase "public religion" seems more closely to approximate what Witherspoon had in mind regarding the relationship between religion and politics, I have used it rather than the more common term "civil religion." For a discussion of civil religion in the context of the American Revolution, see Robert N. Bellah, "The Revolution and the Civil Religion," in Jerald C. Brauer, ed., *Religion and the American Revolution* (Philadelphia: Fortress Press, 1976), 55–73. The reader might also wish to see Jean-Jacques Rousseau, *The Social Contract*, Book IV, Chap. VIII, in *Basic Political Writings*, trans. and ed. Donald A. Cress (Indianapolis: Hackett Publishing Co., 1987), 226, for Rousseau's recommendations for "the dogmas of the civil religion."

26. "Let reverence for the laws, be breathed by every American mother, to the lisping babe, that prattles on her lap—let it be taught in schools, in seminaries, and in colleges . . . in short, let it become the *political religion* of the nation; and let the old and the young, the rich and the poor, the grave and the gay, of all sexes and tongues, and colors and conditions, sacrifice unceasingly upon its altars." Lincoln, "Address Before the Young Men's Lyceum of Springfield, Illinois," January 27, 1838, in *The Collected Works of Abraham Lincoln*, ed. Roy P. Basler, 9 vols. (New Brunswick, NJ: Rutgers University Press, 1953–55), 1:112 [emphasis in original].

27. "The cause [independence] is sacred, and the champions for it ought to be holy." See "Dominion of Providence," in *Selected Writings*, 146.

28. See, for example, "The Nature and Extent of Visible Religion," *Works*, 2:323–51.

29. Gibbon, *Decline and Fall of the Roman Empire*, Chap. XX, 1:639.

30. "Dominion of Providence," in *Selected Writings*, 137.

31. Ibid., 147.

32. In Matthew L. Davis, ed., *Memoirs of Aaron Burr*, 2 vols. (New York: Harper and Bros., 1836), 1:28.

33. See Ebenezer Bradford to Joseph Bellamy, April 18, 1772, in Noll, *Princeton and the Republic*, 44.

34. Joseph Bellamy, "True Religion Delineated" (1750), in *The Works of Joseph Bellamy*, 2 vols. (Boston: Doctrinal Tract and Book Society, 1853; reprint ed., New York: Garland, 1987), 1:135.

35. "Lecture IV," in *Lectures on Moral Philosophy*, 87.

36. On Whitefield, see Murray, *Revival and Revivalism*, 41; on the Jansenists, see Witherspoon, "Lectures on Divinity," in *Works*, 8:25.

37. "Lecture XIV: Jurisprudence," in *Lectures on Moral Philosophy*, 160.

38. From first to last, Witherspoon comes across as a sincere, pious, and orthodox Christian. Throughout his career he was unwavering in his commitment to the truth of Reformed Protestantism even though he was also committed to certain tenets of the Enlightenment.

39. Baron de Montesquieu, *The Spirit of the Laws*, trans. Thomas Nugent, 2 vols. (New York: Hafner, 1949), 2:32.

40. "Dominion of Providence," in *Selected Writings*, 144.

41. "Seasonable Advice to Young Persons," in *Works*, 5:116.

42. "Letters on Education," in *Works*, 8:194.

43. See *David Hume's Political Essays*, ed. Charles W. Hendel (New York: Liberal Arts Press, 1953), 47.

44. Benjamin Franklin, "Autobiography II," in *Benjamin Franklin's Autobiographical Writings*, 624–25.

45. "Dominion of Providence," in *Selected Writings*, 137.

46. "Lectures on Divinity I," in *Works*, 8:12.

47. "Dominion of Providence," in *Selected Writings*, 144 [emphasis added].

48. Ibid., 144.

49. "Dialogue on Civil Liberty; delivered at a Public Exhibition in Nassau-Hall, January 1776," in *Pennsylvania Magazine* (April 1776), 165.

50. "Sermon Delivered at a Public Thanksgiving" (1782), in *Works*, 5:266.

51. Ibid., 5:269–70.

52. See, generally, Max Weber, *The Protestant Ethic and the Spirit of Capitalism*, trans. Talcott Parsons (London: HarperCollins, 1991 [1930]).

53. John Adams, diary entry of February 22, 1756, in *The Selected Writings of John and John Quincy Adams*, ed. Adrienne Koch and William Peden (New York: Alfred A. Knopf, 1946), 5.

54. John Adams, Massachusetts Constitution of 1780, Chap. 6, Sect. 2, in McCullough, *John Adams*, 223.

55. John Adams to Zabdiel Adams, June 21, 1776, in *Works*, 9:401.

56. Washington, Farewell Address, September 19, 1796, in *Writings of George Washington*, ed. Fitzpatrick, 35:229.

57. See Hood, *Reformed America*, 10, 17. Hood provides no specific citations to either the Farewell Address or Witherspoon's *Works* to support this assertion.

58. In William Henry Foote, ed., *Sketches of Virginia: Historical and Biographical* (Philadelphia: William S. Martien, 1850; reprint ed., Richmond: John Knox Press, 1966), 337.

59. Thanksgiving Day Proclamation of October 20, 1779, in *Journals of the Continental Congress*, 15:1191–92.

60. In Herbert J. Storing, ed., *The Complete Anti-Federalist*, 7 vols. (Chicago: University of Chicago Press, 1981), 1:23 [emphasis in original].

61. "On the Religious Education of Children," in *Works*, 4:144.

62. "Dominion of Providence," in *Selected Writings*, 145.

63. "Sermon Delivered at a Public Thanksgiving After Peace," in *Works*, 5:269.

64. "Dominion of Providence," in *Selected Writings*, 144.

65. Scotch Confession of Faith (1560), Article XXIV, in Philip Schaff, ed., *The Creeds of Christendom*, 6th ed., 3 vols. (Grand Rapids, MI: Baker Book House, 1990), 3:475–76 [spelling modernized].

66. George Washington, Farewell Address, in *Writings of George Washington*, 35:229.

67. "Lecture XIV: Jurisprudence," in *Lectures on Moral Philosophy*, 159–60.

68. The Westminster Confession of Faith (1647), Chap. XX, Art. II, in Schaff, *Creeds of Christendom*, 3:644.

69. James Madison, "Memorial and Remonstrance" (1785), Article 1, in Robert S. Alley, ed., *James Madison on Religious Liberty* (Buffalo, NY: Prometheus Books, 1985), 56. In the prior sentence, Madison quotes Article XVI of the Virginia Declaration of Rights (1776) by George Mason: "Religion or the duty which we owe to our Creator and the manner of discharging it, can be directed only by reason and conviction, not by force or violence."

70. Ibid., 57; see also *The Complete Madison: His Basic Writings*, ed. Saul K. Padover (New York: Harper and Brothers, 1953), 301.

71. "Memorial of the Presbytery of Hanover, Virginia," October 24, 1776, in Foote, *Sketches of Virginia*, 323–24. The Virginia General Assembly was at that time considering religious liberty and religious establishment under the new state constitution; the Presbytery opposed any establishment or curtailment of religious liberty and consequently sent up this Memorial to argue its position.

72. "Lecture XIV: Jurisprudence," in *Lectures on Moral Philosophy*, 160.

73. Ibid., 161.

74. See Collins, *President Witherspoon*, 2:25.

75. In Johnson, *A History of the American People*, 210.

76. "In fact, Witherspoon believed that a policy of toleration could have adverse effects if not offset by active state support of Protestant Christianity." Hood, *Reformed America*, 18.

77. "[T]he most active Protestants among America's founding fathers all tried at first to devise some scheme for having governments support the churches. John Witherspoon, the Presbyterian president of Princeton, was the only clergyman to sign the United States' Declaration of Independence in 1776. Soon thereafter he proposed a plan for government to establish more than one religion in a single region, a plan similar to one advocated in Virginia by the patriotic orator Patrick Henry, an active Anglican. But these proposals did not succeed." Mark A. Noll, *The Old Religion in a New World: The History of North American Christianity* (Grand Rapids, MI: Eerdmans, 2002), 54. Witherspoon's scheme is not described, nor is the claim footnoted. Also, see Noll, "Evangelicals in the American Founding and Evangelical Political Mobilization Today," in James H. Hutson, ed., *Religion and the New Republic: Faith in the Founding of America* (Lanham, MD: Rowman and Littlefield, 2000), 146: "Several of the leaders whose beliefs came closest to the modern meaning of evangelical, like John Witherspoon of New Jersey and Patrick Henry of Virginia, were advocates of religious establishments who thought that state support of the churches was essential for their health and the health of society."

78. "Dominion of Providence," in *Selected Writings*, 140–41.

79. See Jean-Jacques Rousseau, *The Social Contract*, Book IV, Chap. VIII, in *Basic Political Writings*, 226. The echo of Rousseau is faint because, so far as I know,

Witherspoon never once mentioned Rousseau; he preferred the more sensible (and pro-British) Frenchman, Montesquieu.

80. "Dialogue on Civil Liberty," 165. Witherspoon conveniently forgets the repressions of the Roman empire in the early years of the Christian church.

81. "Dominion of Providence," in *Selected Writings*, 147.

82. The Westminster Confession of Faith (1647), Chap. XX, Art. II, in Schaff, *Creeds of Christendom*, 3:644.

83. "Introduction, The Form of the Government and Discipline of the Presbyterian Church in the United States of America," in *Constitution of the Presbyterian Church in the United States of America*, cxxxiii–cxxxiv. The Constitution of the Presbyterian Church was drafted in 1787 and ratified in 1788. (The description of liberty of conscience as an "alienable" right is probably a typographical error; the context dictates that it read "inalienable.")

84. "Lecture XIV: Jurisprudence," in *Lectures on Moral Philosophy*, 161.

85. For the argument that Madison's authorship of the First Amendment is doubtful, see, generally, Donald L. Drakeman, "Religion and the Republic: James Madison and the First Amendment," *Journal of Church and State*, 25, no. 3 (Autumn 1983): 427–45. At p. 427, Drakeman asserts that "[Madison] probably did not draft the language adopted as the First Amendment."

86. "After graduating from the College of New Jersey in 1771, Madison spent an extra year at Princeton studying Hebrew under President John Witherspoon, a commitment that suggests he was contemplating the ministry." John Murrin, "Religion and Politics in America from the First Settlements to the Civil War," in Mark A. Noll, ed., *Religion and American Politics: From the Colonial Period to the 1980s* (New York: Oxford University Press, 1990), 41–42n. Even Gore Vidal recounts this episode; see his *Burr: A Novel* (New York: Bantam Books, 1974), 241.

87. See Noll, *Princeton and the Republic*, 44n; Tait, *The Piety of John Witherspoon*, 239n; and "James Madison's Autobiography," ed. Douglass Adair, *William and Mary Quarterly*, 3d ser., 2 (April 1945): 197.

88. A reviewer of Irving Brant's *Life of James Madison* detected in the fourth president a "spiritual amplitude unsurpassed on this continent." See Ketcham, "James Madison and Religion," 181.

89. See James Madison to Robert Walsh, March 2, 1819, in Merrill D. Peterson, ed., *James Madison: A Biography in His Own Words* (New York: Harper and Row, 1974), 369–71.

90. See "Madison's 'Detatched [*sic*] Memoranda,'" ed. Elizabeth Fleet, *William and Mary Quarterly*, 3d ser., vol. 3, no. 4 (October 1946): 534–68.

91. See Ketcham, "James Madison and Religion," 182, 180.

92. In Alley, *James Madison on Religious Liberty*, 87. This lifelong interest in religious topics, evidenced by his correspondence and papers until near the end of his life in 1833, makes puzzling Lance Banning's assertion that "religious topics simply disappear from his writings after 1776." See Banning, *The Sacred Fire of*

Liberty: James Madison and the Founding of the Federal Republic (Ithaca, NY: Cornell University Press, 1995), 80, 430n.

93. See Ketcham, "James Madison and Religion," 180.

94. James Madison to Thomas Jefferson, May 1, 1791, in *The Writings of James Madison,* ed. Gaillard Hunt, 9 vols. (New York: G. P. Putnam's Sons, 1900–10), 6:46.

95. "Such was the character he [Madison] acquired while at college, that Dr. Wetherspoon [*sic*] said of him to Mr. Jefferson (from whom I received the anecdote) that during the whole time he was under his tuition he never knew him to do nor to say an improper thing." Benjamin Rush to James Rush, May 25, 1802, in *Letters of Benjamin Rush,* 2:850.

96. See Robert Allen Rutland, *James Madison: The Founding Father* (New York: Macmillan, 1987), 9.

97. A recent article on Madison's church-state theory points out: "Madison's understanding of the proper relationship between church and state continues to be debated vigorously." See Vincent Phillip Muñoz, "James Madison's Principle of Religious Liberty," *American Political Science Review* 97 (2003): 17.

98. Ketcham, "James Madison and Religion," 180.

99. See, for example, Augustine's *City of God,* Bk. XV, Chap. 1: "everyone, since he takes his origin from a condemned stock, is inevitably evil and carnal to begin with, by derivation from Adam." St. Augustine, *Concerning the City of God against the Pagans,* trans. Henry Bettenson (New York: Penguin Books, 1984), 596. Augustine was the most cited theologian of the Reformers.

100. See James Madison to William Bradford, January 24, 1774, in *The Papers of James Madison,* ed. William T. Hutchinson et al., 17 vols. (Chicago and Charlottesville: University of Chicago Press and University Press of Virginia, 1962–91), 1:106 [hereinafter *Papers of James Madison*].

101. In "James Madison's Autobiography," ed. Adair, 199 [emphasis in original].

102. In Alley, *James Madison on Religious Liberty,* 51–52. For the same reason Madison objected to religious "toleration" in the Virginia Declaration of Rights, one might prefer to see another term such as "cooperationist" replace the term "accommodationist" in contemporary church-state parlance; "accommodate," like "tolerate," implies condescension on the part of civil government toward religion.

103. "On the Georgia Constitution" (1789), in *Works,* 9:220–21.

104. James Madison, "Observations on the 'Draught of a Constitution for Virginia,'" ca. October 15, 1788, in *Papers of James Madison,* 11:288.

105. Mark DeWolfe Howe, *The Garden and the Wilderness* (Chicago: University of Chicago Press, 1965), 8.

106. "Someone has said that the American government and constitution are based on the theology of Calvin and the philosophy of Thomas Hobbes. This at least is true, that there is a hearty puritanism in the view of human nature which pervades the instrument of 1787. It is the work of men who believed in original sin and were resolved to leave open for transgressors no door which they could possibly

shut." James Bryce, *The American Commonwealth,* quoted in Reinhold Niebuhr, *The Irony of American History* (New York: Charles Scribner's Sons, 1952), 23. See also Horace White, quoted in Richard Hofstadter, "The Founding Fathers: An Age of Realism," in *The Moral Foundations of the American Republic,* ed. Robert H. Horwitz, 3d ed. (Charlottesville: University Press of Virginia, 1986), 62: "[The Constitution] is based upon the philosophy of Hobbes and the religion of Calvin. It assumes that the natural state of mankind is a state of war, and that the carnal mind is at enmity with God."

107. Alexander Hamilton, James Madison, and John Jay, *The Federalist Papers,* ed. Clinton Rossiter (New York: New American Library, 1961), 322 [hereinafter Rossiter, *Federalist*].

108. In Rossiter, *Federalist* 55, 346.

109. "Lectures on Divinity XIV," in *Works,* 8:125–26; "The Druid I," in *Works,* 9:227.

110. In Rossiter, *Federalist* 51, 322.

111. In Rossiter, *Federalist* 10, 79.

112. See Rossiter, *Federalist* 51, 324.

113. In Adair, *Fame and the Founding Fathers,* 128; and "James Madison's Autobiography," ed. Adair, 198.

114. "Lecture I," in *Lectures on Moral Philosophy,* 66.

115. See *Papers of Thomas Jefferson,* 2:556. Madison introduced the bill, which was endorsed by Jefferson, on October 31, 1785.

116. James Madison, "Detached Memoranda" (ca. 1819?), in "Madison's 'Detatched [*sic*] Memoranda,'" 560–61. A fuller quotation reads: "Religious proclamations by the Executive recommending thanksgivings & fasts are shoots from the same root with the legislative acts reviewed [that is, congressional chaplaincies]. Altho' recommendations only, they imply a religious agency, making no part of the trust delegated to political rulers. . . . They seem to imply and certainly nourish the erronious [*sic*] idea of a *national* religion. The idea just as it related to the Jewish nation under a theocracy, having been improperly adopted by so many nations which have embraced Xnity, is too apt to lurk in the bosoms even of Americans, who in general are aware of the distinction between religious & political societies. . . . The 1st proclamation of Genl Washington dated Jany 1. 1795 (see if this was the 1st) recommending a day of thanksgiving, embraced all who believed in a supreme ruler of the Universe. That of Mr Adams called for a *Xn* worship. Many private letters reproached the Proclamations issued by J. M. [Madison] for using general terms, used in that of Presidt W——n [Washington]; and some of them for not inserting particulars according with the faith of certain Xn sects. The practice if not strictly guarded naturally terminates in a conformity to the creed of the majority and a single sect, if amounting to a majority." See also *James Madison: Writings,* ed. Jack N. Rakove (New York: Library of America, 1999), 764–65.

117. "Lecture I," in *Lectures on Moral Philosophy,* 65.

118. For recent books that challenge the influence of religion on Madison and the impact of Witherspoon on Madison, see Frank Lambert, *The Founding Fathers and the Place of Religion in America* (Princeton: Princeton University Press, 2003), 10 and 15; and especially James H. Hutson, *Forgotten Features of the Founding: The Recovery of Religious Themes in the Early American Republic* (Lanham, MD: Lexington Books, 2003), 155–85. For another statement of Madison's debt to Witherspoon, see Leo Pfeffer, *Church, State, and Freedom* (Boston: Beacon Press, 1967), 101: "Madison was quite likely influenced by the teachings of the Presbyterian president of Princeton, John Witherspoon, who strongly advocated separation of church and state, and taught that every church should be supported by its own members or funds without help from the taxing power of the state."

119. In "Madison's 'Detatched [*sic*] Memoranda,'" 558.

120. See James Madison to Jasper Adams, September 1833, in Daniel L. Dreisbach, ed., *Religion and Politics in the Early Republic: Jasper Adams and the Church-State Debate* (Lexington: University Press of Kentucky, 1996), 120.

121. Daniel L. Dreisbach, "'Sowing Useful Truths and Principles': The Danbury Baptists, Thomas Jefferson, and the 'Wall of Separation,'" *Journal of Church and State* 39, no. 3 (Summer 1997): 497.

122. For a sustained argument that the deep structure of Madison's thought was indebted to Reformed Protestantism and reinforced by John Witherspoon, see, generally, Garrett Ward Sheldon, *The Political Philosophy of James Madison* (Baltimore: Johns Hopkins University Press, 2001). See also James H. Smylie, "Madison and Witherspoon: Theological Roots of American Political Thought," *Princeton University Library Chronicle* 22 (Spring 1961): 118–32; and Ralph L. Ketcham, "James Madison at Princeton," *Princeton University Library Chronicle* 28 (Autumn 1966): 24–54.

123. *Everson v. Board of Education*, 330 U.S. 1, 18 (1947). For a discussion of the Court's use of Jefferson, see, generally, Dreisbach, "'Sowing Useful Truths and Principles,'" 455–501.

124. James Hutson says that the conviction that "holiness was prerequisite for secular happiness" was a legacy of the Confederation as a whole from 1774 to 1789, the exact years of Witherspoon's political career. See Hutson, *Religion and the Founding of the American Republic*, 58.

Chapter Three. "Plain Common Sense": Educating Patriots at Princeton

1. Northwest Ordinance, July 13, 1787 [reaffirmed 1789], in *United States Code*, 1:liii.

2. Thomas Jefferson to P. S. Dupont de Nemours, April 24, 1816, in *Thomas Jefferson: Writings*, ed. Merrill D. Peterson (New York: Library of America, 1984), 1387.

3. "Pinckney Plan," May 29, 1787, in Farrand, *Records of the Federal Convention of 1787*, 3:598.

4. See Washington's eighth annual message to Congress, December 7, 1796, in *Writings of George Washington*, 35:316; Washington to Thomas Jefferson, March 15, 1795, ibid., 34:146–49; Washington to Alexander Hamilton, September 1, 1796, ibid., 35:204–5; Last Will and Testament, July 9, 1799, ibid., 37:279–81.

5. Richard Brookhiser, *Founding Father: Rediscovering George Washington* (New York: The Free Press, 1996), 141.

6. Benjamin Rush to Richard Price, May 25, 1786, in *Letters of Benjamin Rush*, 2:388–89 [emphasis in original].

7. In Thomas Jefferson Wertenbaker, *Princeton: 1746–1896* (Princeton: Princeton University Press, 1946), 19–20.

8. Charter of the College of New Jersey (1746), in Richard Hofstadter and Wilson Smith, eds., *American Higher Education: A Documentary History*, 2 vols. (Chicago: University of Chicago Press, 1961), 1:83.

9. "Address to the Inhabitants of Jamaica, and other West-India Islands, in Behalf of the College of New-Jersey" (1772), in *Works*, 8:328, 329.

10. Freneau (1752–1832) later fought in the Revolution, wrote anti-British satire, and today enjoys a reputation as "the most significant poet of eighteenth-century America." See George McMichael, ed., *Anthology of American Literature*, 2 vols. (New York: Macmillan, 1974), 1:513 ff. Jefferson described him as the man who "saved our constitution which was fast galloping into monarchy"; Washington called him "that rascal Freneau," a "wretched and insolent dog." In 1791, Freneau was persuaded by Jefferson and Madison to found and edit the blatantly Republican *National Gazette* in Philadelphia, daily copies of which he impertinently sent to President Washington. Brackenridge (1748–1816) was ordained a Presbyterian minister after graduation, became a Revolutionary chaplain, brought out *Six Political Discourses Founded on the Scripture* in 1778, and in later years became a novelist, playwright, and jurist. His political novel *Modern Chivalry* has been called "permanently significant" and the first "to use the novel form seriously as a vehicle of social and political criticism." See Perry Miller, "Preface," in *Major Writers of America, Shorter Edition*, ed. Perry Miller (New York: Harcourt, Brace and World, 1966), xvii; and Marius Brawley, "James Fenimore Cooper 1789–1851; William Cullen Bryant 1794–1878," in ibid., 113.

11. *New-Jersey Gazette*, April 23, 1783, n.p. This toast was raised on April 19, 1783, in Princeton during a celebration after peace was declared.

12. In Scott, "Introduction," *Lectures on Moral Philosophy*, 16.

13. "On the Religious Education of Children" (1789), in *Works*, 4:139.

14. For a biography of Smith (including the correct date of his birth), see McLachlan et al., *Princetonians: A Biographical Dictionary*, 2:42–51. Smith, who graduated from Princeton in 1772, was Witherspoon's son-in-law and succeeded him to the presidency in early 1795, although he seems to have lacked Witherspoon's leadership qualities and left the College in poor shape at his own retirement.

15. "Address to the Inhabitants of Jamaica, and other West-India Islands, in Behalf of the College of New-Jersey" (1772), in *Works*, 8:309.

16. "While in Congress, he [Witherspoon] did not relinquish his direction of the college. He attended every meeting of the Board of Trustees and presided at every Commencement, and the newspapers of the day contain his frequent notices of term openings, his plain hints to schoolmasters, his homely advice to parents and students; and every time he felt that he could properly be absent from his seat he rode back to Princeton and his classes." Collins, ed., "Introduction," in Collins, *Lectures on Moral Philosophy*, xvii.

17. See Scott, "Introduction," *Lectures on Moral Philosophy*, 25.

18. Collins, ed., "Introduction," in Collins, *Lectures on Moral Philosophy*, xxi [emphasis added]. This volume was one in a series published under the auspices of the American Philosophical Association that reprinted "significant and important" early American philosophical works, including Samuel Johnson's "Elements of Philosophy" and selections from Jonathan Edward's writings. These reprints were intended to be reflective of the "deeper currents of American thinking in the early period." See "Prefatory Note," in ibid., iv.

19. "Lecture XII: Of Civil Society," in *Lectures on Moral Philosophy*, 144.

20. Several sets of eighteenth-century student copies of the Lectures are preserved. They are substantially identical, although there are slight variations, usually in word choice, between them. In 1912, V. L. Collins noted some of the variations between three manuscripts dated 1772, 1782, and 1795, in the Princeton University archives. See, generally, Collins, *Lectures on Moral Philosophy*.

21. See Green, *Life of the Revd. John Witherspoon*, 126. On Witherspoon's reliance on Hutcheson's *System of Moral Philosophy*, see, generally, Scott, *Lectures on Moral Philosophy*. Scott's edition, especially its excellent introductory chapter, is the best treatment of Witherspoon as a moral philosopher.

22. "In justice to the memory of DR. WITHERSPOON, it ought to be stated that he did not intend these lectures [on moral philosophy] for the press, and that he once compelled a printer who, without his knowledge, had undertaken to publish them, to desist from the design, by threatening a prosecution as the consequence of persisting in it." Ashbel Green, "Advertisement to the Second American Edition," in *The Works of the Rev. John Witherspoon*, (1802), 1:n.p.

23. "Recapitulation," in *Lectures on Moral Philosophy*, 187. See also Jack Scott's helpful appendix, which he titles Witherspoon's "Bibliography of Chief Writers on Ethical and Political Thought," in ibid., 189–91.

24. "Lecture I," in *Lectures on Moral Philosophy*, 64.

25. Ibid., 65.

26. See Scott, "Introduction," in *Lectures on Moral Philosophy*, 27.

27. "The outline of Hutcheson's *System* is virtually identical to Pufendorf's *On the Law of Nature and Nations*." Frank D. Balog, "The Scottish Enlightenment

and the Liberal Political Tradition," in Allan Bloom and Steven J. Kautz, eds., *Confronting the Constitution* (Washington, DC: AEI Press, 1990), 503n.

28. In Page Smith, *A New Age Now Begins,* 2 vols. (New York: McGraw-Hill, 1976), 1:144.

29. "The Scottish method was brought to America by President John Witherspoon of Princeton, and came into absolute domination of academic curricula by about 1820." Perry Miller, "Introduction," in Perry Miller, ed., *American Thought: Civil War to World War I* (San Francisco: Rinehart Press, 1954), ix.

30. For the transatlantic impact of Scots such as these, see Sher and Smitten, *Scotland and America in the Age of the Enlightenment.*

31. See "Editor's Preface," *The Encyclopaedia Britannica,* 14th ed., 24 vols. (London: The Encyclopaedia Britannica Co., 1937), 1:vii.

32. On Hutcheson, see Daniel Sommer Robinson, *The Story of Scottish Philosophy* (New York: Exposition Press, 1961), 29–31; James McCosh, *The Scottish Philosophy* (Hildesheim: Georg Olms, 1966 [1875]), 49–85; and *Lectures on Moral Philosophy,* especially 25–61.

33. At this point we would do well to keep in mind that Reid, Stewart, and the other common sense philosophers did not primarily intend to engage the "infidel" Hume in a theological debate. That the philosophy of common sense was promulgated in Scotland by Reid, Beattie, Oswald, and Dugald Stewart, and in America by Witherspoon, most of whom were Presbyterian ministers, should not obscure the fact that the common sense dispute with Hume was primarily a dispute over epistemology and method, not over theology. Reid, the founder and subtlest reasoner of the common sense school, faulted Hume for not deriving his faculty psychology properly, according to the Baconian scientific method, and never for Hume's well-known impiety. Thus, Reid's philosophy is not merely, as Edwin Boring put it, "good doctrine for a Presbyterian philosopher." See Edwin G. Boring, *A History of Experimental Psychology* (New York: Appleton-Century-Crofts, 1950), 205.

34. "Lecture VI," in *Lectures on Moral Philosophy,* 96–97.

35. Robinson, *The Story of Scottish Philosophy,* 126. On Reid generally, see *Philosophical Works,* ed. Sir William Hamilton, 2 vols. (Hildesheim: Georg Olms, 1967 [1895]).

36. With the exception of Hume, who called Providence into question.

37. Thomas Hobbes, "Author's Introduction" to *Leviathan,* ed. Michael Oakeshott (New York: Macmillan, 1962), 19.

38. Jefferson to John Trumbull, February 15, 1789, in *Papers of Thomas Jefferson,* 14:561. Jefferson wanted the painter Trumbull to copy their three portraits together "into a knot on the same canvas, that they may not be confounded at all with the herd of other great men."

39. "Lecture II," in *Lectures on Moral Philosophy,* 73.

40. "Lecture III," in *Lectures on Moral Philosophy*, 78. Apparently, Witherspoon would have agreed with Kant that "though all our knowledge begins with experience, it does not follow that it all arises out of experience." See Kant's "Introduction," in *Immanuel Kant's Critique of Pure Reason*, trans. Norman Kemp Smith (New York: St. Martin's Press, 1965), 41.

41. *Opticks*, III.i.31, in Selwyn A. Grave, *The Scottish Philosophy of Common Sense* (Oxford: Oxford University Press, 1966), 7.

42. John Locke, *An Essay Concerning Human Understanding*, Book IV, Chap. III, Sec. 18, in *An Essay Concerning Human Understanding*, ed. Peter H. Nidditch (Oxford: Clarendon Press, 1975), 549 [emphasis in original].

43. "Recapitulation," in *Lectures on Moral Philosophy*, 186.

44. In Douglas Sloan, *The Scottish Enlightenment and the American College Ideal* (New York: Teachers College Press, Columbia University, 1971), 124.

45. Reid, *Inquiry*, Sect. IV, in Daniel N. Robinson, "The Scottish Enlightenment and Its Mixed Bequest," *Journal of the History of the Behavioral Sciences* 22 (1986): 174.

46. "Lecture I," in *Lectures on Moral Philosophy*, 66.

47. "Lecture VII," in *Lectures on Moral Philosophy*, 102.

48. See *Federalist* 5 by Jay, and *Federalist* 22, 29, 31, 83, and 84 by Hamilton. Number 83 alone contains four references to "common sense."

49. "Let all, therefore, who wish or hope to be eminent, remember, that as the height to which you can raise a tower depends upon the size and solidity of its base, so they ought to lay the foundation of their future fame deep and strong in . . . *plain common sense*." "Druid IV" (1781?), in *Works*, 9:266–67 [emphasis in original]; see also *Works*, 9:252.

50. "The truth is, the immaterial system, is a wild and ridiculous attempt to unsettle the principles of common sense by metaphysical reasoning, which can hardly produce any thing but contempt in the generality of persons who hear it, and which I verily believe, never produced conviction even on the persons who pretend to espouse it." See "Lecture II," in *Lectures on Moral Philosophy*, 76.

51. Jefferson to Peter Carr, August 10, 1787, in *Papers of Thomas Jefferson*, 12:15. We might also note that other founders expressed views of the moral sense very similar to that shared by Jefferson and Witherspoon. James Wilson, for example, wrote that "[f]ar from being rivals or enemies, religion and law are twin sisters, friends, and mutual assistants. Indeed, these two sciences run into each other. The divine law, as discovered by reason and the moral sense, forms an essential part of both." See Wilson, "Lectures on Law," in *The Works of James Wilson*, ed. Robert McCloskey, 2 vols. (Cambridge, MA: Harvard University Press, 1967), 1:125.

52. Thomas Jefferson to Thomas Law, June 13, 1814, in *The Writings of Thomas Jefferson*, 14:139, 142.

53. "Lecture III," in *Lectures on Moral Philosophy*, 78.

54. "Lecture IV," in *Lectures on Moral Philosophy*, 90. We noted earlier that in this passage Witherspoon was replicating the positions of Joseph Bellamy, the Connecticut New Light revivalist and disciple of Jonathan Edwards, in his 1750 *Nature of True Religion Delineated.*

55. Jefferson originally wrote "sacred & undeniable," then changed it to read "self-evident." See "Original Rough Draft" of the Declaration in *Papers of Thomas Jefferson*, 1:423, 427–28n. Although the change is sometimes attributed to Benjamin Franklin, the editors of Jefferson's *Papers* say that this attribution "rests on no conclusive evidence, and there seems to be even stronger evidence that the change was made by TJ." See editor's note, *Papers of Thomas Jefferson*, 1:427–28n.

56. Thomas Jefferson to John Adams, March 14, 1820, in *The Writings of Thomas Jefferson*, 15:239–40. I am indebted to Professor Daniel N. Robinson at Oxford University for bringing this passage to my attention.

57. "Even Jefferson, who never used a plow, would take extreme pride in his one truly original invention, the formulae for a moldboard's 'curve of least resistance'; and, like Thomas Reid, he used 'a ploughman' as his test of the moral sense that is equal in all men." Wills, *Inventing America*, 100.

58. "Lectures on Eloquence," in *Works*, 7:165.

59. "Aristides," in *Works*, 9:91.

60. Thomas Paine, *Common Sense*, ed. Isaac Kramnick (London: Penguin Books, 1986), 81.

61. See "Aristides," in Plutarch, *The Lives of the Noble Grecians and Romans*, trans. John Dryden (New York: Modern Library, n.d.), 391–411.

62. Aelius Aristides, *Platonic Oration* ii, in Reid, *Philosophical Works*, 2:801.

63. See Plutarch, *Lives*, 393.

64. "Speech in Congress on the Convention with General Burgoyne," in *Works*, 9:113.

65. Ibid.

66. Alexander Hamilton, ["The Farmer Refuted" (1776)], in Michael Novak, *On Two Wings: Humble Faith and Common Sense at the American Founding* (San Francisco: Encounter Books, 2002), 3.

67. Caroline Robbins has traced the transatlantic influence of the moral sense epistemology in "'When It Is That Colonies May Turn Independent': An Analysis of the Environment and Politics of Francis Hutcheson (1694–1746)," *William and Mary Quarterly*, 3d ser., 11 (1954): 214–51.

68. See Novak, *On Two Wings*, 43.

69. See I. Woodbridge Riley, *American Philosophy: The Early Schools* (New York: Russell and Russell, 1958 [1907]), 483–96; and Herbert W. Schneider, *A History of American Philosophy* (New York: Columbia University Press, 1946), 246–50. Elizabeth Flower and Murray Murphey have attempted to revise this singularly "jaundiced" view of Scottish realism in America, and Witherspoon's part in it. See

Elizabeth Flower and Murray G. Murphey, *A History of Philosophy in America*, 2 vols. (New York: Putnam's Sons, 1977), 1:203–73. Flower and Murphey "hold that so far from being a drag on the American Enlightenment, Common Sense Realism was a part of it." See ibid., 1:204.

70. Schneider, *History of American Philosophy*, 246.

71. John E. Bentley, *An Outline of American Philosophy* (Totowa, NJ: Littlefield, Adams and Co., 1965), 40.

72. Vincent Buranelli, "Colonial Philosophy," *William and Mary Quarterly*, 3d ser., 16 (1959): 353–54. Conspicuously absent from this list are the more "philosophical" of the founders such as Jefferson and Franklin.

73. Eric Voegelin, *Autobiographical Reflections*, ed. Ellis Sandoz (Baton Rouge: Louisiana State University Press, 1987), 28–29.

74. See Douglass Adair, "'That Politics May be Reduced to a Science': David Hume, James Madison and the Tenth Federalist," in *Fame and the Founding Fathers*, ed. Trevor Colbourn (New York: W. W. Norton, 1974), 93–106. Adair saw Hume especially clearly in Madison's formulation of the extended republic, and he quoted from Hume's "Idea of a Perfect Commonwealth" as follows: "[t]hough it is more difficult to form a republican government in an extensive country than in a city; there is more facility, when once it is formed, of preserving it steady and uniform, without tumult and faction." See ibid., 98.

75. Balog, "The Scottish Enlightenment," 504n. The "work" to which Balog refers is Adams's *Discourse on Davila.*

76. See Green, *Life of the Revd. John Witherspoon*, 132–33. Witherspoon's essay was "Remarks on an Essay on Human Liberty," *Scots Magazine* 15 (April 1753): 165–70, which does indeed predate much of Reid's published work, but his claim, particularly to have anticipated "any other author of their views" (for example, Shaftesbury or Hutcheson), has been brought into serious question.

77. "The Berklean [*sic*] system of Metaphysics was in repute in the college when he entered on his office. The tutors were zealous believers in it, and waited on the President, with some expectation of either confounding him, or making him a proselite [*sic*]. They had mistaken their man. He first reasoned against the System, and then ridiculed it, till he drove it out of the college." Green, *Life of the Revd. John Witherspoon*, 132.

78. There seems to have been no hard feelings between Edwards, Jr., and Witherspoon, however. The Beineke Library at Yale University contains an 1800 edition of Witherspoon's *Works* inscribed by their owner, Jonathan Edwards, Jr.

79. The phrase "one and a half centuries" is used because the Pragmatists of the early twentieth century can be seen as the legitimate heirs of Scottish realism. See Flower and Murphey, *A History of Philosophy in America*, 1:216, for the assertion that "the Common Sense Realists were a bridge between the Enlightenment and the pragmatists, not least because they helped determine the way the Kantian philosophy was to be utilized."

80. Claude M. Newlin, *Philosophy and Religion in Colonial America* (New York: Philosophical Library, 1962), 176.

81. Ibid., 178.

82. Thomas Jefferson to Peter Carr, August 10, 1787, in *Papers of Thomas Jefferson*, 12:15. Note that Jefferson repeats the "bungling" language about the Creator in his letter to Thomas Law on June 13, 1814; see *The Writings of Thomas Jefferson*, 14:142.

83. Thomas Jefferson to John Witherspoon, January 12, 1792, in *Papers of Thomas Jefferson*, 23:40.

84. "Recapitulation," in *Lectures on Moral Philosophy*, 186.

85. Jefferson to Henry Lee, May 8, 1825, in *The Life and Selected Writings of Thomas Jefferson*, ed. Adrienne Koch and William Peden (New York: The Modern Library, 1993), 656–57.

86. Morton White, *The Philosophy of the American Revolution* (Oxford: Oxford University Press, 1978), 3.

87. Frederick Mayer, *A History of American Thought: An Introduction* (Dubuque, IA: Wm. C. Brown Co., 1951), 1.

88. There is reason to question this characterization of the Calvinists. Calvinist New England produced many of America's best scientific minds. John Winthrop IV (1714–1779), for example, was our greatest astronomer (with the possible exception of David Rittenhouse of Philadelphia), and he was "generally conceded to be the best that America had yet offered in the Newtonian line." See Daniel J. Boorstin, *The Americans: The Colonial Experience* (New York: Vintage Books, 1958), 245. And Jonathan Edwards, the most "severely orthodox" of Calvinists, as a young man wrote very perceptive treatises on the motion of spiders and on optics.

89. All three men were university professors of moral philosophy, and all three published (Witherspoon posthumously) works in moral philosophy. Yet Smith's *Theory of Moral Sentiments* continues to attract attention even today, and *The Wealth of Nations* is looked upon as one of the finest examples of political economy from the eighteenth or any other century. And while Witherspoon was busy helping found the American republic during the 1780s, Kant was producing some of the most influential formal treatises of the modern era.

90. Jefferson to John Trumbull, February 15, 1789, in *Papers of Thomas Jefferson*, 14:561.

91. On Stewart and Locke, see Frederick Copleston, *A History of Philosophy*, 9 vols. (Garden City, NY: Doubleday, 1962–77), 5:375–83.

92. Buranelli, "Colonial Philosophy," 354.

93. Tocqueville, *Democracy in America*, 429.

94. Adams to Jefferson, July 16, 1814, in Lester J. Cappon, ed., *The Adams-Jefferson Letters*, 2 vols. (Chapel Hill: University of North Carolina Press, 1959), 2:437.

95. Jefferson to Peter Carr, August 10, 1787, in *Papers of Thomas Jefferson*, 12:15.

96. See *Chisholm* v. *Georgia*, 2 U.S. 419 (1793); also *United States Supreme Court Reports*, Law. Ed., 100 vols. (Rochester, NY: Lawyer's Co-Operative Publishing Co., 1926–56), 1:440 ff. Wilson quoted Reid as follows: "Dr. Reid, in his excellent enquiry into the human mind, on the principles of common sense, speaking of the sceptical and illiberal philosophy, which under bold, but false pretensions to liberality, prevailed in many parts of Europe before he wrote, makes the following judicious remark: 'The language of philosophers, with regard to the original faculties of the mind, is so adapted to the prevailing system, that it cannot fit any other; like a coat that fits the man for whom it was made, and shows him to advantage, which yet will fit very awkward upon one of a different make, although as handsome and well-proportioned. It is hardly possible to make any innovation in our philosophy concerning the mind and its operations, without using new words and phrases, or giving a different meaning to those that are received.' With equal propriety may this solid remark be applied to the great subject, on the principles of which the decision of this court is to be founded." *Chisholm* v. *Georgia* (1793), in *United States Supreme Court Reports*, Law. Ed., 1:455.

97. Copleston, *History of Philosophy*, 5:140.

98. Alexis de Tocqueville, *The Old Régime and the French Revolution*, trans. Stuart Gilbert (New York: Doubleday, 1955), 153.

Chapter Four. "An Animated Son of Liberty": Revolution

1. "Reflections on the Present State of Public Affairs," in *Works*, 9:71–72.

2. See, for example, Charles Leonard Lundin, *Cockpit of the Revolution* (Princeton: Princeton University Press, 1940).

3. Mitchell, *Alexander Hamilton*, 44.

4. "Witherspoon, of College of N.J., was earlier than local compatriots in advancing from remonstrance to rebellion." Ibid., 495n.

5. Diary entry of September 3, 1774, in *Diary and Autobiography of John Adams*, 2:121. Early the next year, on February 15, 1777, Adams, Witherspoon, Benjamin Rush, Elbridge Gerry, and others dined beneath a portrait of George III turned upside-down. See Adams, diary entry of February 16, 1777, in *Works*, 2:434.

6. Elias Boudinot, who was himself opposed to independence at the time, recorded that Witherspoon made the "first attempt to try the pulse of the People of New Jersey on the Subject of Independence" on April 19, 1776. (Boudinot incorrectly recorded the date, which was actually April 18.) See Elias Boudinot, *Journal, or Historical Recollections of American Events during the Revolutionary War* (Philadelphia: Frederick Bourquin, 1894), 8.

7. Dickinson, although he refused to sign the Declaration of Independence, nevertheless volunteered for the army; Galloway ultimately sided with the Tories; Hancock, of course, went on to become president of the Continental Congress, and

Witherspoon dedicated his most famous (and most political) sermon to him seven years later in 1776.

8. Newspaper account of July 13, 1770, in Collins, *President Witherspoon*, 1:132.

9. Madison to James Madison, Sr., July 23, 1770, in *The Writings of James Madison*, 1:7.

10. Major James Witherspoon (1751–1777) was killed at Germantown on October 4, 1777, by the same cannonball that struck down Brigadier General Francis Nash (c. 1742–1777). Three days later, the elder Witherspoon was back in his seat in Congress. See Green, *Life of the Revd. John Witherspoon*, 31n; Collins, *President Witherspoon*, 2:31n; Dumas Malone, ed., *Dictionary of American Biography*, 20 vols. (New York: Charles Scribner's Sons, 1928–58), 13:386–87. In December 1777, Continental Congressman James Duane of New York told William Smith, president of the College of Philadelphia, that he "would not be his [Witherspoon's] Son—That the Day of the News of his [James's] Death in the Field he spoke long & dropped Jokes." See William Smith, diary entry of December 23, 1777, in *Historical Memoirs of William Smith*, 2:277.

11. Marvin Olasky, *Fighting for Liberty and Virtue: Political and Cultural Wars in Eighteenth-Century America* (Washington, DC: Regnery, 1996), 129.

12. "Mr. William Livingston and he [Witherspoon] labored, he says, to procure an instruction that the tea should not be paid for." John Adams, diary entry of August 27, 1774, in *Works*, 2:356. Parliament had decided to aid the failing East India Company by granting it a near-monopoly on the tea trade.

13. George Washington to Bryan Fairfax, July 4, 1774, in *Writings of George Washington*, 3:229.

14. See "Reflections on the Present State of Public Affairs," in *Works*, 9:66–72; "Thoughts on American Liberty," in *Works*, 9:73–77.

15. "Pastoral Letter," in *Works*, 5:167–75.

16. Witherspoon doubtless chose the date so that a recommendation for independence could be announced the following day, April 19, 1776, exactly one year after the battles of Lexington and Concord.

17. Boudinot, *Journal*, 5–6.

18. See Collins, *President Witherspoon*, 1:211. William Franklin was held in Connecticut until 1778, when he was exchanged with the British, and then went to England where he lived out the rest of his life.

19. *Journals of the Continental Congress*, 5:489.

20. See appendix A, this volume.

21. See Collins, *President Witherspoon*, 1:219–21; and Louis F. Benson, "What Did Witherspoon Say?" *Journal of the Presbyterian Historical Society* 12 (1927): 389–97. Portions of the speech are reproduced in Rev. William Breed's *Presbyterians and the Revolution* (Decatur, MS: Issacharian Press, 1993 [1876]), which also contains the fraudulent version of the "Mecklenburg Declaration," thereby casting further doubt on the speech's authenticity.

22. "In the clause of the original draught that upbraids George III. with the hiring and sending foreign mercenary troops to invade America, among those mentioned, the *Scotch* are specified. It was said that Dr. Witherspoon, the learned president of Nassau College, who was a *Scotchman* by birth, moved to strike out the word '*Scotch*,' which was accordingly done." Richard H. Lee, ed., *Memoir of the Life of Richard Henry Lee*, 2 vols. (Philadelphia: H. C. Carey and I. Lea, 1825), 1:176 [emphasis in original]. Roger G. Kennedy, in his *Burr, Hamilton, and Jefferson* (New York: Oxford University Press, 2000) asserts on p. 226 that "[o]nly a last-minute action by Burr's Princeton friend John Witherspoon prevented the Continental Congress from demonstrating the planters' animosities by including in the Declaration of Independence an attack upon Scots *merchants* as well as upon the Hanoverian King George [emphasis added]." Presumably this is a mistaken reference to Witherspoon's successful effort to have the language about Scots *mercenaries* stricken from the Declaration. Regarding James Wilson's probable aid, Ezra Stiles of Yale College recorded that "[t]here are only two Scotchmen in Congress viz., Dr. Witherspoon Presidt of Jersey College, & Mr. Wilson, Pennsylva, a Lawyer. Both strongly national & can't bear any Thing in Congress which reflects on Scotland." Stiles, diary entry from July 1777, in Collins, *President Witherspoon*, 2:188.

23. See Benjamin Rush, "Travels Through Life," in *The Autobiography of Benjamin Rush: His "Travels Through Life," Together with His Commonplace Book for 1789–1813*, ed. George W. Corner (Princeton: Princeton University Press, 1948), 147.

24. Collins, *President Witherspoon*, 1:219.

25. "Dominion of Providence," in *Selected Writings*, 136.

26. "Pastoral Letter," in *Works*, 5:171–73.

27. "On Conducting the American Controversy," in *Works*, 9:83. Witherspoon had been ridiculed as a "Preacher of Sedition" by an anonymous Edinburgh pamphleteer in 1776. See Collins, *President Witherspoon*, 1:230.

28. John Adams to Timothy Pickering, August 6, 1822, in *Works*, 2:514n.

29. Collins, *President Witherspoon*, 2:181.

30. See Tait, *The Piety of John Witherspoon*, 46. Tait notes that "[t]ax records show that for a number of years he owned one or two slaves to help him farm his 500-plus acres at Tusculum."

31. "Lecture X: Of Politics," in *Lectures on Moral Philosophy*, 125.

32. See Tait, *The Piety of John Witherspoon*, 219n.

33. In Collins, *President Witherspoon*, 167–68.

34. "Some believe the phrase 'with a firm Reliance on the protection of Divine Providence' in the final sentence [of the Declaration] was his contribution." John Eidsmoe, *Christianity and the Constitution: The Faith of Our Founding Fathers* (Grand Rapids, MI: Baker Book House, 1987), 86.

35. *Papers of Thomas Jefferson*, 1:427.

36. See the version of the Declaration in Jefferson's "Notes of Proceedings in the Continental Congress," *Papers of Thomas Jefferson*, 1:315, 319. At p. 319, Jefferson represents the "Original Rough Draft" and the congressional additions in parallel columns.

37. For full citations, see chapter 1, notes 68–70, this volume.

38. Collins, *President Witherspoon*, 2:229.

39. See Wilson Carey McWilliams, "The Bible in the American Political Tradition," in Myron J. Aronoff, ed., *Religion and Politics* (New Brunswick, NJ: Transaction Books, 1984), 11–45.

40. "The Bible . . . has been the second voice in the grand dialogue of American political culture, an alternative to the 'liberal tradition' set in the deepest foundations of American life." McWilliams, "The Bible in the American Political Tradition," 11.

41. In Michael Wynn Jones, *The Cartoon History of the American Revolution* (New York: G. P. Putnam's Sons, 1975), 38–39.

42. John Adams to Dr. J. Morse, December 2, 1815, in *Works*, 10:185.

43. John Adams to H. Niles, February 13, 1818, in *Works*, 10:282–83 [emphasis in original].

44. "Though by now the Revolution has been voluminously, and one might suppose exhaustively, studied, we still do not realize how effective were generations of Protestant preaching in evoking patriotic enthusiasm. No interpretation of the religious utterances as being merely sanctimonious window dressing will do justice to the facts or to the character of the populace. Circumstances and the nature of the dominant opinion in Europe made it necessary for the official statement to be released in primarily 'political' terms — the social compact, inalienable rights, the right of revolution. But those terms, in and by themselves, would never have supplied the drive to victory, however mightily they weighed with the literate minority." Miller, *Nature's Nation* (Cambridge, MA: The Belknap Press of Harvard University Press, 1967), 97.

45. William G. McLoughlin, "The Role of Religion in the Revolution: Liberty of Conscience and Cultural Cohesion in the New Nation," in Stephen G. Kurtz and James H. Hutson, eds., *Essays on the American Revolution* (Chapel Hill: University of North Carolina Press, 1973), 198.

46. See Jefferson to Henry Lee, May 8, 1825, in *The Life and Selected Writings of Thomas Jefferson*, 657.

47. See Julian H. Franklin, ed., "Introduction," in *Constitutionalism and Resistance in the Sixteenth Century: Three Treatises by Hotman, Beza, and Mornay* (New York: Pegasus, 1969), 11–12.

48. See Calvin, *Commentary on Genesis 39:2*, in *Institutes of the Christian Religion*, trans. Ford Lewis Battles, ed. John T. McNeill, 2 vols. (Philadelphia: Westminster Press, 1960), 2:1494n.

49. *Institutes*, Book IV, Chap. XX, 2:1519.

50. "Letters on Education" (1775), in *Works*, 8:170.

51. This is precisely the conclusion reached by Page Smith: "the Revolution was not the work of a few middle-class radical intellectuals like Sam Adams and John Hancock; nor was it the consequence of a quarrel over the profits from the colonial trade. It was a profound popular movement of a people, or a substantial portion of those people, against the state of dependence and subordination in which they found themselves in relation to the mother country." Smith, *A New Age Now Begins*, 1:8–9.

52. "Sermon Delivered at a Public Thanksgiving" (1782), in *Works*, 5:254–55.

53. "Pastoral Letter" (1775), in *Works*, 5:171–73.

54. "On the Contest Between Great Britain and America," Witherspoon to unnamed correspondent, September 3, 1778, in *Works*, 9:169–70.

55. "On the Affairs of the United States," Witherspoon to unnamed correspondent in Scotland, March 20, 1780, in *Works*, 9:174–75.

56. "Thoughts on American Liberty" (1774), in *Works*, 9:73–74.

57. See Franklin, *Constitutionalism and Resistance in the Sixteenth Century*; Harold J. Laski, ed., *A Defence of Liberty Against Tyrants: A Translation of the Vindiciae contra Tyrannos by Junius Brutus* (London: G. Bell and Sons, 1924) (note that the authorship of the *Vindiciae* is debated and only attributed to Mornay); George Buchanan, *De jure regni apud Scotos, or, A Dialogue Concerning the Due Privilege of Government* (Philadelphia: Andrew Steuart, 1766); and Samuel Rutherford, *Lex, Rex, or, The Law and the Prince* (London: John Field, 1644; reprint ed., Harrisonburg, VA: Sprinkle Publications, 1982).

58. Gibbon noted that "Buchanan is the earliest, or at least the most celebrated, of the reformers, who has justified the theory of resistance. See his Dialoge de Jure Regni apud Scotos, tom. ii. p. 28, 30, edit. fol. Ruddiman." In Gibbon, *Decline and Fall of the Roman Empire*, Chap. XX, 1:641n.

59. See "Appendix 2: John Witherspoon's Personal Library in 1794," in *Lectures on Moral Philosophy*, 192–203.

60. Herbert D. Foster, "International Calvinism through Locke and the Revolution of 1688," *American Historical Review* 32 (April 1927): 487.

61. John Neville Figgis, *The Divine Right of Kings*, 2d ed. (Cambridge: Cambridge University Press, 1934), 114n. For a discussion of the *Vindiciae*, see Laski, editor's "Introduction," in *A Defence*. The *Vindiciae* is arranged in four questions: "I. Whether Subjects are bound and ought to obey Princes, if they command that which is against the Law of God"; "II. Whether it be lawful to resist a Prince which doth infringe the Law of God, or ruine [*sic*] the Church, by whom, how, and how far it is lawful"; "III. Whether it be lawful to resist a Prince which doth oppress or ruine a publick State, and how far such resistance may be extended, by whom, how, and by what right or law it is permitted"; "IV. Whether neighbour Princes or States may be, or are, bound by Law to give succour to the subjects of other

Princes, afflicted for the cause of True Religion, or oppressed by manifest Tyranny."
See Laski, *Defence*, 61.

62. See Laski, editor's "Introduction," in ibid., 54.

63. In Foster, "International Calvinism," 475.

64. In Schaff, *Creeds of Christendom*, 2:277.

65. Ibid.

66. See Peter Laslett, ed., "Appendix B: Sources of 'Two Treatises' in Locke's
Reading," in *Two Treatises of Government: A Critical Edition*, rev. ed. (New York:
Mentor, 1965), 151, 156. Locke listed the *Vindiciae* among his "A Catalogue of my
Books at Oxford," which appears in his journal between the entries for July 14 and 19,
1681 (see pp. 148, 151). But it is Laslett's thesis that Locke actually wrote the *Two
Treatises* in the late 1670s, not after the Glorious Revolution of 1688, in which case
the fact that Locke had the *Vindiciae* by 1681 loses some of its force. Locke could
still have owned the *Vindiciae* before 1681 and not recorded it—his list might not
be exhaustive—or he could have read it without owning it. However, Laslett also
records that the *Vindiciae* was printed in the 1643 Latin edition of Machiavelli's
Prince, which Locke owned, although we do not know when it came into his possession (see p. 156). Thus, it is entirely possible that Locke had read Brutus's *Vindiciae* (see note 57) before composing his *Two Treatises*, even if Laslett's supposition about the earlier date of composition is correct.

67. See Winthrop S. Hudson, "John Locke: Heir of Puritan Political Theorists,"
in George L. Hunt and John T. McNeill, eds., *Calvinism and the Political Order*
(Philadelphia: Westminster Press, 1965), 108–29.

68. The elder John Locke (1606–1663) was a captain of cavalry in the Parlia-
mentary army during the English Civil War, and Locke himself recalled his mother
Agnes Keene (1597–1654), who was also descended from Puritan stock, as a "very
pious woman." See Maurice William Cranston, *John Locke: A Biography* (New York:
Macmillan, 1957), 13; see also Thomas I. Cook, ed., "Introduction," in John Locke,
Two Treatises of Government (New York: Hafner Publishing Co., 1947), vii. At this
point we should also recall that the English Civil War was called by many contemporaries the "Puritan Rebellion," just as non-Americans during the Revolution referred to it as a "Presbyterian rebellion." In England, Zachary Gray was convinced
that "[t]he presbyterians . . . preached the people into rebellion [in 1649]," and one
Rev. Dr. South reminded his flock that "[i]t was the [Presbyterian] pulpit that supplied the field with swordsmen, and the parliament-house with incendiaries." See
J. A. St. John, ed., *The Prose Works of John Milton*, 4 vols. (London: George Bell and
Sons, 1889), 2:3n. Edmund Burke had made a similar distinction between rebellion,
revolution, and reformation. In his 1777 "Address to the British Colonists in North
America," Burke said: "[w]e do not call you rebels and traitors" because the Americans were in his view fighting to uphold the principles of "the fair [English] consti-
tution." In Michael Freeman, *Edmund Burke and the Critique of Political Radicalism*
(Chicago: University of Chicago Press, 1980), 174.

69. Concerning the influence of his Puritan ancestors, one of whom had been a judge at the Salem witch trials, Hawthorne wrote: "either of these stern and black-browed Puritans would have thought it quite a sufficient retribution for his sins, that, after so long a lapse of years, the old trunk of the family tree . . . should have borne, as its topmost bow [*sic*], an idler like myself. . . . And yet, let them scorn me as they will, strong traits of their nature have intertwined themselves with mine." Nathaniel Hawthorne, *The Scarlet Letter,* in E. Digby Baltzell, *Puritan Boston and Quaker Philadelphia* (New York: The Free Press, 1979), 52. In one of his best-known short stories, Hawthorne describes a "settlement of Puritans, most dismal wretches," who, when "they met in conclave, it was never to keep up the old English mirth, but to hear sermons three hours long, or to proclaim bounties on the heads of wolves and the scalps of Indians." Nathaniel Hawthorne, "The Maypole of Merry Mount," in *Major Writers of America, Shorter Edition,* ed. Perry Miller (New York: Harcourt, Brace and World, 1966), 380.

70. Gibbon, *Decline and Fall of the Roman Empire,* Chap. XX, Sect. III, 1:651.

71. Foster, "International Calvinism," 476. Foster may exaggerate the Calvinism of his group—Richard Hooker, Thomas Bilson, John Milton, Philip Hunton, Henry Ainsworth, John Selden, Hugo Grotius, Alexander Barclay—but his larger point remains valid.

72. "Locke became, in terms of his own medical profession, a 'carrier' of Calvinism from the Reformation to the revolutions of 1688 and 1776." Foster, "International Calvinism," 485.

73. See *Selected Writings,* 126–47; Sandoz, *Political Sermons of the American Founding Era,* 529–58; and *Works,* 5:176–236.

74. There is a significant body of literature that follows the line of John Adams and sees the roots of the Revolution sown in the Great Awakening and the climate of religious enthusiasm that preceded the actual fighting. Prominent examples are Alan Heimert, *Religion and the American Mind* (Cambridge, MA: Harvard University Press, 1966); William G. McLoughlin, "'Enthusiasm for Liberty': The Great Awakening as the Key to the Revolution," in *Preachers and Politicians: Two Essays on the Origins of the American Revolution,* ed. McLoughlin, 47–73 (Worcester, MA: American Antiquarian Society, 1977); and Perry Miller, *Nature's Nation.* Miller writes, "[t]hough by now the Revolution has been voluminously, and one might suppose exhaustively, studied, we still do not realize how effective were generations of Protestant preaching in evoking patriotic enthusiasm." See ibid., 97. Jon Butler, on the other hand, suggests that colonial preaching had little to do with Revolutionary politics. See Butler, *Awash in a Sea of Faith: Christianizing the American People* (Cambridge, MA: Harvard University Press, 1990), 203.

75. Anonymous Glasgow editor's notes, "The Dominion of Providence Over the Passions of Men" (Glasgow, 1777), in Collins, *President Witherspoon,* 1:227.

76. "Dominion of Providence," in *Selected Writings,* 140.

77. "Witherspoon's unnamed counsellor was George Whitefield, with whom he conferred before leaving Britain." See Murray, *Revival and Revivalism*, 41–42.

78. Rev. Thomas Randall to John Witherspoon, March 4, 1767, in L. H. Butterfield, ed., *John Witherspoon Comes to America: A Documentary Account Based Largely on New Materials* (Princeton: Princeton University Press, 1953), 29 [emphasis in original]. This was a common sentiment among preachers on both sides of the Atlantic during the Revolutionary era. In 1776, Rev. Samuel West gave a prognosis nearly identical to Randall's and to Witherspoon's: "yet I cannot help hoping, and even believing, that Providence has designed this continent for to be the asylum of liberty and true religion." In Miller, *Nature's Nation*, 106.

79. Witherspoon to Archibald Wallace, February 28, 1767, in Butterfield, *John Witherspoon Comes to America*, 28.

80. "Dominion of Providence," in *Selected Writings*, 140–41; also *Works*, 5:203.

81. See Olasky, *Fighting for Liberty and Virtue*; see also Miller, *Nature's Nation*, 108.

82. "Ignorance of the British with Respect to America," in *Works*, 8:306.

83. "Dominion of Providence" (1776), in *Selected Writings*, 146.

84. "On the Contest Between Great Britain and America" (1778), in *Works*, 9:167.

85. "Thanksgiving Sermon," in *Works*, 5:261–62.

86. "Dominion of Providence," in *Selected Writings*, 141 [emphasis added].

87. Ibid., 142.

88. "Address to the Natives of Scotland Residing in America," in *Works*, 5:217–18 [hereinafter "Address"].

89. "Address," in *Works*, 5:22.

90. Ibid., 5:218n. See also chapter 6, note 56, this volume.

91. Ibid., 5:224.

92. "On Conducting the American Controversy" (1773), in *Works*, 9:87.

93. "Reflections on the Present State of Public Affairs," in *Works*, 9:66–67.

94. John Jay's language in *Federalist* 2 is reminiscent of such a cautionary tone: "it *appears* as if it was the design of Providence that an inheritance so proper and convenient for a band of brethren, united to each other by the strongest ties, should never be split into a number of unsocial, jealous, and alien sovereigns." In Rossiter, *Federalist* 2, 38 [emphasis added].

95. "Reflections on the Present State of Public Affairs," in *Works*, 9:71.

96. See *Works*, 9:154–65. This document, although in the name of the United States, was apparently written by Witherspoon on his own initiative, since it does not appear in either the *Journals of the Continental Congress* or *The Revolutionary Diplomatic Correspondence of the United States*.

97. "Memorial and Manifesto," in *Works*, 9:154–55 [emphasis in original]. Once again Witherspoon was expressing a common American sentiment of the

Revolutionary era. In 1765 a Rhode Islander writing as "A Plain Yeoman" in the *Providence Gazette* of May 11, 1765, "denied any connection between Great Britain and the colonies except 'that we are all the common subjects of the same King.'" See Edmund S. Morgan, *The Birth of the Republic, 1763–89*, 3d ed. (Chicago: University of Chicago Press, 1992), 26.

98. "Memorial and Manifesto," in *Works*, 9:158–60.

99. Ibid., 9:160–61.

100. See Philip F. Detweiler, "The Changing Reputation of the Declaration of Independence: The First Fifty Years," *William and Mary Quarterly*, 3d ser., 19 (1962): 557–74; and Detweiler, "Congressional Debate on Slavery and the Declaration of Independence," *American Historical Review* 63 (1958): 598–616.

101. "Lecture XII: Of Civil Society," in *Lectures on Moral Philosophy*, 145.

102. For the use of "Nature's God," "Creator," and "divine Providence" in the Westminster Confession, see Chap. I, Art. I, in Schaff, *Creeds of Christendom*, 3:600, which reads: "the light of nature, and the works of creation and providence, do so far manifest the goodness, wisdom, and power of God, as to leave men inexcusable." More specifically, for God as "Creator," see Chap. IV, Art. II, in ibid., 3:611, which says: "[i]t hath pleased God . . . to create or make of nothing the world, and all things therein." For God as "Supreme Judge of the World," see Chap. I, Art. X, in ibid., 3:605–6, which says: "[t]he Supreme Judge, by which all controversies . . . and private spirits, are to be examined, and in whose sentence we are to rest, can be no other but the Holy Spirit"; see also Chap. XXIII, Art. I, in ibid., 3:652 for God as "Supreme Lord and King of all the world." Finally, for God as "divine Providence," see Chap. I, Art. I, in ibid., 3:600 on God's "works of creation and providence." "Providence" for the Westminster divines meant God's ongoing activity toward the world and was contrasted with his creation. This seems to be what the founders meant as well: Providence was not used as a name for God, as were the other three terms in the Declaration, and the protecting aspect of providence is stressed in the Declaration's final paragraph.

103. See Westminster Confession of Faith (1647), Chap. I, Art. I, in Schaff, *Creeds of Christendom*, 3:600.

104. Wilson Carey McWilliams suggests that the Declaration contains an "equivocal religiosity" that was "designed to be acceptable to deists and orthodox believers alike," although he denies that the Creator or Nature's God of the Declaration is the "distinctly biblical God." See McWilliams, "The Bible in the American Political Tradition," 21.

105. Westminster Confession of Faith (1647), Chap. I, Art. X, in Schaff, *Creeds of Christendom*, 3:605–6.

106. "There is a day coming in which there will be a general righteous judgment of the whole world, by Jesus Christ. In speaking upon this subject, I shall show, That God is the Supreme Judge of the world. That there is a time coming, when God will, in the most public and solemn manner, judge the whole world. That the

person by whom he will judge it is Jesus Christ. That the transactions of that day will be greatly interesting and truly awful. That all shall be done in righteousness. And finally, I shall take notice of those things which shall be immediately consequent upon the judgment." Jonathan Edwards, "The Final Judgment: or, The World Judged Righteously by Jesus Christ," in *The Works of Jonathan Edwards*, ed. Edward Hickman, 2 vols. (Edinburgh: Banner of Truth Trust, 1834; reprint ed., 1974), 2:101 [emphasis in original].

107. In Schama, *Citizens*, 167.

108. "Lecture IV," in *Lectures on Moral Philosophy*, 85.

109. See Mark A. Noll, Nathan O. Hatch, and George M. Marsden, *The Search for Christian America* (Westchester, IL: Crossway Books, 1983), 72 ff.

110. Jefferson to Maria Cosway, October 12, 1786, in *Thomas Jefferson: Writings*, 875 [emphasis added].

111. "Lecture I," in *Lectures on Moral Philosophy*, 65.

112. Westminster Confession of Faith, Chap. I, Art. I, in Schaff, *Creeds of Christendom*, 3:600–601.

113. Tocqueville was quick to realize that Reformed Protestantism in early America was "almost as much a political theory as a religious doctrine." *Democracy in America*, 38.

114. "Speech on the Conference Proposed by Lord Howe," in *Works*, 9:104.

**Chapter Five.   "An Equal Republican Consitution": Confederation,
Union, and Nationhood**

1. See Willmoore Kendall and George W. Carey, *The Basic Symbols of the American Political Tradition*, rev. ed. (Washington, DC: Catholic University Press, 1995 [1970]), 90: "what it [the Declaration] did was to establish a baker's dozen of new sovereignties."

2. This despite the fact that the Declaration is listed as the first of the Organic Laws of the United States. See *United States Code*, 1:xli–xliii.

3. Luther Martin, June 19, 1787, in Madison, *Notes of Debates in the Federal Convention*, 153.

4. "Part of a Speech in Congress upon the Confederation" (1776), in *Works*, 9:138 [emphasis added].

5. "Memorial and Manifesto of the United States," in *Works*, 9:155 [emphasis in original].

6. See "Lecture XIII: Of the Law of Nature and of Nations," in *Lectures on Moral Philosophy*, 150–56, 156n.

7. Ibid., 150. Witherspoon here reiterated what was said in a prior lecture, namely, that "distinct societies or states independent, are at this moment in a state of nature, or natural liberty, with regard to each other." See "Lecture X: Of Politics,"

in *Lectures on Moral Philosophy*, 122. This fact was taken to be a proof of the present existence of a state of nature, regardless of whether there had ever been an actual historical state of nature before civil societies were formed.

8. Witherspoon in Congress, July 30, 1776, in Thomas Jefferson, "Notes of Proceedings in the Continental Congress," in *Papers of Thomas Jefferson*, 1:323.

9. See "Speech in Congress upon the Confederation," in *Works*, 9:135–41; also in Paul H. Smith et al., eds., *Letters of Delegates to Congress, 1774–1789*, 25 vols. (Washington, DC: Library of Congress, 1976–98), 4:584–87. Notes of the speech, including extemporaneous remarks not included in the version in Witherspoon's *Works*, were also made by John Adams and Jefferson. See Adams, "Notes of Debates in the Continental Congress, in 1775 and 1776," in *Works*, 2:496; and Jefferson, "Notes of Proceedings in the Continental Congress," in *Papers of Thomas Jefferson*, 1:324–25.

10. See *Journals of the Continental Congress*, March 1, 1781, 19:214.

11. "Speech in Congress upon the Confederation," in *Works*, 9:135–36.

12. Ibid., 9:136.

13. "[W]hy is it suggested that three or four confederacies would be better than one?" In Rossiter, *Federalist* 1, 41. See also Hamilton's mention of the possibility of "three confederacies—one consisting of the four Northern, another of the four Middle, and a third of the five Southern States," in Rossiter, *Federalist* 13, 97.

14. "Aristides," in *Works*, 9:97–98. Article III of the Articles of Confederation created a "firm league of friendship" between the states.

15. "Speech in Congress upon the Confederation," in *Works*, 9:136.

16. Witherspoon in Congress, February 3, 1781, in *Journals of the Continental Congress*, 19:110.

17. See *Journals of the Continental Congress*, 19:100. Witherspoon's continuing interest in the western lands was what prompted the uncommonly long letter from George Washington noted in chapter 1. See Washington to John Witherspoon, March 10, 1784, in *Writings of George Washington*, 27:348–52.

18. In Collins, *President Witherspoon*, 2:73.

19. Ibid.

20. Witherspoon in Congress, July 30, 1776, in *Papers of Thomas Jefferson*, 1:322.

21. See *Papers of Thomas Jefferson*, 1:324–25.

22. Articles of Confederation, Art. V, in *United States Code*, 1:xlvi.

23. "Address to the Natives of Scotland Residing in America" (1777), in *Works*, 5:226.

24. In Humphrey, *Nationalism and Religion in America*, 85.

25. See Monaghan, "Stare Decisis and Constitutional Adjudication," *Columbia Law Review* 88 (1988): 725 [emphasis in original].

26. James Madison to Henry Lee, June 25, 1824, in *The Writings of James Madison*, 9:191.

27. Alexander Hamilton, "Opinion on the Constitutionality of an Act to Establish a Bank" (1791), in *Papers of Alexander Hamilton*, 8:111.

28. "Through the summer and into the fall of 1781, countered at every turn by Witherspoon and opposed by the French and the frightened delegates from the deep South, Madison fought a losing battle to make the western claims of the United States . . . part of the peace ultimata." Lance Banning, "James Madison and the Nationalists, 1780–1783," *William and Mary Quarterly*, 3d ser., 40 (1983): 236.

29. See Carol Berkin, *A Brilliant Solution: Inventing the American Constitution* (New York: Harcourt, 2002), 224.

30. H. Jefferson Powell notes that "[a]s one of the prime movers in the Philadelphia convention of 1787 and in the Virginia ratifying convention the following year, as one of the authors of *The Federalist*, and as the draftsman of both the Virginia Resolutions of 1798 and the Report of 1800, Madison played a critical role both in the process of framing and ratifying the Constitution and in the formulation of a consensus about its meaning." Powell, "The Original Understanding of Original Intent," *Harvard Law Review* 98 (1985): 935.

31. See Adair, *Fame and the Founding Fathers*, 124.

32. See "Madison Chronology," in *Papers of James Madison*, 9:xxiv; also James Madison to James Monroe, August 12, 1786, in ibid., 9:90.

33. See Merrill Jensen et al., eds., *The Documentary History of the Ratification of the Constitution*, 18 vols. (Madison: State Historical Society of Wisconsin, 1976–95), 3:371.

34. See Henry Knox to Nathan Dane, November 21, 1787, in ibid., Supplement to Vol. 2, 64.

35. See James Madison to Edmund Randolph, November 18, 1787, in ibid.

36. Green, *Life of the Revd. John Witherspoon*, 172–73.

37. Collins, *President Witherspoon*, 2:73.

38. See *Papers of James Madison*, 9:91n.

39. "When a majority of the New York Assembly, to their eternal infamy, attempted to break the union of the colonies, by refusing to approve the proceedings of the Congress, and applying to Parliament by separate petition—because they presumed to make mention of the principal grievance of taxation, it was treated with ineffable contempt." See "On the Controversy About Independence" (ca. 1776), in *Works*, 9:81.

40. Collins, *President Witherspoon*, 2:15. See also Wharton, *Revolutionary Diplomatic Correspondence of the United States*, 1:461. "[W]hen . . . Witherspoon, or Harrison, was in the ascendant on the committee, Franklin was treated as from the nature of things at the head of our diplomatic system."

41. Wharton, *Revolutionary Diplomatic Correspondence of the United States*, 2:470.

42. "The faculty psychology Publius employed was representative of a large and distinguished school of thought which included the Scottish moral philosopher

John Witherspoon, who emigrated to America to become president of Princeton, a signer of the Declaration of Independence, and the teacher of James Madison." See Daniel Walker Howe, *Making the American Self: Jonathan Edwards to Abraham Lincoln* (Cambridge, MA: Harvard University Press, 1997), 80. See also Robinson, "The Scottish Enlightenment and Its Mixed Bequest," 171, for the claim that "Madison's writings . . . are fully indebted to Witherspoon's instruction at Princeton in the years preceding the Revolution." For a discussion of the Scottish faculty psychology, see Boring, *A History of Experimental Psychology*, 203–9.

43. "Dominion of Providence," in *Selected Writings*, 147.

44. In Rossiter, *Federalist* 51, 324.

45. In Rossiter, *Federalist* 49, 314.

46. "On the Federal City," in *Works*, 9:217. We can hear a similar note in Madison's *Federalist* 51, which says that the body of people may from time to time need to have their views enlarged and refined by passing them through "the medium of a chosen body of citizens." See Rossiter, *Federalist* 10, 82.

47. "Address to the Natives of Scotland Residing in America" (1776), in *Works*, 5:226.

48. In Rossiter, *Federalist* 1, 33.

49. In Rossiter, *Federalist* 55, 346.

50. In Rossiter, *Federalist* 51, 322.

51. In Rossiter, *Federalist* 6, 54.

52. "Speech in Congress upon the Confederation," in *Works*, 9:139.

53. In Rossiter, *Federalist* 38, 237.

54. In Rossiter, *Federalist* 85, 523.

55. "Speech in Congress upon the Confederation," in *Works*, 9:139.

56. Ibid., 9:140.

57. Montesquieu was, according to Ashbel Green, Witherspoon's favorite French author, and he listed Montesquieu's *Spirit of the Laws* and *Considerations on the Cause of the Grandeur and Declension of the Romans* in his "Bibliography of Chief Writers on Ethical and Political Thought" at the end of his Lectures on Moral Philosophy. See Scott, *Lectures on Moral Philosophy*, 44, 191. For the influence of Montesquieu on early American political thought, see, generally, Paul O. Carrese, *The Cloaking of Power: Montesquieu, Blackstone, and the Judicializing of Liberalism* (Chicago: University of Chicago Press, 2002).

58. "No State shall . . . make any Thing but gold and silver Coin a Tender in Payment of Debts." U.S. Constitution, Art. I, Sect. 10, in *United States Code*, 1:lvii.

59. *Essay on Money*, in *Works*, 9:9–10.

60. Ibid., 9:35.

61. Ibid., 9:49, 52.

62. Ibid., 9:56, 57n.

63. Ibid., 9:65 [emphasis added].

64. Ibid., 9:64.

65. See "Druid V" (1781), in *Works*, 9:269–70, for Witherspoon's analysis of "Americanisms, or ways of speaking peculiar to this country."

66. "Speech on the Conference Proposed by Lord Howe," in *Works*, 9:104 [emphasis added].

67. Humphrey, *Nationalism and Religion in America*, 1.

68. Ibid., 440.

69. A preliminary draft of "a system of discipline and church government" was written during the Synod of 1786, only "part of which was read" on May 22. See *Records of the Presbyterian Church*, 524. The real work of constitution-making was done in the Synod of 1787, and the constitution was ratified in 1788.

70. Westminster Confession of Faith (1647), Chap. XXIII, Art. III, in Schaff, *Creeds of Christendom*, 3:653.

71. "The Confession of Faith," Chap. XXIII, Art. III, in *Constitution of the Presbyterian Church in the United States of America* (Philadelphia: Thomas Bradford, 1789), 35 [emphasis in original].

72. "Aristides" (1776), in *Works*, 9:95.

73. "Introduction," Art. II, in *Constitution of the Presbyterian Church in the United States of America*, cxxxiv.

74. "Introduction, The Form of the Government and Discipline of the Presbyterian Church in the United States of America," in *Constitution of the Presbyterian Church in the United States of America*, cxxxiii–cxxxv. The full quotation from the Westminster Confession reads: "God alone is Lord of the conscience; and hath left it free from the doctrine and commandments of men; which are in any thing contrary to his word; or beside it in matters of faith or worship." See Westminster Confession of Faith, Chap. XX, Art. II, in Schaff, *Creeds of Christendom*, 3:644. This hedging-in of freedom of the conscience by the biblical standards of faith and worship thus enabled the Presbyterian church itself to regulate the faith and practice of its professing members. To the American Presbyterians (and indeed to the Westminster divines) the conscience could never be autonomous given the grave effects of the Fall on all human faculties, including the conscience.

75. Edmund Randolph in the Virginia Convention, June 10, 1788, in Farrand, *Records of the Federal Convention of 1787*, 3:310.

76. Publius called the proposed government "partly national" and "partly federal"; see Rossiter, *Federalist* 39, 246.

77. The Presbyterian General Assembly was an innovative form of church government in that there had never been any such national body prior to its creation by the Presbyterian constitution. General Assemblies had, of course, been used by British Protestants long before the American Presbyterian General Assembly.

78. For a discussion of the federal aspects of the Presbyterian church, see John Willson, *John Witherspoon and the Presbyterian Constitution* (Hillsdale, MI: Hillsdale College Press, 1994), 18–19. Others have noticed the natural affinity between Presbyterianism and our system of federal government. "Clearly Presbyterianism

is good schooling for complex, larger-than-local representative government. . . . It is certainly not a farfetched hypothesis to suggest that the Presbyterian experience was influential in the forging of the viable political structure of government visible in the Constitution, especially considering the influence of Presbyterianism on James Wilson, Witherspoon, and his student Madison." See Flower and Murphey, *A History of Philosophy in America*, 1:216–17.

79. "Form of the Government," Chap. XI, Sect. II, in *Constitution of the Presbyterian Church in the United States of America*, 147. The number of ministers in each presbytery was determined by the number of congregations, and so indirectly by population.

80. "A Few Reflections, Humbly Submitted to the Consideration of the Public in General, and in Particular to the Congress of the United States, on the Federal City," in *Works*, 9:216 [emphasis added].

81. Ibid., 9:214.

82. "It is even uncertain whether the bare residence of Congress during their annual sessions (which it is to be hoped in a few years will be but short) independent of other circumstances, will ever raise a great commercial city at all." See ibid., 9:217.

83. Thomas Jefferson to James Madison, September 6, 1789, in *Thomas Jefferson: Writings*, 449. Here, Jefferson took his cues from John Locke, who held that government attended solely to the worldly affairs of the commonwealth.

84. "Lecture XIV: Jurisprudence," in *Lectures on Moral Philosophy*, 159. In this context, "constitution" means not merely the ordering document but the form of the government as well.

85. Recall that Witherspoon considered the "public credit of religion" to be "more powerful than the most sanguinary laws." See "On the Religious Education of Children," in *Works*, 4:144. Thus, laws — even good laws — were less powerful than religion to make men moral.

86. "In framing a government which is to be administered by men over men, the great difficulty lies in this: You must first enable the government to control the governed: and in the next place, oblige it to control itself." In Rossiter, *Federalist* 51, 322.

87. "Sermon Delivered at a Public Thanksgiving" (1782), in *Works*, 5:269.

Chapter Six. John Witherspoon and Early American Political Thought

1. Again, I quote Tocqueville: "There is no country in the world in which the boldest political theories of the eighteenth-century philosophers are put so effectively into practice as in America." In *The Old Régime and the French Revolution*, 153.

2. Madison, *Notes of Debates in the Federal Convention of 1787*, 46.

3. "Col. MASON observed that a vote had already passed, he found—he was out at the time—for vesting the executive powers in a single person. Among these powers was that of appointing to offices in certain cases. The probable abuses of a negative [veto] had been well explained by Doctor FRANKLIN, as proved by experience, the best of all tests. Will not the same door be opened here?" George Mason in the Convention, June 4, 1787, in ibid., 64.

4. In Rossiter, *Federalist* 1, 33.

5. In Rossiter, *Federalist* 85, 526–27 [emphasis in original]. The founders generally meant three things by "experience": cumulative American experience up to the founding, their own personal experience, and history. See Donald S. Lutz, *A Preface to American Political Theory* (Lawrence: University Press of Kansas, 1992), 116.

6. In Rossiter, *Federalist* 34, 206.

7. Madison, *Notes of Debates in the Federal Convention of 1787*, 221.

8. Ellsworth wrote as "The Landholder," excoriating Martin for "a speech which held during two days, and which might have continued two months, but for those marks of fatigue and disgust you saw strongly expressed on whichever side of the house you turned your mortified eyes." See Farrand, *Records of the Federal Convention of 1787*, 3:271–72.

9. In *Benjamin Franklin's Autobiographical Writings*, 258. The pamphlet was his "Dissertation on Liberty and Necessity, Pleasure and Pain" (1725).

10. In Rossiter, *Federalist* 37, 227.

11. In Rossiter, *Federalist* 49, 315.

12. See Donald S. Lutz, *The Origins of American Constitutionalism* (Baton Rouge and London: Louisiana State University Press, 1988), 138–49.

13. John Adams to Thomas Jefferson, July 16, 1814, in *Adams-Jefferson Letters*, 2:437.

14. Ibid.

15. Thomas Jefferson to William Short, October 31, 1819, in *The Portable Thomas Jefferson*, ed. Merrill D. Peterson (New York: Penguin Books, 1975), 564.

16. Thomas Jefferson to John Adams, July 5, 1814, in *Adams-Jefferson Letters*, 2:432–33.

17. In *The Republic of Plato*, Chap. XXII, trans. Francis MacDonald Cornford (London: Oxford University Press, 1941), 209.

18. "Recapitulation," in *Lectures on Moral Philosophy*, 186.

19. Selwyn A. Grave, "Common Sense," in *The Encyclopedia of Philosophy*, ed. Paul Edwards, 8 vols. (New York: Macmillan Publishing and The Free Press, 1967), 2:157.

20. See "Appendix 2: John Witherspoon's Personal Library in 1794," in *Lectures on Moral Philosophy*, 192–203.

21. See *Works*, 9:199–211.

22. See Boorstin, *The Americans: The Colonial Experience*, 6.

23. See, generally, J. I. Packer, *A Quest for Godliness: The Puritan Vision of the Christian Life* (Wheaton, IL: Crossway Books, 1994).

24. Marvin Olasky has argued that Americans were fighting for virtue every bit as much as they were for liberty. See his *Fighting for Liberty and Virtue.*

25. Witherspoon recommended that a resolution be issued to "declare, not only that we esteem the claim of the British Parliament to be illegal and unconstitutional, but that we are firmly determined never to submit to it, and do deliberately prefer war with all its horrors, and even extermination itself, to slavery rivetted on us and our posterity." See "Thoughts on American Liberty," in *Works,* 9:75–76.

26. When a Revolutionary War veteran, Capt. Levi Prescott of Danvers, Massachusetts, was interviewed by the historian Mellen Chamberlain in 1837, he claimed never to have heard of Locke, Sydney, or James Harrington. "Young man," Prescott said, "what we meant in going for those red-coats, was this: we always had governed ourselves and we always meant to. They didn't mean we should." In Charles Warren, *The Making of the Constitution* (Boston: Little, Brown and Co., 1937), 4.

27. Compare Allan Bloom, *The Closing of the American Mind* (New York: Simon and Schuster, 1987), 97: "This is a regime founded by philosophers and their students"; and Thomas L. Pangle, "The Philosophic Understanding of Human Nature Informing the Constitution," in Bloom and Kautz, *Confronting the Constitution,* 9: "The American Constitution is a product not of philosophers but of statesmen and lawgivers."

28. Henry used this metaphor, of course, in his famous "Liberty or Death" speech before the Virginia Assembly (1775).

29. "Sermon Delivered at a Public Thanksgiving" (1782), in *Works,* 5:265.

30. The literature on the founding is vast, and getting more vast all the time; there have been a number of works that have chronicled its historiography. For a succinct catalogue of the relevant literature, see Dale S. Kuehne, *Massachusetts Congregational Political Thought, 1760–1790* (Columbia: University of Missouri Press, 1996), 1–21. For elegant summaries of the political historiography, see Garrett Ward Sheldon, *The Political Philosophy of Thomas Jefferson* (Baltimore: Johns Hopkins University Press, 1991); and Michael P. Zuckert, *The Natural Rights Republic* (Notre Dame, IN: University of Notre Dame Press, 1996).

31. Louis Hartz's *The Liberal Tradition in America* (New York: Harcourt, Brace and World, 1955) is the classic statement of this position.

32. See Robbins, *The Eighteenth-Century Commonwealthman: Studies in the Transmission, Development, and Circumstance of English Liberal Thought from the Restoration of Charles II until the War with the Thirteen Colonies* (Cambridge, MA: Harvard University Press, 1959).

33. See Bailyn, *The Ideological Origins of the American Revolution* (Cambridge, MA: Harvard University Press, 1967). J. G. A. Pocock's *Machiavellian Moment* (Princeton: Princeton University Press, 1975) sees American classical republi-

canism filtered through an Italian Renaissance lens; and several volumes by Gordon Wood, including his most recent *The American Revolution* (New York: Modern Library, 2002), argue for a classical republican understanding of the founding.

34. On the Scottish Enlightenment, see, for example, Adair, *Fame and the Founding Fathers*, 93–106, 124–40; and Wills, *Inventing America*. On Reformed Christianity, the most forceful single volume is Barry Alan Shain, *The Myth of American Individualism: The Protestant Origins of American Political Thought* (Princeton: Princeton University Press, 1994).

35. See Sheldon, *The Political Philosophy of James Madison*, xi. An interpretation of the founding that stands somewhat outside these three schools is Kendall and Carey, *The Basic Symbols of the American Political Tradition*.

36. Concerning founding historiography generally, Fischer writes: "Paul Revere's idea of liberty was not the same as our modern conception of individual autonomy and personal entitlement. It was not a form of 'classical Republicanism,' or 'English Opposition Ideology,' or 'Lockean Liberalism,' or any of the learned anachronisms that scholars have invented to explain a way of thought that is alien to their own world." David Hackett Fischer, *Paul Revere's Ride* (New York: Oxford University Press, 1994), xvii.

37. John Locke, "Second Treatise of Civil Government," Sect. 136, in *Two Treatises of Government: A Critical Edition*, 404 [emphasis in original].

38. "Lecture X: Of Politics," in *Lectures on Moral Philosophy*, 122–23. Witherspoon appropriated the Lockean formula ("Second Treatise," Sect. 95) of the social compact as represented by Hutcheson (*System of Moral Philosophy*). See editor's note, *Lectures on Moral Philosophy*, 129n.

39. "Lecture X: Of Politics," in *Lectures on Moral Philosophy*, 122–23.

40. "Druid II" (1776), in *Works*, 9:234.

41. "Lecture VI," in *Lectures on Moral Philosophy*, 95.

42. "The Dominion of Providence Over the Passions of Men," in *Selected Writings*, 137, 138.

43. See "Lecture III: Of the Law of Nature and Nations," in *Lectures on Moral Philosophy*, 150–56. Locke himself had borrowed this phrase and concept from Pufendorf, whose *On the Law of Nature and Nations* (1672) lent its title to Witherspoon's Lecture III as well as its structure to Witherspoon's Lectures as a whole, mediated through Hutcheson's *System of Moral Philosophy*, which served as a model for the Lectures.

44. "Lecture VIII," in *Lectures on Moral Philosophy*, 110.

45. "Lecture X: Of Politics," in *Lectures on Moral Philosophy*, 123, 122.

46. Ibid., 122–23.

47. Ibid., 123.

48. Witherspoon owned the 1713 edition of Locke's *Two Treatises,* and he included the 1690 edition of that work in his "Bibliography of Chief Writers on

Ethical and Political Thought" at the end of the *Lectures on Moral Philosophy.* See *Lectures on Moral Philosophy*, 191, 195.

49. See *Lectures on Moral Philosophy*, 187, 92, 189–91. Every title listed by Witherspoon in that bibliography dates from the second millennium A.D., and there is only one figure, John Selden, who predates Hobbes.

50. "Lectures on Divinity," in *Works*, 8:25–26. Among the principal writings of Ralph Cudworth (1617–1688), a Cambridge divine, was *The True Intellectual System of the Universe* (1678).

51. "Lecture XIV: Jurisprudence," in *Lectures on Moral Philosophy*, 159.

52. Jean-Jacques Rousseau, "Discourse on the Sciences and the Arts [First Discourse]," in *Basic Political Writings*, 12.

53. A contemporary of Witherspoon's once dryly lamented that more Ciceronian productions had not issued from the place to justify its name.

54. Esther Forbes, *Paul Revere and the World He Lived In* (Boston: Houghton Mifflin Co., 1969 [1942]), 378.

55. Epaminondas was a famous Theban general who defeated the Spartans at the battle of Leuctra in 371 B.C. He is mentioned extensively in Plutarch's *Lives;* see Plutarch, *The Lives of the Noble Grecians and Romans*, 353 ff.

56. See "Lecture XIV: Jurisprudence," in *Lectures on Moral Philosophy*, 161. Witherspoon also mentioned "the ancients" in several other historical, and never prescriptive, contexts. For example, he explained why they stressed prudence in their discussions of virtue: "Another reason why prudence seems to have held such a place among the ancients was, that their chief foundation for virtue was interest, or what will produce happiness. The inquiry upon this subject was, what is the *summum bonum.* Now to this, prudence is very necessary. Agreeably to all this they commonly called the virtuous man, the *wise man,* and he was always an hero." See "Lecture IX," in *Lectures on Moral Philosophy*, 115.

57. Hutson, *Religion and the Founding of the American Republic*, 46.

58. "On Conducting the American Controversy" (1773), in *Works*, 9:85; see also David Walker Woods, Jr., *John Witherspoon* (New York: Fleming H. Revell, 1906), 193.

Appendix A. Witherspoon and the Debate in Congress on Independence, July 1776

1. Green, *Life of the Revd. John Witherspoon*, 159–60.

2. John Dickinson, "Vindication," in John H. Hazelton, *The Declaration of Independence: Its History* (New York: Da Capo Press, 1970 [1906]), 353 [emphasis in original].

3. See *Journals of the Continental Congress*, 5:489–518.

4. Ibid., 5:505, 506–7, 510.

5. Ibid., 5:489–90, 515. Witherspoon possibly signed the Declaration some-time in August, along with other members of Congress. Jefferson's statement that "every member present except Mr. Dickinson" signed in "the evening of the last [July 4]" has been brought into question by modern scholarship. See *Papers of Thomas Jefferson*, 1:315. However, Benjamin Rush implied that he and the other members of Congress did indeed sign it on July 4, although he recalled that it was done in the morning: "Scarcely a word was said [during the celebration on July 4, 1811] of the solicitude and labors and fears and sorrows and sleepless nights of the men who projected, proposed, defended, and subscribed the Declaration of Inde-pendence. Do you recollect your memorable speech upon the day on which the vote was taken? Do you recollect the pensive and awful silence which pervaded the house when we were called up, one after another, to the table of the President of Congress to subscribe what was believed by many at that time to be our own death warrants? The silence and the gloom of the morning were interrupted, I well recollect, only for a moment by Colonel Harrison of Virginia, who said to Mr. Gerry at the table: 'I shall have a great advantage over you, Mr. Gerry, when we are all hung for what we are now doing. From the size and weight of my body I shall die in a few minutes, but from the lightness of your body you will dance in the air an hour or two before you are dead.' This speech procured a transient smile, but it was soon succeeded by the solemnity with which the whole business was conducted." See Rush to John Adams, July 20, 1811, in *Letters of Benjamin Rush*, 2:1090. Benjamin Harrison's mor-bid joke was verified by Elbridge Gerry himself in 1811. See Rush to John Adams, September 4, 1811, in ibid., 2:1102: "A Mr. Richardson from Charleston visited me a few days ago. . . . He told me among other things that Governor Gerry, who intro-duced him to you [Adams], acquiesced in the correctness of B. Harrison's speech to him upon their subscribing the Declaration of Independence."

6. *Papers of Thomas Jefferson*, 1:309.

7. Ibid., 1:313. The "final decision" in question was whether to approve the Resolution for Independence introduced by Richard Henry Lee of Virginia on June 7, not the Declaration, which had not yet been submitted by Jefferson.

8. Ibid., 1:313–14.

9. John Adams to Thomas McKean, July 30, 1815, in Hazelton, *The Declara-tion of Independence*, 466.

10. See John Adams, "Notes of Debates in the Continental Congress, in 1775 and 1776," in *Works*, 2:443–502.

11. "Dominion of Providence," in *Selected Writings*, 144.

12. *Works*, 5:265.

13. "Memorial and Manifesto of the United States of North-America, to the Mediating Powers in the Conferences for Peace, to the Other Powers in Europe, and in General to All Who Shall See the Same," in *Works*, 9:164–65.

Appendix B. Dating the "Sermon Delivered at a Public Thanksgiving After Peace," November 1782

1. *Works,* 5:237–70.
2. Collins, *President Witherspoon,* 2:125.
3. *Works,* 5:237, 239 [emphasis added].
4. Ibid., 5:237.
5. See *Journals of the Continental Congress,* 25:699–701.
6. Ibid., 22:137–38.
7. Ibid., 23:647; and *Works,* 5:237, 239.
8. *Works,* 5:238.
9. Ibid., 5:238–39.

bibliography

Adair, Douglass. *Fame and the Founding Fathers*. Ed. Trevor Colbourn. New York: W. W. Norton, 1974.

Adams, John. *The Diary and Autobiography of John Adams*. Ed. L. H. Butterfield. 4 vols. Cambridge, MA: The Belknap Press of Harvard University Press, 1961.

———. *The Selected Writings of John and John Quincy Adams*. Ed. Adrienne Koch and William Peden. New York: Alfred A. Knopf, 1946.

———. *The Works of John Adams*. Ed. Charles Francis Adams. 10 vols. Boston: Little, Brown and Co., 1850–56.

Ahlstrom, Sydney E. *A Religious History of the American People*. New Haven: Yale University Press, 1972.

Alexander, Samuel Davies. *Princeton College during the Eighteenth Century*. New York: Anson D. F. Randolph and Co., 1872.

Alley, Robert S., ed. *James Madison on Religious Liberty*. Buffalo, NY: Prometheus Books, 1985.

Anderson, Paul R., and Max H. Fisch. *Philosophy in America from the Puritans to James, With Representative Selections*. New York: D. Appleton-Century Co., 1939.

Axelrad, Jacob. *Philip Freneau, Champion of Democracy*. Austin: University of Texas Press, 1967.

Bailyn, Bernard. *The Ideological Origins of the American Revolution*. Cambridge, MA: Harvard University Press, 1967.

Balog, Frank D. "The Scottish Enlightenment and the Liberal Political Tradition." In *Confronting the Constitution*, ed. Allan Bloom and Steven J. Kautz, 191–208. Washington, DC: AEI Press, 1990.

Baltzell, E. Digby. *Puritan Boston and Quaker Philadelphia*. New York: The Free Press, 1979.

Bancroft, George. *History of the American Revolution*. 3 vols. London: Richard Bentley, 1852.

———. *History of the Formation of the Constitution of the United States of America*. 2 vols. New York: D. Appleton and Co., 1882.

————. *History of the United States, From the Discovery of the Continent.* 6 vols. New York: D. Appleton and Co., 1886.

Banning, Lance. "James Madison and the Nationalists, 1780–1783." *William and Mary Quarterly,* 3d ser., 40 (1983): 227–55.

————. *The Sacred Fire of Liberty: James Madison and the Founding of the Federal Republic.* Ithaca, NY: Cornell University Press, 1995.

Bartley, David D. "John Witherspoon and the Right of Resistance." Ph.D. dissertation, Ball State University, 1989.

Bell, Whitfield J. "Scottish Emigration to America: A Letter of Dr. Charles Nisbet to Dr. John Witherspoon, 1784." *William and Mary Quarterly,* 3d ser., 11 (1954): 276–89.

Bellah, Robert N. *The Broken Covenant: American Civil Religion in Time of Trial.* 2d ed. Chicago: University of Chicago Press, 1992.

————. "The Revolution and the Civil Religion." In *Religion and the American Revolution,* ed. Jerald C. Brauer, 55–73. Philadelphia: Fortress Press, 1976.

Bellamy, Joseph. *The Works of Joseph Bellamy.* 2 vols. Boston: Doctrinal Tract and Book Society, 1853; reprint ed., New York: Garland, 1987.

Benson, Louis F. "What Did Witherspoon Say?" *Journal of the Presbyterian Historical Society* 12 (1927): 389–97.

Bentley, John E. *An Outline of American Philosophy.* Totawa, NJ: Littlefield, Adams and Co., 1965.

Bergman, Marvin. "Public Religion in Revolutionary America: Ezra Stiles, Devereux Jarratt, and John Witherspoon." Ph.D. dissertation, University of Chicago Divinity School, 1990.

Berkin, Carol. *A Brilliant Solution: Inventing the American Constitution.* New York: Harcourt, 2002.

Berns, Walter. *The First Amendment and the Future of American Democracy.* New York: Basic Books, 1976.

————. "Religion and the Founding Principle." In *The Moral Foundations of the American Republic,* 3d ed., ed. Robert H. Horwitz, 204–29. Charlottesville: University Press of Virginia, 1986.

Blake, John Lauris, ed. *Anecdotes of the American Revolution: Selected from Garden's Anecdotes.* Hartford, CT: C. M. Wells, 1850 [1844].

Bloom, Allan. *The Closing of the American Mind.* New York: Simon and Schuster, 1987.

Bloom, Allan, and Steven J. Kautz, eds. *Confronting the Constitution.* Washington, DC: AEI Press, 1990.

Bodo, John R. *The Protestant Clergy and Public Issues, 1812–1848.* Princeton: Princeton University Press, 1954.

Boettner, Loraine. *The Reformed Doctrine of Predestination.* Philadelphia: Presbyterian and Reformed Publishing Co., 1971 [1932].

Boller, Paul F., Jr. "George Washington and Religious Liberty." *William and Mary Quarterly,* 3d ser., 17 (1960): 486–506.

Bonomi, Patricia U. *Under the Cope of Heaven: Religion, Society, and Politics in Colonial America.* New York: Oxford·University Press, 1986.

Boorstin, Daniel J. *The Americans: The Colonial Experience.* New York: Vintage Books, 1958.

Boring, Edwin G. *A History of Experimental Psychology.* New York: Appleton-Century-Crofts, 1950.

Bork, Robert. *The Tempting of America: The Political Seduction of the Law.* New York: The Free Press, 1990.

Boudinot, Elias. *Journal, or Historical Recollections of American Events during the Revolutionary War.* Philadelphia: Frederick Bourquin, 1894.

Bowen, Catherine Drinker. *Miracle at Philadelphia: The Story of the Constitutional Convention, May to September 1787.* Boston: Little, Brown and Co., 1966.

Boyd, Julian P. *The Declaration of Independence: The Evolution of the Text.* Rev. ed. Washington, DC: Library of Congress, 1999 [1943].

Bozeman, Theodore Dwight. *Protestants in an Age of Science: The Baconian Ideal and Antebellum American Religious Thought.* Chapel Hill: University of North Carolina Press, 1977.

Brackenridge, Hugh Henry. *Modern Chivalry.* Ed. Claude M. Newlin. New York: Hafner Publishing Co., 1968.

Brackett, William Oliver. "John Witherspoon, His Scottish Ministry." Ph.D. dissertation, New College of Divinity, Edinburgh, 1948.

Brant, Irving. *The Fourth President: A Life of James Madison.* Indianapolis: Bobbs-Merrill, 1970.

Breed, W. P. *Presbyterians and the Revolution.* Decatur, MS: Issacharian Press, 1993 [1876].

Broderick, Francis L. "Pulpit, Physics, and Politics: The Curriculum of the College of New Jersey, 1746–1794." *William and Mary Quarterly,* 3d ser., 6 (1949): 58–68.

Brookhiser, Richard. *Founding Father: Rediscovering George Washington.* New York: The Free Press, 1996.

Brown, Richard D. "The Founding Fathers of 1776 and 1787: A Collective View." *William and Mary Quarterly,* 3d ser., 33 (1976): 465–80.

Bryson, Gladys. *Man and Society: The Scottish Inquiry of the 18th Century.* Princeton: Princeton University Press, 1945.

Buchanan, George. *De jure regni apud Scotos, or, A Dialogue Concerning the Due Privilege of Government.* Philadelphia: Andrew Steuart, 1766.

Buckley, Thomas E. *Church and State in Revolutionary Virginia, 1775–1787.* Charlottesville: University Press of Virginia, 1977.

Buranelli, Vincent. "Colonial Philosophy." *William and Mary Quarterly,* 3d ser., 16 (1959): 343–62.

Burnett, Edmund C., ed. *Letters of Members of the Continental Congress.* 8 vols. Washington, DC: Carnegie Institute of Washington, 1921–36.

Bushman, Richard L., ed. *The Great Awakening: Documents on the Revival of Religion, 1740–1745.* Chapel Hill: University of North Carolina Press, 1969.

Butler, Jon. *Awash in a Sea of Faith: Christianizing the American People.* Cambridge, MA: Harvard University Press, 1990.

Butterfield, Lyman Henry, ed. *John Witherspoon Comes to America: A Documentary Account Based Largely on New Materials.* Princeton: Princeton University Press, 1953.

Calhoun, David B. *Princeton Seminary.* 2 vols. Edinburgh: Banner of Truth Trust, 1994.

Calvin, John. *Institutes of the Christian Religion.* Trans. Ford Lewis Battles. Ed. John T. McNeill. 2 vols. Philadelphia: Westminster Press, 1960.

Cappon, Lester J., ed. *The Adams-Jefferson Letters.* 2 vols. Chapel Hill: University of North Carolina Press, 1959.

Carrese, Paul O. *The Cloaking of Power: Montesquieu, Blackstone, and the Judicializing of Liberalism.* Chicago: University of Chicago Press, 2002.

Cassirer, Ernst. *The Philosophy of the Enlightenment.* Princeton: Princeton University Press, 1951.

Cohen, I. Bernard. *Science and the Founding Fathers: Science in the Political Thought of Jefferson, Franklin, Adams, and Madison.* New York: W.W. Norton, 1995.

Collins, Varnum Lansing. *The Continental Congress at Princeton.* Princeton: Princeton University Library, 1908.

———. *President Witherspoon: A Biography.* 2 vols. Princeton: Princeton University Press, 1925; reprint ed., New York: Arno Press, 1969.

The Constitution of the Presbyterian Church in the United States of America: Containing the Confession of Faith, the Catechisms, the Government and Discipline, and the Directory for the Worship of God. Philadelphia: Thomas Bradford, 1789.

Copleston, Frederick. *A History of Philosophy.* 9 vols. Garden City, NY: Doubleday, 1962–77.

Corwin, Edward S. *French Policy and the American Alliance of 1778.* New York: Burt Franklin, 1970 [1916].

Cousins, Norman, ed. *"In God We Trust": The Religious Beliefs and Ideas of the American Founding Fathers.* New York: Harper and Brothers, 1958.

Cranston, Maurice William. *John Locke: A Biography.* New York: Macmillan, 1957.

Daiches, David. "John Witherspoon, James Wilson, and the Influence of Scottish Rhetoric on America." *Eighteenth-Century Life* 15 (1991): 167–80.

Daud, Charles Hendry. *The Mighty Affair: How Scotland Lost Her Parliament.* Edinburgh: Oliver and Boyd, 1972.

Davis, Derek H. *Religion and the Continental Congress, 1774–1789: Contributions to Original Intent.* New York: Oxford University Press, 2000.

Davis, Matthew L., ed. *Memoirs of Aaron Burr.* 2 vols. New York: Harper and Bros., 1836.

Detweiler, Philip F. "The Changing Reputation of the Declaration of Independence: The First Fifty Years." *William and Mary Quarterly,* 3d ser., 19 (1962): 557–74.

———. "Congressional Debate on Slavery and the Declaration of Independence." *American Historical Review* 63 (1958): 598–616.

Diamond, Martin. *The Founding of the Democratic Republic.* Itasca, IL: F. E. Peacock, 1981.

Diamond, Peter J. "Witherspoon, William Smith, and the Scottish Philosophy in Revolutionary America." In *Scotland and America in the Age of the Enlightenment,* ed. Richard B. Sher and Jeffrey R. Smitten, 115–32. Princeton: Princeton University Press, 1990.

Dienstag, Joshua F. "Serving God and Mammon: The Lockean Sympathy in Early American Political Thought." *American Political Science Review* 90 (1996): 497–511.

Diggins, John Patrick. *The Lost Soul of American Politics: Virtue, Self-Interest, and the Foundation of Liberalism.* New York: Basic Books, 1984.

Dodds, Harold W. *John Witherspoon, 1723–1794.* Princeton: Princeton University Press, 1944.

Drakeman, Donald L. "Religion and the Republic: James Madison and the First Amendment." *Journal of Church and State* 25, no. 3 (Autumn 1983): 427–45.

Dreisbach, Daniel L. *Real Threat and Mere Shadow: Religious Liberty and the First Amendment.* Westchester, IL: Crossway Books, 1987.

———. "'Sowing Useful Truths and Principles': The Danbury Baptists, Thomas Jefferson, and the 'Wall of Separation.'" *Journal of Church and State* 39, no. 3 (Summer 1997): 455–501.

———. *Thomas Jefferson and the Wall of Separation between Church and State.* New York: New York University Press, 2002.

Dreisbach, Daniel L., ed. *Religion and Politics in the Early Republic: Jasper Adams and the Church-State Debate.* Lexington: University Press of Kentucky, 1996.

Dreisbach, Daniel L., Mark D. Hall, and Jeffry H. Morrison, eds. *The Founders on God and Government.* Lanham, MD: Rowman and Littlefield, 2004.

East, Robert A., and Jacob Judd, eds. *The Loyalist Americans: A Focus on Greater New York.* Tarrytown, NY: Sleepy Hollow Restorations, 1975.

Eckenrode, H. J., ed. *Separation of Church and State in Virginia: A Study in the Development of the Revolution.* Richmond: Virginia State Library, 1910.

Edwards, Jonathan. *The Works of Jonathan Edwards.* Ed. Edward Hickman. 2 vols. Edinburgh: Banner of Truth Trust, 1834; reprint ed., 1974.

Eidsmoe, John. *Christianity and the Constitution: The Faith of Our Founding Fathers.* Grand Rapids, MI: Baker Book House, 1987.

Elkins, Stanley M., and Eric L. McKitrick. *The Age of Federalism.* New York: Oxford University Press, 1993.

Elliot, Jonathan, ed. *The Debates in the Several State Conventions on the Adoption of the Federal Constitution*. 5 vols. Philadelphia: J. B. Lippincott Co., 1891.

Ellis, Joseph J. *American Sphinx: The Character of Thomas Jefferson*. New York: Alfred A. Knopf, 1997.

―――. *Founding Brothers: The Revolutionary Generation*. New York: Alfred A. Knopf, 2000.

Farrand, Max, ed. *The Records of the Federal Convention of 1787*. Rev. ed. 4 vols. New Haven: Yale University Press, 1966.

Fechner, Roger J. "The Godly and Virtuous Commonwealth of John Witherspoon." In *Ideas in America's Cultures from Republic to Mass Society*, ed. Hamilton Cravens, 7–25. Ames: Iowa State University Press, 1982.

―――. "The Moral Philosophy of John Witherspoon and the Scottish-American Enlightenment." Ph.D. dissertation, University of Iowa, 1974.

Ferris, Robert E., ed. *Signers of the Constitution*. Washington, DC: United States Department of the Interior, 1976.

Figgis, John Neville. *The Divine Right of Kings*. 2d ed. Cambridge: Cambridge University Press, 1934.

―――. "Political Thought in the Sixteenth Century." In *The Cambridge Modern History: The Wars of Religion*. New York: Macmillan, 1934.

Finke, Roger, and Rodney Stark. *The Churching of America, 1776–1990: Winners and Losers in Our Religious Economy*. New Brunswick, NJ: Rutgers University Press, 1992.

Fischer, David Hackett. *Paul Revere's Ride*. New York: Oxford University Press, 1994.

Fithian, Philip Vickers. *Journal & Letters of Philip Vickers Fithian, 1773–1774: A Plantation Tutor of the Old Dominion*. Ed. Hunter Dickinson Farish. Williamsburg, VA: Colonial Williamsburg, 1943.

Fleming, Donald, and Bernard Bailyn, eds. *Perspectives in American History* No. 4. Boston: Little, Brown, 1970.

Flower, Elizabeth and Murray G. Murphey. *A History of Philosophy in America*. 2 vols. New York: Putnam's Sons, 1977.

Foote, William Henry, ed. *Sketches of Virginia: Historical and Biographical*. Philadelphia: William S. Martien, 1850; reprint ed., Richmond: John Knox Press, 1966.

Foster, Herbert D. "International Calvinism through Locke and the Revolution of 1688." *American Historical Review* 32 (April 1927): 475–99.

Franklin, Benjamin. *Benjamin Franklin's Autobiographical Writings*. Ed. Carl Van Doren. New York: Viking Press, 1945.

―――. *The Papers of Benjamin Franklin*. Ed. Leonard W. Labaree, Whitfield J. Bell, Jr., et al. 33 vols. to date. New Haven: Yale University Press, 1959–.

Franklin, Julian H., ed. *Constitutionalism and Resistance in the Sixteenth Century: Three Treatises by Hotman, Beza, and Mornay*. New York: Pegasus, 1969.

Freeman, Michael. *Edmund Burke and the Critique of Political Radicalism.* Chicago: University of Chicago Press, 1980.

Gaustad, Edwin Scott, and Philip L. Barlow. *New Historical Atlas of Religion in America.* New York: Oxford University Press, 2001.

Gay, Peter. *The Enlightenment: An Interpretation, the Rise of Modern Paganism.* New York: Random House, 1966.

Geissler, Suzanne. *Jonathan Edwards to Aaron Burr, Jr.: From the Great Awakening to Democratic Politics.* New York: E. Mellen Press, 1981.

Gibbon, Edward. *The History of the Decline and Fall of the Roman Empire.* 3 vols. New York: Modern Library, n.d.

Grave, Selwyn A. *The Scottish Philosophy of Common Sense.* Oxford: Oxford University Press, 1966.

Green, Ashbel. *Life of the Revd. John Witherspoon, D.D., LL.D.* Ed. Henry Lyttleton Savage. Princeton: Princeton University Press, 1973.

Griffin, Keith L. *Revolution and Religion: American Revolutionary War and the Reformed Clergy.* New York: Paragon House, 1994.

Hall, Mark David. *The Political and Legal Philosophy of James Wilson, 1742–1798.* Columbia: University of Missouri Press, 1997.

Hamilton, Alexander. *The Papers of Alexander Hamilton.* Ed. Harold C. Syrett. 27 vols. New York: Columbia University Press, 1961–87.

Hamilton, Alexander, James Madison, and John Jay. *The Federalist Papers.* Ed. Clinton Rossiter. New York: New American Library, 1961.

Hamilton, John C. *Alexander Hamilton: Portrait in Paradox.* New York: Harper and Row, 1959.

Hamilton, Marci A. "The Calvinist Paradox of Distrust and Hope at the Constitutional Convention." In *Christian Perspectives on Legal Thought,* ed. Michael W. McConnell, Robert F. Cochran, Jr., and Angela C. Carmella, 293–306. New Haven: Yale University Press, 2001.

———. "The Reverend John Witherspoon and the Constitutional Convention." In *Law and Religion: A Critical Anthology,* ed. Stephen M. Feldman, 54–66. New York: New York University Press, 2000.

Hanzsche, William Thomson. *Forgotten Founding Fathers of the American Church and State.* Boston: Christopher Publishing House, 1954.

Hartz, Louis. *The Liberal Tradition in America.* New York: Harcourt, Brace and World, 1955.

Hazelton, John H. *The Declaration of Independence: Its History.* New York: Da Capo Press, 1970 [1906].

Heimert, Alan. *Religion and the American Mind.* Cambridge, MA: Harvard University Press, 1966.

Heimert, Alan, and Andrew Delbanco, eds. *The Puritans in America: A Narrative Anthology.* Cambridge, MA: Harvard University Press, 1985.

Henderson, H. James. "The Structure of Politics in the Continental Congress." In *Essays on the American Revolution*, ed. Stephen G. Kurtz and James H. Hutson, 157–96. Chapel Hill: University of North Carolina Press, 1973.

Herman, Arthur. *How the Scots Invented the Modern World.* New York: Crown Publishers, 2001.

Hindle, Brooke. "Witherspoon, Rittenhouse, and Sir Isaac Newton." *William and Mary Quarterly*, 3d ser., 15 (1958): 365–72.

Hobbes, Thomas. *Leviathan.* Ed. Michael Oakeshott. New York: Macmillan, 1962.

Hofstadter, Richard. "The Founding Fathers: An Age of Realism." In *The Moral Foundations of the American Republic*, 3d ed., ed. Robert H. Horwitz, 62–74. Charlottesville: University Press of Virginia, 1986.

Hofstadter, Richard, and Wilson Smith, eds. *American Higher Education: A Documentary History.* 2 vols. Chicago: University of Chicago Press, 1961.

Hood, Fred J. *Reformed America: The Middle and Southern States, 1783–1837.* University, AL: University of Alabama Press, 1980.

Howe, Daniel Walker. *Making the American Self: Jonathan Edwards to Abraham Lincoln.* Cambridge, MA: Harvard University Press, 1997.

Howe, Mark DeWolfe. *The Garden and the Wilderness: Religion and Government in American Constitutional History.* Chicago: University of Chicago Press, 1965.

Hudson, Winthrop S. "Democratic Freedom and Religious Faith in the Reformed Tradition." *Church History* 18 (1949): 153–71.

———. "John Locke: Heir of Puritan Political Theorists." In *Calvinism and the Political Order*, ed. George L. Hunt and John T. McNeill, 108–29. Philadelphia: Westminster Press, 1965.

Hume, David. *David Hume's Political Essays.* Ed. Charles W. Hendel. New York: Liberal Arts Press, 1953.

———. *Dialogues Concerning Natural Religion.* Ed. Norman Kemp Smith. Oxford: Clarendon Press, 1935.

Humphrey, Edward Frank. *Nationalism and Religion in America, 1774–1789.* New York: Russell and Russell, 1965.

Hunt, Gaillard. *James Madison and Religious Liberty.* Washington, DC: U.S. Government Printing Office, 1902.

Hunt, George L., and John T. McNeill, eds. *Calvinism and the Political Order.* Philadelphia: Westminster Press, 1965.

Hunter, James Davison, and Os Guinness, eds. *Articles of Faith, Articles of Peace: The Religious Liberty Clauses and the American Public Philosophy.* Washington, DC: The Brookings Institution, 1990.

Hutcheson, Francis. *A System of Moral Philosophy.* New York: A. M. Kelley, 1968.

Hutson, James H. *Forgotten Features of the Founding: The Recovery of Religious Themes in the Early American Republic.* Lanham, MD: Lexington Books, 2003.

Hutson, James H., ed. *Religion and the Founding of the American Republic.* Washington, DC: Library of Congress, 1998.

————, ed. *Religion and the New Republic: Faith in the Founding of America.* Lanham, MD: Rowman and Littlefield, 2000.

Huyler, Jerome. *Locke in America: The Moral Philosophy of the Founding Era.* Lawrence: University Press of Kansas, 1995.

Hyneman, Charles S., and Donald S. Lutz, eds. *American Political Writing during the Founding Era, 1760–1805.* 2 vols. Indianapolis: Liberty Press, 1983.

Index, Journals of the Continental Congress, 1774–1789. Ed. Kenneth E. Harris and Steven D. Tilley. Washington, DC: General Services Administration, National Archives and Records Service, 1976.

Index, The Papers of the Continental Congress, 1774–1789. Compiled by John P. Butler. 5 vols. Washington, DC: U.S. Government Printing Office, 1978.

James, Charles Fenton. *Documentary History of the Struggle for Religious Liberty in Virginia.* Lynchburg, VA: J. P. Bell Co., 1900.

Jefferson, Thomas. *Jefferson's Memorandum Books: Accounts, with Legal Records and Miscellany, 1767–1826.* Ed. James A. Bear, Jr., and Lucia C. Stanton. 2 vols. Princeton: Princeton University Press, 1997.

————. *The Papers of Thomas Jefferson.* Ed. Julian P. Boyd et al. 30 vols. to date. Princeton: Princeton University Press, 1950–.

————. *The Portable Thomas Jefferson.* Ed. Merrill D. Peterson. New York: Penguin Books, 1975.

————. *Thomas Jefferson: Writings.* Ed. Merrill D. Peterson. New York: Library of America, 1984.

————. *The Works of Thomas Jefferson.* Ed. Paul Leicester Ford. 12 vols. New York: G. P. Putnam's Sons, 1904–5.

————. *The Writings of Thomas Jefferson.* Ed. Andrew A. Lipscomb and Albert Ellery Bergh et al. 20 vols. Washington, DC: Thomas Jefferson Memorial Association of the United States, 1903–4.

Jensen, Merrill et al., eds. *The Documentary History of the Ratification of the Constitution.* 18 vols. Madison: State Historical Society of Wisconsin, 1976–95.

Johnson, Paul. *A History of the American People.* New York: HarperCollins, 1997.

Jones, Michael Wynn. *The Cartoon History of the American Revolution.* New York: G. P. Putnam's Sons, 1975.

Jones, Olin McKendra. *Empiricism and Intuitionism in Reid's Common Sense Philosophy.* Princeton: Princeton University Press, 1927.

Journal of the Proceedings of the Convention of New-Jersey. Burlington, NJ: Isaac Collins, 1776.

Journals of the Continental Congress, 1774–1789. Ed. Worthington Chauncey Ford et al. 34 vols. Washington, DC: U.S. Government Printing Office, 1904–37.

Kant, Immanuel. *Immanuel Kant's Critique of Pure Reason.* Trans. Norman Kemp Smith. New York: St. Martin's Press, 1965.

————. *Prolegomena To Any Future Metaphysics That Can Qualify as a Science.* La Salle, IL: Open Court, 1902.

Kemeny, P. C. *Princeton in the Nation's Service: Religious Ideals and Educational Practice, 1868–1928.* New York: Oxford University Press, 1998.

Kendall, Willmoore, and George W. Carey. *The Basic Symbols of the American Political Tradition.* Rev. ed. Washington, DC: Catholic University Press: 1995 [1970].

Kennedy, Roger G. *Burr, Hamilton, and Jefferson.* New York: Oxford University Press, 2000.

Ketcham, Ralph L. *James Madison: A Biography.* New York: Macmillan, 1971.

———. "James Madison and Religion—A New Hypothesis." In *James Madison on Religious Liberty,* ed. Robert S. Alley, 175–96. Buffalo, NY: Prometheus Books, 1985.

———. "James Madison at Princeton." *Princeton University Library Chronicle* 28 (Autumn 1966): 24–54.

Koch, Adrienne, and William Peden, eds. *The Life and Selected Writings of Thomas Jefferson.* New York: Modern Library, 1993.

Koch, Gustav A. *Republican Religion: The American Revolution and the Cult of Reason.* New York: Henry Holt and Co., 1948.

Kramer, Leonard J. "Muskets in the Pulpit, 1776–1783." *Journal of the Presbyterian Historical Society* 32 (1954): 37–51.

Kuehn, Manfred. *Scottish Common Sense in Germany, 1768–1800.* Kingston, ON: McGill-Queen's University Press, 1987.

Kuehne, Dale S. *Massachusetts Congregational Political Thought, 1760–1790.* Columbia: University of Missouri Press, 1996.

Kuklick, Bruce. *Churchmen and Philosophers: From Jonathan Edwards to John Dewey.* New Haven: Yale University Press, 1985.

Lambert, Frank. *The Founding Fathers and the Place of Religion in America.* Princeton: Princeton University Press, 2003.

Lancaster, Bruce. *The American Heritage History of the American Revolution.* New York: American Heritage, 1984.

———. *From Lexington to Liberty: The Story of the American Revolution.* Garden City, NY: Doubleday and Co., 1955.

Landsman, Ned C. "Presbyterians and Provincial Society: The Evangelical Enlightenment in the West of Scotland, 1740–1775." *Eighteenth-Century Life* 15 (1991): 194–209.

———. *Scotland and Its First American Colony, 1683–1765.* Princeton: Princeton University Press, 1985.

Laski, Harold J., ed. *A Defence of Liberty Against Tyrants: A Translation of the Vindiciae contra Tyrannos by Junius Brutus.* London: G. Bell and Sons, 1924.

Leavelle, Arnaud Bruce. "James Wilson and the Relation of the Scottish Metaphysics to American Political Thought." *Political Science Quarterly* 57 (1942): 394–410.

Lee, Richard H., ed. *Memoir of the Life of Richard Henry Lee.* 2 vols. Philadelphia: H. C. Carey and I. Lea, 1825.

Lincoln, Abraham. *The Collected Works of Abraham Lincoln.* Ed. Roy P. Basler. 9 vols. New Brunswick, NJ: Rutgers University Press, 1953–55.

Lindsay, Thomas. "James Madison on Religion and Politics." *American Political Science Review* 85 (1991): 1321–37.

Lipset, Seymour Martin. "American Exceptionalism Reaffirmed." In *Is America Different?: A New Look at American Exceptionalism*, ed. Byron E. Shafer, 1–45. Oxford: Clarendon Press, 1991.

Locke, John. *An Essay Concerning Human Understanding.* Ed. Peter H. Nidditch. Oxford: Clarendon Press, 1975.

———. *Two Treatises of Government.* Ed. Thomas I. Cook. New York: Hafner Publishing Co., 1947.

———. *Two Treatises of Government: A Critical Edition.* Rev. ed. Ed. Peter Laslett. New York: Mentor, 1965.

Lossing, Benson John. *Biographical Sketches of the Signers of the Declaration of American Independence.* New York: George F. Cooledge and Brother, 1848.

Love, Mary. "John Witherspoon in Scotland: An Eighteenth Century Evangelical." *Princeton Theological Review* 2 (1913): 461–87.

Lundin, Charles Leonard. *Cockpit of the Revolution: The War for Independence in New Jersey.* Princeton: Princeton University Press, 1940.

Lutz, Donald S. *The Origins of American Constitutionalism.* Baton Rouge: Louisiana State University Press, 1988.

———. *A Preface to American Political Theory.* Lawrence: University Press of Kansas, 1992.

Maclean, John. *History of the College of New Jersey, From Its Origin in 1746 to the Commencement of 1854.* 2 vols. Philadelphia: J. B. Lippincott, 1877.

Madison, James. *The Complete Madison: His Basic Writings.* Ed. Saul K. Padover. New York: Harper and Brothers, 1953.

———. "James Madison's Autobiography." Ed. Douglass Adair. *William and Mary Quarterly*, 3d ser., 2 (April 1945): 191–209.

———. *James Madison: Writings.* Ed. Jack N. Rakove. New York: Library of America, 1999.

———. "Madison's 'Detatched [*sic*] Memoranda.'" Ed. Elizabeth Fleet. *William and Mary Quarterly*, 3d ser., vol. 3, no. 4 (October 1946): 534–68.

———. *Notes of Debates in the Federal Convention of 1787.* Ed. Adrienne Koch. New York: W. W. Norton, 1987 [1966].

———. *The Papers of James Madison.* Ed. William T. Hutchinson et al. 17 vols. Chicago and Charlottesville: University of Chicago Press and University Press of Virginia, 1962–91.

———. *The Writings of James Madison.* Ed. Gaillard Hunt. 9 vols. New York: G. P. Putnam's Sons, 1900–1910.

Maier, Pauline. *American Scripture: Making the Declaration of Independence.* New York: Knopf, 1997.

Malone, Dumas, ed. *Dictionary of American Biography.* 22 vols. New York: Charles Scribner's Sons, 1928–58.

Marty, Martin. *Religion, Awakening, and Revolution.* Wilmington, NC: Consortium, 1977.

May, Henry F. *The Enlightenment in America.* New York: Oxford University Press, 1976.

Mayer, Frederick. *A History of American Thought: An Introduction.* Dubuque, IA: Wm. C. Brown Co., 1951.

McAllister, James L. "Francis Alison and John Witherspoon: Political Philosophers and Revolutionaries." *Journal of Presbyterian History* 54 (Spring 1976): 33–60.

———. "John Witherspoon: Academic Advocate for American Freedom." In *A Miscellany of American Christianity,* ed. Stuart C. Henry, 183–224. Durham, NC: Duke University Press, 1963.

McCormick, Richard P. *Experiment in Independence: New Jersey in the Critical Period, 1781–1789.* New Brunswick, NJ: Rutgers University Press, 1950.

McCosh, James. *John Witherspoon and His Times.* Philadelphia: Presbyterian Board of Publication, 1890.

———. *The Scottish Philosophy.* Hildesheim: Georg Olms, 1966 [1875].

McCullough, David. *John Adams.* New York: Simon and Schuster, 2001.

McIlwain, Charles H., ed. *The Political Works of James I.* Cambridge, MA: Harvard University Press, 1918.

McLachlan, James et al., eds. *Princetonians: A Biographical Dictionary.* 5 vols. Princeton: Princeton University Press, 1976–91.

McLoughlin, William G. "'Enthusiasm for Liberty': The Great Awakening as the Key to the Revolution." In *Preachers and Politicians: Two Essays on the Origins of the American Revolution,* ed. McLoughlin, 47–73. Worcester, MA: American Antiquarian Society, 1977.

———. "The Role of Religion in the Revolution: Liberty of Conscience and Cultural Cohesion in the New Nation." In *Essays on the American Revolution,* ed. Stephen G. Kurtz and James H. Hutson, 197–255. Chapel Hill: University of North Carolina Press, 1973.

McMichael, George, ed. *Anthology of American Literature.* 2 vols. New York: Macmillan, 1974.

McWilliams, Wilson Carey. "The Bible in the American Political Tradition." In *Religion and Politics,* ed. Myron J. Aronoff, 11–45. New Brunswick, NJ: Transaction Books, 1984.

Mead, Sidney E. "Neither Church nor State: Reflections on James Madison's 'Line of Separation.'" *Journal of Church and State* 10 (1968): 349–64.

Mecklin, Joseph M. *The Story of American Dissent.* New York: Harcourt, Brace and Co., 1934.

Meyers, Marvin, ed. *The Mind of the Founder: Sources of the Political Thought of James Madison.* Hanover, NH: University Press of New England, 1982.

Miller, Perry. *Nature's Nation*. Cambridge, MA: The Belknap Press of Harvard University Press, 1967.

Miller, Thomas P. "Witherspoon, Blair and the Rhetoric of Civic Humanism." In *Scotland and America in the Age of the Enlightenment*, ed. Richard B. Sher and Jeffrey R. Smitten, 100–114. Princeton: Princeton University Press, 1990.

Minutes of the Convention of the State of New-Jersey, Holden at Trenton the 11th Day of December 1787. Trenton, NJ: n.p., 1788.

Mitchell, Broadus. *Alexander Hamilton: Youth to Maturity, 1755–1788*. New York: Macmillan, 1957.

Monaghan, Henry Paul. "Stare Decisis and Constitutional Adjudication." *Columbia Law Review* 88 (1988): 723–73.

Montague, Mary Louise. *John Witherspoon, Signer of the Declaration of Independence; George Washington's Closest Friend and Sponsor*. Washington, DC: McQueen, 1932.

Montesquieu, Baron de. *The Spirit of the Laws*. Trans. Thomas Nugent. 2 vols. New York: Hafner, 1949.

Morgan, Edmund S. *The Birth of the Republic, 1763–89*. 3d ed. Chicago: University of Chicago Press, 1992.

Morrill, John, ed. *The Scottish National Covenant in Its British Context, 1638–51*. Edinburgh: Edinburgh University Press, 1990.

Morrison, Jeffry H. "John Witherspoon and 'The Public Interest of Religion.'" *Journal of Church and State* 41 (1999): 551–73.

Muñoz, Vincent Phillip. "James Madison's Principle of Religious Liberty." *American Political Science Review* 97 (2003): 17–32.

Murray, Iain H. *Revival and Revivalism: The Making and Marring of American Evangelicalism, 1750–1858*. Edinburgh: Banner of Truth Trust, 1994.

Murrin, John M. "The Great Inversion, or Court versus Country: A Comparison of the Revolution Settlements in England (1688–1721) and America (1776–1816)." In *Three British Revolutions: 1641, 1688, 1776*, ed. J. G. A. Pocock, 368–453. Princeton: Princeton University Press, 1980.

———. "Religion and Politics in America from the First Settlements to the Civil War." In *Religion and American Politics: From the Colonial Period to the 1980s*, ed. Mark A. Noll, 19–43. New York: Oxford University Press, 1990.

Newlin, Claude M. *Philosophy and Religion in Colonial America*. New York: Philosophical Library, 1962.

Nichols, James Hastings. *Democracy and Churches*. Philadelphia: Westminster Press, 1951.

———. "John Witherspoon on Church and State." In *Calvinism and the Political Order*, ed. George L. Hunt and John T. McNeill, 130–39. Philadelphia: Westminster Press, 1965.

Noll, Mark A. *Christians in the American Revolution*. New York: Christian University Press, 1977.

————. "Evangelicals in the American Founding and Evangelical Political Mobilization Today." In *Religion and the New Republic: Faith in the Founding of America*, ed. James H. Hutson, 137–58. Lanham, MD: Rowman and Littlefield, 2000.

————. *The Old Religion in a New World: The History of North American Christianity*. Grand Rapids, MI: Eerdmans, 2002.

————. *Princeton and the Republic, 1768–1822: The Search for a Christian Enlightenment in the Era of Samuel Stanhope Smith*. Princeton: Princeton University Press, 1989.

Noll, Mark A., ed. *Religion and American Politics: From the Colonial Period to the 1980s*. New York: Oxford University Press, 1990.

Noll, Mark A., Nathan O. Hatch, and George M. Marsden. *The Search for Christian America*. Westchester, IL: Crossway Books, 1983.

Novak, Michael. *On Two Wings: Humble Faith and Common Sense at the American Founding*. San Francisco: Encounter Books, 2002.

Olasky, Marvin. *The American Leadership Tradition: Moral Vision from Washington to Clinton*. New York: The Free Press, 1999.

————. *Fighting for Liberty and Virtue: Political and Cultural Wars in Eighteenth-Century America*. Washington, DC: Regnery, 1996.

Packer, J. I. *A Quest for Godliness: The Puritan Vision of the Christian Life*. Wheaton, IL: Crossway Books, 1994.

Paine, Thomas. *The Complete Writings of Thomas Paine*. Ed. Philip S. Foner. 2 vols. New York: The Citadel Press, 1945.

Paltsits, Victor Hugo, ed. *Washington's Farewell Address*. New York: The New York Public Library, 1935.

Pangle, Lorraine Smith, and Thomas L. Pangle. *The Learning of Liberty: The Educational Ideas of the American Founders*. Lawrence: University Press of Kansas, 1993.

Pangle, Thomas L., "The Philosophic Understanding of Human Nature Informing the Constitution." In *Confronting the Constitution*, ed. Allan Bloom and Steven J. Kautz, 9. Washington DC: AEI Press, 1990.

————. *The Spirit of Modern Republicanism: The Moral Vision of the American Founders and the Philosophy of Locke*. Chicago: University of Chicago Press, 1988.

Parrington, Vernon L. *The Colonial Mind, 1620–1800*. New York: Harcourt, Brace, 1954.

Paterson, William. *Glimpses of Colonial Society and the Life at Princeton College, 1766–1773, by One of the Class of 1763*. Ed. W. Jay Mills. Philadelphia: J. B. Lippincott, 1903.

Peterson, Merrill D., ed. *James Madison: A Biography in His Own Words*. New York: Harper and Row, 1974.

Peterson, Richard J. "Scottish Common Sense in America, 1768–1850: An Evaluation of Its Influence." Ph.D. dissertation, American University, 1963.

Pfeffer, Leo. *Church, State, and Freedom*. Boston: Beacon Press, 1967.

Plato. *The Republic of Plato.* Trans. Francis MacDonald Cornford. London: Oxford University Press, 1941.

Plutarch. *The Lives of the Noble Grecians and Romans.* Trans. John Dryden. New York: Modern Library, n.d.

Pocock, J. G. A. *The Machiavellian Moment.* Princeton: Princeton University Press, 1975.

Powell, J. H., ed. "Speech of John Dickinson Opposing the Declaration of Independence, 1 July, 1776." *The Pennsylvania Magazine of History and Biography* 65 (1941): 458–81.

Powell, H. Jefferson. "The Original Understanding of Original Intent." *Harvard Law Review* 98 (1985): 885–948.

Presbyterians and the American Revolution: A Documentary Account. Journal of Presbyterian History 52, no. 4, special edition (Winter 1974).

Rahe, Paul A. *Republics Ancient and Modern: Classical Republicanism and the American Revolution.* Chapel Hill: University of North Carolina Press, 1992.

Ramsay, David. *The History of the American Revolution.* Ed. Lester H. Cohen. 2 vols. Indianapolis: Liberty Classics, 1990.

Records of the Presbyterian Church in the United States of America, Embracing the Minutes of the General Presbytery and General Synod, 1706–1788. Philadelphia: Presbyterian Board of Publication, 1904.

Reid, Thomas. *Philosophical Works.* Ed. Sir William Hamilton. 2 vols. Hildesheim: Georg Olms, 1967 [1895].

Rich, George. "John Witherspoon: His Scottish Intellectual Background." Ph.D. dissertation, Syracuse University, 1964.

Riley, I. Woodbridge. *American Philosophy: The Early Schools.* New York: Russell and Russell, 1958 [1907].

Robbins, Caroline. *The Eighteenth Century Commonwealthman: Studies in the Transmission, Development and Circumstance of English Liberal Thought from the Restoration of Charles II until the War with the Thirteen Colonies.* Cambridge, MA: Harvard University Press, 1959.

———. "'When It Is That Colonies May Turn Independent': An Analysis of the Environment and Politics of Francis Hutcheson (1694–1746)." *William and Mary Quarterly,* 3d ser., 11 (1954): 214–51.

Robinson, Daniel N. "The Scottish Enlightenment and Its Mixed Bequest." *Journal of the History of the Behavioral Sciences* 22 (1986): 171–77.

Robinson, Daniel Sommer. *The Story of Scottish Philosophy.* New York: Exposition Press, 1961.

Robinson, Stewart MacMaster. "Notes on the Witherspoon Pamphlets." *Princeton University Library Chronicle* 27 (1965): 53–59.

Rossiter, Clinton. *1787: The Grand Convention.* New York: Macmillan, 1966.

———. *Seedtime of the Republic—The Origin of the American Tradition of Political Liberty.* New York: Harcourt, Brace and Co., 1953.

Rousseau, Jean-Jacques. *Basic Political Writings: Jean-Jacques Rousseau.* Trans. and ed. Donald A. Cress. Indianapolis: Hackett Publishing Co., 1987.

———. *Political Writings.* Trans. and ed. Frederick Watkins. New York: Thomas Nelson and Sons, 1953.

Rush, Benjamin. *The Autobiography of Benjamin Rush: His "Travels Through Life," Together with His Commonplace Book for 1789–1813.* Ed. George W. Corner. Princeton: Princeton University Press, 1948.

———. *Letters of Benjamin Rush.* Ed. L. H. Butterfield. 2 vols. Princeton: Princeton University Press, 1951.

Rutherford, Samuel. *Lex, Rex, or, The Law and the Prince.* London: John Field, 1644; reprint ed., Harrisonburg, VA: Sprinkle Publications, 1982.

Rutland, Robert Allen. *The Birth of the Bill of Rights, 1776–1791.* Chapel Hill: University of North Carolina Press, 1955.

———. *James Madison: The Founding Father.* New York: Macmillan, 1987.

Safire, William, ed. *Lend Me Your Ears: Great Speeches in History.* New York: W. W. Norton and Co., 1992.

Sandeen, Ernest R., and Frederick Hale. *American Religion and Philosophy: A Guide to Information Sources.* Detroit: Gale, 1978.

Sandoz, Ellis. "Foundations of American Liberty and Rule of Law." *Presidential Studies Quarterly* 24 (1994): 605–17.

———. *A Government of Laws: Political Theory, Religion, and the American Founding.* Baton Rouge: Louisiana State University Press, 1990.

Sandoz, Ellis, ed. *Political Sermons of the American Founding Era, 1730–1805.* Indianapolis: Liberty Press, 1991.

Schachner, Nathan. "Alexander Hamilton Viewed by His Friends: The Narratives of Robert Troup and Hercules Mulligan." *William and Mary Quarterly,* 3d ser., 4 (1947): 203–25.

Schaedler, Louis C. "James Madison, Literary Craftsman." *William and Mary Quarterly,* 3d ser., 3 (1946): 515–33.

Schaff, Philip, ed. *The Creeds of Christendom.* 6th ed. 3 vols. Grand Rapids, MI: Baker Book House, 1990.

Schama, Simon. *Citizens: A Chronicle of the French Revolution.* New York: Alfred A. Knopf, 1989.

Schneider, Herbert W. *A History of American Philosophy.* New York: Columbia University Press, 1946.

Schultz, Roger. "Covenanting in America: The Political Theology of John Witherspoon." Master's Thesis, Trinity Evangelical Divinity School, Deerfield, Illinois, 1985.

Schutz, John A., and Douglass Adair, eds. *The Spur of Fame: Dialogues of John Adams and Benjamin Rush, 1805–1813.* San Marino, CA: Huntington Library, 1966.

Schwartz, Bernard. *The Roots of the Bill of Rights.* 5 vols. New York: Chelsea House, 1980.

Secret Journals of the Acts and Proceedings of Congress: From the First Meeting Thereof to the Dissolution of the Confederation. 4 vols. Boston: Thomas B. Wait, 1820–21.

Shain, Barry Alan. *The Myth of American Individualism: The Protestant Origins of American Political Thought.* Princeton: Princeton University Press, 1994.

Shalhope, Robert E. "Toward a Republican Synthesis: The Emergence of an Understanding of Republicanism in American Historiography." *William and Mary Quarterly*, 3d ser., 29 (1972): 49–80.

Sheldon, Garrett Ward. *The Political Philosophy of James Madison.* Baltimore: Johns Hopkins University Press, 2001.

———. *The Political Philosophy of Thomas Jefferson.* Baltimore: Johns Hopkins University Press, 1991.

Shepard, Robert Stephen. *God's People in the Ivory Tower: Religion in the Early American University.* Brooklyn, NY: Carlson, 1991.

Sher, Richard B., and Jeffrey R. Smitten, eds. *Scotland and America in the Age of the Enlightenment.* Princeton: Princeton University Press, 1990.

Shuffelton, Frank, ed. *The American Enlightenment.* Rochester, NY: University of Rochester Press, 1993.

Skinner, Quentin. *The Foundations of Modern Political Thought.* Cambridge: Cambridge University Press, 1978.

Sloan, Douglas. *The Scottish Enlightenment and the American College Ideal.* New York: Teachers College Press, Columbia University, 1971.

Smith, Goldwin. *A History of England.* 2d ed. New York: Charles Scribner's Sons, 1957 [1949].

Smith, Page. *John Adams.* 2 vols. Garden City, NY: Doubleday, 1962.

———. *A New Age Now Begins.* 2 vols. New York: McGraw-Hill, 1976.

Smith, Paul H. et al., eds. *Letters of Delegates to Congress, 1774–1789.* 25 vols. Washington, DC: Library of Congress, 1976–98.

Smith, Samuel Stanhope. "John Witherspoon, D.D." In *Annals of the American Pulpit*, ed. William B. Sprague. New York: Robert Carter and Brothers, 1869; reprint ed., New York: Arno Press, 1969.

Smith, William. *Historical Memoirs of William Smith.* Ed. William H. W. Sabine. 2 vols. New York: Colburg and Tegg, 1956–58.

Smoot, John Murray. "Presbyterianism in Revolutionary Pennsylvania: Constitutionalism and Freedom." Ph.D. dissertation, St. Mary's Seminary and University, 1982.

Smylie, James H. "Madison and Witherspoon: Theological Roots of American Political Thought." *Princeton University Library Chronicle* 22 (Spring 1961): 118–32.

Sowerby, E. Millicent, ed. *Catalogue of the Library of Thomas Jefferson.* 5 vols. Charlottesville: University Press of Virginia, 1983.

Spalding, Matthew, and Patrick J. Garrity. *A Sacred Union of Citizens: George Washington's Farewell Address and the American Character.* Lanham, MD: Rowman and Littlefield, 1996.

Spinoza, Benedict de. *A Theologico-Political Treatise and A Political Treatise* (*Tractatus Theologico-Politicus*). Trans. R. H. M. Elwes. New York: Dover Publications, 1951.

Sprague, William B., ed. *Annals of the American Pulpit.* 9 vols. New York: Robert Carter and Brothers, 1857–69.

Stephen, Leslie et al., eds. *Dictionary of National Biography.* 22 vols. London: Oxford University Press, 1921–22.

Stevens, Ellis. *Sources of the Constitution of the United States Considered in Relation to Colonial and English History.* New York: MacMillan and Co., 1929.

St. John, J. A., ed. *The Prose Works of John Milton.* 4 vols. London: George Bell and Sons, 1889.

Stohlman, Martha Lou Lemmon. *John Witherspoon: Parson, Politician, Patriot.* Philadelphia: Westminster Press, 1976.

Storing, Herbert J., ed. *The Complete Anti-Federalist.* 7 vols. Chicago: University of Chicago Press, 1981.

Stourzh, Gerald. *Alexander Hamilton and the Idea of Republican Government.* Stanford, CA: Stanford University Press, 1970.

Stout, Harry. "Rhetoric and Reality in the Early Republic: The Case of the Federalist Clergy." In *Religion and American Politics: From the Colonial Period to the 1980s,* ed. Mark A. Noll, 62–76. New York: Oxford University Press, 1990.

Sweet, William Warren. *Religion in the Development of American Culture, 1765–1840.* Gloucester, MA: Peter Smith, 1963 [1952].

Swiggett, Howard. *The Forgotten Leaders of the Revolution.* Garden City, NY: Doubleday, 1955.

Swindler, William F., ed. *Sources and Documents of United States Constitutions.* 10 vols. Dobbs Ferry, NY: Oceana Publications, 1973–79.

Tait, L. Gordon. "John Witherspoon: The Making of a Patriot, 1768–1776." *Ohio Journal of Religious Studies* 4 (1976): 54–63.

———. *The Piety of John Witherspoon: Pew, Pulpit, and Public Forum.* Louisville, KY: Geneva Press, 2001.

Tansill, C. C., ed. *Documents Illustrative of the Formation of the Union of the American States.* Washington, DC: U.S. Government Printing Office, 1827.

Tocqueville, Alexis de. *Democracy in America.* Trans. George Lawrence. Ed. J. P. Mayer. New York: Harper and Row, 1969.

———. *The Old Régime and the French Revolution.* Trans. Stuart Gilbert. New York: Doubleday, 1955.

Trevelyan, George Otto. *The American Revolution.* New York: Longmans, Green and Co., 1899–1913.

Trinterud, Leonard J. *The Forming of an American Tradition: A Re-examination of Colonial Presbyterianism.* Freeport, NY: Books for Libraries Press, 1970 [1949].

Tyler, Moses Coit. "President Witherspoon in the American Revolution." *American Historical Review* 1 (1896): 671–79.

United States Code: Containing the General and Permanent Laws of the United States, in Force on January 4, 1995. 35 vols. Washington, DC: U.S. Government Printing Office, 1995.

United States Supreme Court Reports. Law. Ed. 100 vols. Rochester, NY: Lawyer's Co-Operative Publishing Co., 1926–56.

Voegelin, Eric. *Autobiographical Reflections.* Ed. Ellis Sandoz. Baton Rouge: Louisiana State University Press, 1987.

Walpole, Horace. *Horace Walpole's Correspondence.* Ed. W. S. Lewis et al. 48 vols. New Haven: Yale University Press, 1937–83.

Warren, Charles. *The Making of the Constitution.* Boston: Little, Brown and Co., 1937.

Washington, George. *George Washington: A Collection.* Ed. W. B. Allen. Indianapolis: Liberty Classics, 1988.

———. *The Papers of George Washington.* Ed. W. W. Abbot et al. 30 vols. Charlottesville: University Press of Virginia, 1983–98.

———. *The Writings of George Washington, From the Original Manuscript Sources, 1745–1799.* Ed. John C. Fitzpatrick. 39 vols. Washington, DC: U.S. Government Printing Office, 1931–44.

Weber, Max. *The Protestant Ethic and the Spirit of Capitalism.* Trans. Talcott Parsons. London: HarperCollins, 1991 [1930].

Webster, Noah. *An American Dictionary of the English Language.* 2 vols. New York: Johnson Reprint Corp., 1970 [1828].

Wertenbaker, Thomas Jefferson. *Princeton: 1746–1896.* Princeton: Princeton University Press, 1946.

Wharton, Francis, ed. *The Revolutionary Diplomatic Correspondence of the United States.* 6 vols. Washington, DC: U.S. Government Printing Office, 1889.

White, Morton. *The Philosophy of the American Revolution.* Oxford: Oxford University Press, 1978.

———. *Philosophy, The Federalist, and the Constitution.* New York: Oxford University Press, 1987.

White, R. J. *The Horizon Concise History of England.* New York: American Heritage Publishing Co., 1971.

Whitehead, John W. *An American Dream.* Westchester, IL: Crossway Books, 1987.

Wills, Garry. *Explaining America: The Federalist.* Garden City, NY: Doubleday and Co., 1981.

———. *Inventing America: Jefferson's Declaration of Independence.* New York: Random House, 1979.

Willson, John. *John Witherspoon and the Presbyterian Constitution.* Hillsdale, MI: Hillsdale College Press, 1994.

Wilson, James. *The Works of James Wilson.* Ed. Robert McCloskey. 2 vols. Cambridge, MA: Harvard University Press, 1967.

Witherspoon, John. *An Annotated Edition of Lectures on Moral Philosophy by John Witherspoon.* Ed. Jack Scott. Newark, DE: University of Delaware Press, 1982.

———. "Dialogue on Civil Liberty." *Pennsylvania Magazine* 2 (1776): 157–67.

———. *A Draught of the Form of the Government and Discipline of the Presbyterian Church in the United States of America.* New York: S. and J. Loudon, 1787.

———. *Essay on Money as a Medium of Commerce, with Remarks on the Advantages and Disadvantages of Paper Admitted into General Circulation.* Philadelphia: Young, Stewart, and McCulloch, 1786.

———. *Lectures on Moral Philosophy by John Witherspoon, D.D., LL.D., President of the College of New Jersey.* Ed. Varnum Lansing Collins. Princeton: Princeton University Press, 1912.

———. *The Miscellaneous Works of the Revd. John Witherspoon.* Philadelphia: William W. Woodward, 1803.

———. "Remarks on an Essay on Human Liberty." *Scots Magazine* 15 (1753): 165–70.

———. *The Selected Writings of John Witherspoon.* Ed. Thomas P. Miller. Carbondale: Southern Illinois University Press, 1990.

———. *The Works of the Rev. John Witherspoon.* 4 vols. Philadelphia: William W. Woodward, 1800–1801.

———. *The Works of the Rev. John Witherspoon.* 2d ed. 4 vols. Philadelphia: William W. Woodward, 1802.

———. *The Works of John Witherspoon.* 9 Vols. Edinburgh: Ogle and Aikman et al., 1804–5.

———. *The Works of the Rev. John Witherspoon.* 4 vols. Philadelphia: William W. Woodward, 1804.

Witte, Wayne W. "John Witherspoon: A Servant of Liberty—A Study in Doctrinal History and Political Calvinism." Th. D. dissertation, Princeton Theological Seminary, 1954.

Wood, Gordon S. *The American Revolution.* New York: Modern Library, 2002.

———. *Creation of the American Republic, 1776–1787.* Chapel Hill: University of North Carolina Press, 1969.

Woods, David Walker, Jr. *John Witherspoon.* New York: Fleming H. Revell, 1906.

Wrenn, Lawrence G. "John Witherspoon and Church Law." Dissertation, Pontificia Universitas Lateranensis, Rome.

Wright, Thomas. *England under the House of Hanover.* 2 vols. Port Washington, NY: Kennikat Press, 1971 [1848].

Zuckert, Michael P. *The Natural Rights Republic.* Notre Dame, IN: University of Notre Dame Press, 1996.

index

JEFFRY H. MORRISON

is James Madison Visiting Fellow and visiting assistant
professor of politics at Princeton University. He is also
assistant professor of government at Regent University.

H. Pomarÿ Del.

A North-West Prospect of Naſsau-Hall